INSPIRE / PLAN / DISCOVER / EXPERIENCE

ROME

DK EYEWITNESS

ROME

CONTENTS

DISCOVER 6

EXPERIENCE 60

NEED TO KNOW 328

This page: The Spanish Steps
Previous: Rome skyline seen from the
top of the Victor Emmanuel Monument

DISCOVER

St Peter's Square and colonnade

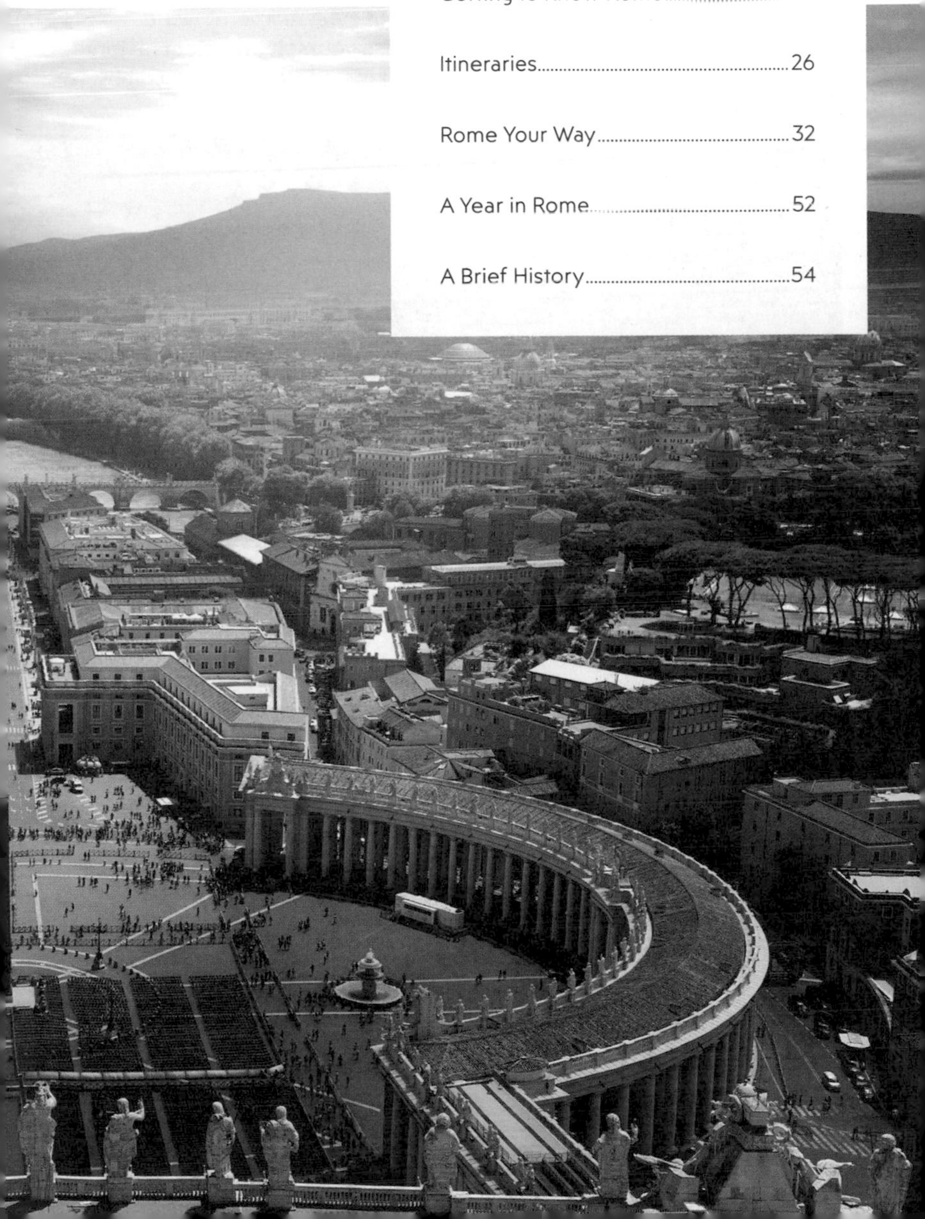

WELCOME TO
ROME

Hugely photogenic, with its spectacular piazzas, cascading fountains and exuberant street life, Rome is a Baroque extravaganza just waiting for you to join in *la dolce vita*. Linger over a Campari Spritz in a pavement café, marvel at world-famous art, immerse yourself in ancient history and spook yourself in underground catacombs.

1 Detail of *The Coronation of the Virgin* mosaic in Santa Maria Maggiore

2 The Roman Forum

3 Fontana dei Quattro Fiumi on Piazza Navona

Rome brings history to life like no other city. Whether visiting the Colosseum, the temples and basilicas of the Forum, or the Pantheon, you can travel back in time to ancient Rome. At the Baths of Caracalla and Palazzo Valentini digital technology restores ancient ruins to their former glory. For spectacular views over the whole city climb to the cupola of St Peter's, then see God create Adam on the world-famous Sistine Chapel ceiling. Immerse yourself in the Baroque euphoria of Piazza Navona, float down the Spanish Steps, throw a coin in the Trevi fountain, dive into the food markets of Campo de' Fiori and Testaccio and experience the vibrant nightlife of Trastevere and the hipster bars and restaurants of Monti. Rome's large central park, Villa Borghese, provides a peaceful green refuge, where you can also see an extraordinary collection of Bernini sculptures in the Museo Borghese. For dramatic modern architecture and art visit Zaha Hadid's MAXXI or MACRO's site in a converted beer factory. The villas of Tivoli and the ancient Roman city of Ostia Antica provide fascinating day trips from the city.

It's not surprising that Rome, with a huge number of ancient sites, museums, churches and galleries, can feel a little overwhelming. To help, our Roman experts have picked out themes and planned detailed itineraries to whet your appetite. The city has been broken down into easily navigable chapters with colourful, comprehensive maps and insider tips to help you plan the perfect visit. Whatever your dream trip includes, this DK Eyewitness Travel Guide to Rome is your ideal companion.

3

REASONS TO LOVE
ROME

This dynamic city is full of ancient ruins, Renaissance palaces, Baroque churches, world-famous art, elegant shops and culinary delights, offering a unique tapestry of history, art and entertainment.

1 MAGNIFICENT SQUARES AND FOUNTAINS

Rome is full of gloriously cinematographic piazzas with cascading fountains, great for people-watching over a coffee.

ANCIENT MONUMENTS 2

Let your imagination run riot as you explore the myriad ruins of one of the world's most ancient cities – splendid palaces, amphi-theatres and triumphal arches, as well as baths and markets.

3 THE APERITIVO

The *aperitivo*, a pre-prandial drink with snacks, is an Italian tradition. Romans love to unwind over a wine, Aperol or Campari Spritz with olives, canapés or a buffet while watching the world go by from a pavement café.

PIAZZA SAN PIETRO AT DAWN 4

Designed by Bernini, Piazza San Pietro is one of the most magnificent public spaces in the world. To see it at its best, get up at the crack of dawn.

DESIGNER SHOPPING 5

Romans would never shop for serious clothes in jeans and trainers, so to truly relish the experience, don your glad rags for an indulgent few hours drifting in and out of boutiques.

DOLCE & GABBANA

EXCEPTIONAL GELATO 6

On a steamy afternoon or balmy night, strolling the cobbled streets of the centro storico with a *coppetta* or *cono* of ice cream is a time-honoured Roman tradition.

21ST-CENTURY ROME 7

Leave history behind for a few hours for contemporary art at the ultra-modern MAXXI, or a jazz or classical concert at state-of-the-art Auditorium Parco della Musica *(p316)*.

THE SISTINE CHAPEL 8

Standing in the Sistine Chapel, looking up at Michelangelo's immense, iconic frescoes on the ceiling, is one of the most awe-inspiring experiences Rome has to offer.

9 SUNSET OVER ROME

Famously built over seven hills, with a skyline defined by the distinctive domes of over 900 churches, Rome has no shortage of viewpoints. The city is most photogenic at sunset.

ROMAN STREET FOOD 10

Don't leave Rome without trying *pizza bianca* (with a base of olive oil and salt). *Supplì* (fried rice balls with fillings) and *polpette di bollito* (meat croquettes) are other staples, best sampled at Testaccio Market *(p51)*.

UNDERGROUND ROME 11

Head underground through layers of history to discover a hidden city of crypts and catacombs featuring spooky mummies, bone sculptures and sites of pagan sacrifice.

VILLA BORGHESE 12

The lush expanse of Villa Borghese is Rome's green lung. Great for picnicking, boating on the lake or going for a bike ride, the large park also has several fascinating museums *(p142)*.

VITTORIA

Tevere

Villa
Giulia

Villa
Ruffo

Santa Maria
del Popolo

CAMPO
MARZIO

PRATI

VATICAN
p280

Vatican
Museums

Castel
Sant'Angelo

BORGO

VATICAN
CITY

Piazza
S. Pietro

St Peters

PONTE

**PIAZZA
NAVONA**
p118

**PIAZZA
DELLA
ROTONDA**
p100

Piazza
Navona

Pantheon

PARIONE

PIGNA

Campo
de' Fiori

Gesù

Palazzo
Farnese

CAMPO DE' FIORI
p158

Villa
Farnesina

JANICULUM
p268

Tevere

ANGELO

Gianicolo

Villa
Abamelek

Piazza S.
Apollonia

Santa Maria
in Trastevere

TRASTEVERE

TRASTEVERE
p254

Villa
Sciarra

Santa
Sabina

AVENTINE

EXPLORE
ROME

AVENTINE
p240

TESTACCIO

This guide divides Rome into
15 colour-coded sightseeing
areas, as shown on this map.
Find out more about each area
on the following pages.

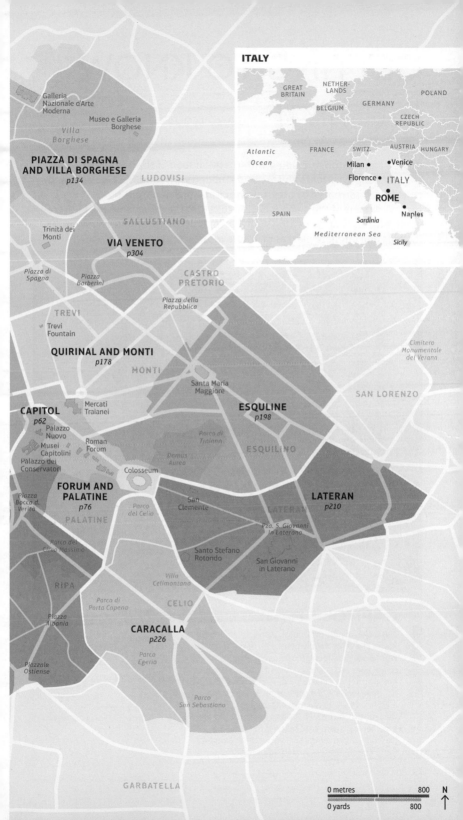

Galleria
Nazionale d'Arte
Moderna

Villa
Borghese

Museo e Galleria
Borghese

PIAZZA DI SPAGNA
AND VILLA BORGHESE
p134

LUDOVISI

Trinità dei
Monti

SALLUSTIANO

VIA VENETO
p304

Piazza di
Spagna

Piazza
Barberini

CASTRO
PRETORIO

Piazza della
Repubblica

TREVI

Trevi
Fountain

QUIRINAL AND MONTI
p178

MONTI

Santa Maria
Maggiore

CAPITOL
p62

Mercati
Traianei

ESQULINE
p198

Palazzo
Nuovo

Musei
Capitolini

Roman
Forum

Parco di
Traiano

ESQUILINO

Palazzo dei
Conservatori

Domus
Aurea

Colosseum

Piazza
Bocca d.
Verita

FORUM AND
PALATINE
p76

San
Clemente

LATERAN
p210

PALATINE

Parco
del Celio

LATERAN

Pza. S. Giovanni
in Laterano

Parco del
Circo Massimo

Santo Stefano
Rotondo

San Giovanni
in Laterano

RIPA

Villa
Celimontana

Piazza
Albania

Parco di
Porta Capena

CELIO

Piazzale
Ostiense

CARACALLA
p226

Parco
Egeria

Parco
San Sebastiano

GARBATELLA

CIMITERO
Monumentale
del Verano

SAN LORENZO

ITALY

GREAT
BRITAIN

NETHER-
LANDS

POLAND

BELGIUM

GERMANY

CZECH
REPUBLIC

Atlantic
Ocean

FRANCE

SWITZ.

AUSTRIA

HUNGARY

Milan •

• Venice

Florence •

ITALY

ROME

SPAIN

• Naples

Sardinia

Mediterranean Sea

Sicily

0 metres		800
0 yards		800

N
↑

GETTING TO KNOW
ROME

Rome's *centro storico*, cradled within a great loop of the Tiber River, is a maze of cobbled streets and piazzas studded with fountains, palaces and churches, interrupted by green swathes in which umbrella pines shade the toothy remains of the ancient city. Across the river, the dome of St Peter's dominates the horizon, rising high above Vatican City and the mellow façades and intimate piazzas of Trastevere.

CAPITOL

PAGE 62

This is the monumental heart of ancient and modern Rome. The white marble behemoth of the Victor Emmanuel Monument, the focus of patriotic ceremonies and political demonstrations, dominates heavily trafficked Piazza Venezia. Behind it, Capitol Hill has been the seat of municipal government since ancient times, with civic marriages still taking place in the registry office of the Palazzo del Senatorio, which, together with the palazzi housing the Capitoline Museums with their treasures of Classical sculpture, frame the elegant Piazza del Campidoglio.

Best for
Seeing iconic Roman sculptures

Home to
The Capitoline Museums

Experience
Views of the Roman Forum from the window in the Tabularium of the Capitoline Museums and from the terrace of the Caffetteria dei Musei Capitolini

FORUM AND PALATINE

Mussolini's Via dei Fori Imperiali slices above the ruins of the temples and basilicas that once formed the centre of political, commercial and judicial life in ancient Rome. By day it is peppered with souvenir stands and lined with coaches from which crocodiles of tourists pour out to follow umbrella-toting guides around the Roman Forum and Colosseum. The Forum is far quieter and more atmospheric at night, when the tour groups have left and the monuments are illuminated. Crowds are easier to avoid at all times in the green, pine-shaded expanses of the Palatine Hill.

Best for
Exploring the ruins of ancient Rome

Home to
Roman Forum; Palatine; Colosseum

Experience
The Colosseum floodlit at night

→

PAGE 100

PIAZZA DELLA ROTONDA

The compact core of cobbled streets and piazza around the Pantheon is crammed with churches and palaces, restaurants, cafés and enticing gelaterias. Businessmen remonstrate into their phones, chauffeurs leap into action as paparazzi pounce on politicians, ice-cream eaters and tourists jam the streets. Hidden in the back streets are fragments from a temple of Isis, shops selling ecclesiastical paraphernalia and the ancient Temple of Hadrian, while the church of Sant'Ignazio di Loyola holds magnificent *trompe l'oeil* frescoes.

Best for
Atmospheric strolling

Home to
The Pantheon; the Gesù

Experience
The ice creams of Giolitti or Grom gelaterias

PAGE 118

PIAZZA NAVONA

An exuberantly Baroque oval dominated by the towering obelisk and cascading waters of Bernini's Fontana dei Quattro Fiumi, Piazza Navona is the social heart of Rome. An outdoor salon fringed with pricey pavement cafés, it is full from morning to night with tourists, Romans, buskers, mime-artists, and itinerant street vendors. The picturesque cobbled streets around it are home to places to sleep, eat and drink that run the gamut from super-chic to super-cheap. Antiques shops, vintage clothes stores and some extremely stylish fashion, shoe and design boutiques are found here too.

Best for
Baroque architecture and exuberant streetlife

Home to
Fontana dei Quattro Fiumi

Experience
The beauty of Piazza Navona at dawn

PAGE 134

PIAZZA DI SPAGNA AND VILLA BORGHESE

The triangle of streets between Piazza del Popolo and Piazza di Spagna are studded with designer boutiques, bijou cosmetics shops, art galleries, antiques shops and upmarket delicatessens. It's an area in which to wander, window-shop and people-watch in between a little leisurely sightseeing. Via del Corso is full of chain shops, transforming into a human river at peak times. For respite, head to the Villa Borghese park, with its green lawns, shady pines, boating lake, museums and cafés.

Best for
Shopping; relaxing in a green space; art treasures

Home to
Piazza di Spagna; Santa Maria del Popolo; Villa Borghese park and the museums of Galleria Borghese and Villa Giulia

Experience
An aperitivo on Piazza del Popolo

PAGE 158

CAMPO DE' FIORI

The area between Corso Vittorio Emanuele and the Tiber River, Campo de' Fiori is dominated by the morning food market in Campo de' Fiori itself. In and around the square the neighbourhood's culinary traditions have spawned some of the city's most authentic places to eat Roman food – some long-established and some contemporary. The area gets very lively at sundown, with students, locals and tourists flooding its eateries and bars.

Best for
Soaking up the market atmosphere; strolling along medieval streets lined with artisan shops

Home to
Campo de' Fiori piazza; frescoes in Palazzo Farnese

Experience
Crisp pizza bianca fresh from the oven from Antico Forno Roscioli

→

PAGE 178

QUIRINAL AND MONTI

A sprawling zone cut through by traffic-clogged Via Nazionale, Quirinal stretches downhill, encompassing the slopes of the Viminal – dominated by the august façade and sombre denizens of the Ministry of the Interior – and across to the Quirinal Hill. Here the Palazzo del Quirinale, residence of the Italian president, dominates a rather desolate piazza. Rome's most famous fountain, the Trevi, is nearby. For coffee, lunch, shopping or an aperitivo, head to the livelier, fashionable Monti district.

Best for
Exploring the streets, shops and cafés of Monti

Home to
Trevi Fountain; Palazzo Massimo alle Terme (Museo Nazionale Romano); Galleria Colonna

Experience
Lunch or a drink on Piazza Madonna dei Monti

PAGE 198

ESQUILINE

Central Rome's most multicultural quarter and one of the poorer areas of the city, the Esquiline's traffic-filled streets evoke gritty urban shabbiness interspersed with 19th-century elegance. Its most famous sights are the churches, whose interiors are mosaicked like jewellery boxes. This is the place for multi-ethnic dining options – take your pick of Eritrean, Chinese, Indian and Thai eateries. The huge, loud Nuovo Mercato Esquilino market represents all the different cultures here, and is full of the smells and colours of exotic spices and a vast array of international foods.

Best for
International eateries; churches with glittering mosaics

Home to
Santa Maria Maggiore; Santa Pudenziana; Santa Prassede

Experience
Eritrean food; multicultural atmosphere

LATERAN

PAGE 210

Traditionally a working-class area, the Lateran retains an unpretentious feel, its left-wing traditions and loyalties still evident in the huge free May Day concert organized every year by the trades unions in the central large Piazza di San Giovanni. Modern avenues open out onto beautiful churches – the Lateran is the site of Rome's oldest basilica, San Giovanni. The area is also home to the huge Via Sannio clothes and shoes market.

Best for
Travelling back through three layers of history in San Clemente

Home to
San Giovanni in Laterano; San Clemente

Experience
The spooky Mithraeum hidden below San Clemente

PAGE 226

CARACALLA

Largely undeveloped except for an immense military hospital and a handful of beguiling churches, the Celian Hill rises, green and tranquil, from the busy thoroughfares that now cut along the valleys at its foot. It's a lovely place to stroll from one little church to the next along quiet roads. The Villa Celimontana park, at its heart, is perfect for a picnic, while anyone who really loves to walk can carry right on beyond the ancient city walls to the Via Appia Antica *(p321)*.

Best for
A quiet stroll on the Celian Hill

Home to
Baths of Caracalla

Experience
A summer jazz concert in Villa Celimontana park

→

PAGE 240

AVENTINE

Rising above the Tiber River to the southwest of
the Palatine, the twin-peaked Aventine Hill is a lush,
leafy residential area with a handful of early Christian
churches scattered among its secluded villas, gardens
and convents. Although in the centre of Rome, it is
remarkably peaceful, and for once the sound of bird-
song is louder than the roar of traffic. On the far side
of the hill, Testaccio, a working-class neighbourhood
defined by the huge market at its heart, is one of
Rome's trendiest areas and the best place in the
city for anyone seriously interested in food.

Best for
Niche fashion and food shops

Home to
Il Mattatoio; the Pyramid
of Caius Cestius; Santa Maria
in Cosmedin

Experience
The take-away food stalls
at the Mercato di Testaccio

TRASTEVERE

PAGE 254

With its picturesque, higgledy-piggledy cobbled streets, mellow rose and ochre façades and intimate piazzas, bohemian Trastevere epitomizes a stranger's romantic notion of Rome. Shrines to the Madonna still protect tiny piazzas housing chic bars, restaurants and boutiques. In the evening this district becomes the centre of Rome's liveliest nightlife, with most of the action concentrated around Piazza Santa Maria in Trastevere. The area to the east of Viale di Trastevere is less gentrified, with warehouses dating back to the days when this was the home of the Tiber's dockers.

Best for
Daytime strolling and shopping and night-time bars

Home to
Santa Maria in Trastevere.

Experience
The centre of Rome's social life

PAGE 268

JANICULUM

The highest of Rome's hills – though not one of the original seven – the Janiculum is a great place to go for a walk and views of the city, and can be approached from either the Vatican or Trastevere. The main focus is Piazzale Giuseppe Garibaldi, a wide, cobbled space with snack vans and a puppet show booth, at its busiest in the early evening as people gather to watch the sunset over the city. Head to Villa Farnesina for beautiful paintings and frescoes by Raphael and his pupils.

Best for
A bracing walk after a day in the Vatican Museums

Home to
The Renaissance Villa Farnesina

Experience
A view of Rome at sunset

→

PAGE 280

VATICAN

With St Peter's basilica, the centre of the Roman Catholic faith, and the Vatican Museums, housing some of the world's greatest art collections, the Vatican is a must for pilgrims and art lovers. The area around the world's smallest sovereign state is full of busy streets lined with souvenir shops selling ecclesiastical memorabilia and hawkers flogging Sistine Chapel T-shirts and plaster Pietàs. Cobbled, pedestrianized Borgo Pio is the most attractive street, retaining some old-world charm and authentic places to eat.

Best for
World-famous art and sculpture

Home to
St Peter's; the Vatican Museums and Sistine Chapel; Castel Sant'Angelo.

Experience
A Papal Audience on Piazza San Pietro

PAGE 304

VIA VENETO

The focus of the decadent and glamorous night scene of the late 1950s and 60s that inspired Fellini's film *La Dolce Vita*, Via Veneto is but a shadow of its former self, though the street retains its elegance and is home to some of the city's most luxurious hotels. The fascinating, though macabre, Capuchin Crypt, with thousands of human bones as well as mummified corpses decorating its walls and ceilings, comes as a surprise underneath the 17th-century Santa Maria della Concezione church.

Best for
Scary skeletal sculptures and mummies

Home to
The Capuchin crypt; Palazzo Barberini; Santa Maria della Vittoria

Experience
A cocktail in Il Giardino rooftop bar at the Hotel Eden

BEYOND THE CENTRE

Rome has a small, compact centre – you can walk from one side to the other in a couple of hours – and keen walkers can easily cover some of the city's peripheral sights on foot too. Ranging from Roman catacombs to the 21st-century MAXXI art gallery, and from ancient churches to the futuristic suburb of EUR and fantasy quarter of Coppedè, delving outside the centre not only brings you to sights off the beaten track, but into residential neighbourhoods where you can get a real sense of everyday life in Rome.

Best for
Discovering the Art Nouveau architecture of the Coppedè Quarter

Home to
Ostia Antica; MAXXI; Villa Ada park; Via Appia Antica

Experience
A classical or jazz concert at the Auditorium Parco della Musica; World Music festival at Villa Ada in July

←
1 Roman Forum at sunrise
2 Interior of the Pantheon
3 Fresh produce at the market on Campo de' Fiori
4 Spanish Steps

Whether you are in Rome for several days or just want a brief flavour of this great city, these itineraries will help you make the most of your time, taking in the key sights and experiences.

24 HOURS

Morning

Do as the Romans do, and breakfast on a coffee and pastry in a café-bar, while you plot a route by foot or by bus to the Colosseum (p88). Try to get there early – it opens at 8.30am. If the queues are long when you arrive, content yourself with a walk around the building to admire its world-famous tiers of arches. Wander past the Roman Forum (p80), and up Capitoline Hill (p63); pop in to see the breathtaking equestrian statue of Marcus Aurelius in the Capitoline Museums (pp66–9), or just admire the replica in the centre of Michelangelo's Piazza del Campidoglio, before treating yourself to a coffee with sweeping views over the Forum from the museums' rooftop bar, Caffetteria dei Musei Capitolini. Head over to Palazzo Valentini (p98) to view the ruins of two Roman houses and see them restored to their former glory through virtual reality headsets, then stroll through the Jewish Ghetto to Campo de' Fiori with its open-air market (p162), stopping for lunch at Ar Galletto restaurant (Piazza Farnese 104).

Afternoon

Wind across to Piazza Navona (p120) to make a circuit of its spectacular fountains before crossing over to visit the Pantheon (p104). Buy an ice cream from Grom (p114), then wander the narrow cobbled streets, window-shopping your way to the Trevi Fountain (p182). Head north to Piazza di Spagna (p138) to join the crowds on the Spanish Steps, then walk along via Trinità dei Monti, from where there are sweeping views over the multi-domed skyline of Rome to St Peter's.

Evening

If it's between April and October reward yourself with an aperitivo on the panoramic terrace of Ciampini al Café du Jardin (Piazza Trinità dei Monti) – it's a bit touristy, but the views at sunset are worth it! In winter, when the café is closed, head back to Piazza di Spagna and join the smart set for a cocktail at the Hotel de Russie's Stravinskij Bar. Then head to Assaggia Roma (Via Margutta 19) for a dinner of Italian cuisine staples.

→

1 St Peter's Square

2 The Colosseum

3 Pavement tables at
Antico Caffè Greco

4 *Rape of Proserpine* by Bernini
in Museo e Galleria Borghese

3 DAYS

Day 1

Morning Get up at dawn for the unforgettable experience of an almost empty Piazza San Pietro, entering the Basilica, along with nuns, priests and pilgrims, at 7am (p228). The spiral steps winding up inside the shell of the dome to the cupola open at 8am – having the views to yourself is magical. Book a slot to the Vatican Museums online in advance (p289), and take in the glories of the Cortile della Pigna over breakfast in the café. See the Sistine Chapel ceiling, then select your other highlights in the museums, breaking for lunch in the pizzeria outside the Carriage Pavilion.

Afternoon Clear your mind with a long, bracing walk up the Janiculum Hill (p269) for fabulous views over the city, winding down past Bramante's Tempietto (p275) into Trastevere (p255) to browse its boutiques. Marvel at the splendid mosaics in the church of Santa Maria in Trastevere (p258).

Evening Enjoy a well-earned aperitivo on Piazza Santa Maria in Trastevere, followed by dinner at Enoteca Ferrara (p265).

Day 2

Morning Explore the Colosseum (p88), then head to the Palatine (p94). With pine trees shading its slopes and wild flowers surrounding its ruins, this is one of the most evocative of Rome's ancient sites. Don't miss the lovely Farnese Gardens or the surviving section of Emperor Nero's Cryptoporticus tunnel (p97). Head downhill into the Roman Forum (p80), and see if you can spot the melted coins fused to the pavement of the Basilica Aemilia and the chequerboards carved into the steps of Basilica Julia. Treat yourself to lunch at the bistro, La Bottega del Caffè, on Monti's traffic-free Piazza Madonna dei Monti.

Afternoon Stroll up past the quirky fashion boutiques of Via dei Serpenti to Trajan's Markets (p92), an ancient Roman shopping mall, and the digitally reconstructed Roman villas below Palazzo Valentini (p98). See superb frescoes at Palazzo Massimo alle Terme (p186).

Evening Collapse over a fine glass of wine at the Trimani Il Wine Bar (p192), followed by a dinner of inventive Italian dishes at L'Asino d'Oro (p194).

Day 3

Morning Start with a leisurely caffè latte at the Antico Caffè Vitti on pretty Piazza San Lorenzo in Lucina, then browse the chic shops of Via Campo Marzio, Via del Leone and Piazzetta della Toretta; strike across Piazza del Parlamento to Piazza del Montecitorio – watch politicians and lobbyists coming and going from the parliament building, then zig-zag down to the Pantheon (p104), taking in little Piazza delle Coppelle. See Caravaggio canvasses in San Luigi dei Francesi (p125) and the ingenious courtyard of Sant'Ivo alla Sapienza (p127), then cross Piazza Navona for lunch at Chiostro del Bramante Bistro (Arco della Pace 5).

Afternoon Head up to Villa Borghese to see world-famous sculptures by Bernini in the Galleria Borghese (p144), and, if you are not too tired, the incredible Etruscan collection at Villa Giulia (p146).

Evening Wind down with an aperitivo on the garden terrace of GNAM's Caffè delle Belle Arti (p143), then walk to Dal Pollarolo restaurant for a dinner of local Italian pasta dishes (Via di Ripetta 4–5).

1

2

3

4

1 Baths of Caracalla

2 Hall of Mirrors, Palazzo Doria Pamphilj

3 Bramante's Tempietto

4 Pavement eatery in Trastevere

5 DAYS

Day 1

Morning Explore the Forum (p80) and walk up through the Imperial ruins of the Palatine Hill (p96). If you are here at the weekend, pick up supplies for sandwiches at the Circo Massimo farmers' market (p51).

Afternoon See iconic ancient sculptures at the Capitoline Museums (p66), then head to the Crypta Balbi museum (p170).

Evening Stroll through the Jewish Ghetto, for an aperitivo at Roscioli, then dine on *cucina romana* at Piperno (p173).

Day 2

Morning Search out traces of the Teatro di Pompeo (164), then dive underground to see the remains of the Roman stadium beneath Piazza Navona (p122). Take an audio tour through Palazzo Doria Pamphilj (p114), narrated by the current Prince, Jonathan. Treat yourself to lunch in the palazzo's café.

Afternoon After marvelling at the dizzying frescoes in Sant'Ignazio di Loyola (p109) indulge in some retail therapy on Via Condotti (p148), then visit the room where John Keats spent his final months at the Keats-Shelley Memorial House (p138) before seeing the wonderful frescoes in Villa Medici (see p149).

Evening Enjoy a cocktail and dinner at Doney Café (p308) on nearby Via Veneto.

Day 3

Morning Take in the splendour of Santa Maria Maggiore (p202), then pick up picnic supplies at nearby Panella (Via Merulana 59) and head through the Parco Oppio, past the ruins of the Baths of Trajan (p208). Stop off for some time travel through the strata of San Clemente (p216) before heading up to the Villa Celimontana park (p233) for a picnic.

Afternoon Continue over the Celian Hill to visit the Baths of Caracalla (p230). Then catch bus 118 along the Via Appia Antica to the Catacombs of San Callisto and continue on foot to the Tomb of Cecilia Metella (p319).

Evening Dine on fine Mediterranean cuisine at Ristorante L'Archeologia (Via Appia Antica 139).

Day 4

Morning Wander past the pretty gardens and villas of the Aventine to Testaccio. After clambering around Monte Testaccio (p248) explore the exhibitions and shops of the fairtrade market in the Mercato di Testaccio (p50). Lunch on delicious street food at the market.

Afternoon Cross the Tiber, walk through Porta Portese market (p50), and along the pine-shaded paths through the Villa Sciarra park (p262) to Bramante's Tempietto (p275).

Evening Dine on Roman dishes at Antica Pesa (Via Garibaldi 18), followed by a nightcap and live jazz at Big Mama (p265).

Day 5

Morning Explore Villa Borghese park on foot, by bike or by rickshaw, making time for a row on the lake and a visit to Museo Carlo Bilotti (p143). Treat yourself to a lunch of handmade ravioli on the elegant travertine terrace of GNAM's Caffè delle Arti (p143).

Afternoon Visit the Museo e Galleria Borghese (p144) before walking through the Salaria neighbourhood to Coppedè for some fanciful architecture (p317). Take tram 3 from nearby Piazza Buenos Aires back into town to Trastevere – the ideal neighbourhood to spend your last evening in Rome.

Evening Sip a Prosecco accompanied by live music at Ombre Rosse (p265), then head to Antico Arco (p275) for a gourmet dinner.

▽ **Ancient Frescoes**

Head to Palazzo Massimo alle Terme *(p186)* to see the exquisite frescos of garden scenes from the house of Emperor Augustus's wife Livia. A sense of the role that art played in the lives of more ordinary Romans can be seen at Ostia Antica in the frescoes depicting carrots and chick peas on the wall of a bar *(p315)*.

△ **Early Christian Mosaics**

Mosaic reached its zenith in the 6th-9th centuries as Rome fell under the influence of Byzantine art. See one of the finest mosaics in Rome in Santa Maria in Domnica's apse *(p233)*, a superb example of Byzantine style in the 9th century.

ROME FOR
ART LOVERS

As a power-centre first of the Roman Empire and then of the Catholic Church Rome has always been a magnet for those with immense wealth and ambition. Over the centuries emperors, popes and aristocrats have displayed their riches by commissioning works from the greatest artists of their time.

△ **Renaissance Masterpieces**

Many major artists of the Renaissance were attracted to Rome. For some of the most splendid art, see the frescoes on the Sistine Chapel ceiling created by Michelangelo for Pope Julius II and Pope Paul III Farnese *(p292)*. Head to Villa Farnesina for glorious mythological frescoes painted by Raphael for super-wealthy banker Agostino Chigi

▽ Early Baroque Painting

Caravaggio worked for both church and aristocracy in Rome, often introducing an iconoclastic secularism to religious works. Look out for the sexualized angel and the very realistic depiction of trees, leaves and stones in *The Flight to Egypt* in the art gallery in Palazzo Doria Pamphilj *(p114)*.

▷ Baroque Flamboyance

Rome's wealth and power were at their height in the late 17th century, propelling a massive restyling of the city. Hundreds of churches, palaces and piazzas were redesigned in a flamboyant Baroque style. Look out in particular for magnificent fountains, many designed by Bernini, such as the Fontana del Tritone, which pepper the centre of the city. To see some of Bernini's most ground-breaking, emotive sculptures, created for Cardinal Scipione Borghese, visit the Museo e Galleria Borghese *(p144)*.

△ Modern and Contemporary Art

For 20th-century art, head to GNAM *(p144)*, which has works by De Chirico, such as *Spettacolo Misterioso* (1971), the Italian Futurists and Giacometti. Museo Carlo Bilotti *(p143)* also has paintings by De Chirico. For contemporary art, visit the futuristic MAXXI *(p316)*.

TOP 4 ARTISTS IN ROME

Michelangelo
(1475–1564)
Remarkable sculptor, painter and architect

Raphael
(1483–1520)
Supreme painter of the High Renaissance

Caravaggio
(1571–1610)
Pioneer of dramatic Baroque painting

Bernini
(1598–1680)
Architect and the leading sculptor of his age

Coffee

The average Italian visits simple café-bars at least twice a day – for breakfast and after lunch. Around Piazzas Navona, Spagna and Rotonda, ordinary café-bars are scarce, but there is one on almost every street corner elsewhere. Most Italians drink while standing up at the bar. For an authentic coffee experience, try Bar del Cappuccino on Via Arenula 50.

Traditional way of drinking coffee, standing at the bar

ROME FOR
FOODIES

There are few more enduring pleasures than lingering over a leisurely al fresco meal in a piazza in the Eternal City. Roman food is tasty, nutritious, simple and extremely varied. Menus tend to be seasonal and food is redolent of aromatic herbs, olive oil, garlic and onion.

INSIDER TIP
Gelato

Legend has it that the art of ice-cream making was brought to Sicily in the 16th century by its medieval Arab rulers who introduced the technique of blending fruit syrups and flower essences with snow taken from the slopes of Mount Etna. Gourmet ice creams made with organic ingredients have taken Rome by storm – try the delicious offerings at San Crespino gelateria on Via della Panetteria 42.

Traditional Roman Dishes

Originating in working-class areas such as Testaccio, traditional Roman food is based on cheap cuts of meat and offal and simple pasta dishes such as *cacio e pepe* (pecorino cheese and black pepper). *Carciofi alla giudia* (deep-fried artichokes) is a key delicacy introduced by the Jewish community of the Ghetto.

A traditional Roman restaurant on Via Arco di San Calisto in Trastevere

↑ Aperitivo drinks at a pavement bar in Trastevere

Aperitivo and Wine Bars

The *aperitivo*, a pre-dinner glass of wine, Aperol or Campari Spritz, served with snacks, is a tradition rooted in northern cities such as Turin and Milan, but is very popular in Rome too. At the very least there will be crisps, olives and peanuts to accompany the drinks, but often there are abundant buffets such as the one in Vin Allegro in Trastevere on Piazza Giuditta Tavani Arquati.

Food to Take Away

Hot take-away food has been a feature of Italian life since Roman times. Taste hot focaccia dripping with Ligurian olive oil or a slice of pizza fresh from the oven *(pizza a taglio)*, topped with anchovies and *puntarella* (chicory shoots) or courgette flowers and ricotta, available at bakeries. Enjoy aubergine *parmigiana* (fried aubergines with cheese and tomato sauce) or herby roast chicken and golden-crusted savoury pies at *rosticcerie*.

↑ Antico Forno Roscioli on Via Chavari 34, famous for superb *pizza a taglio*

EAT

Dine on creative dishes at one of Rome's chic new-wave eateries.

Casa Coppelle

This Franco-Roman restaurant offers a tempting range of dishes. The rack of lamb with vermouth and apple is a highlight.

📍U2 🏠Piazza delle Coppelle 49 🌐casacoppelle.com

$$$

Casa e Bottega

Traditional dishes are brought to new heights by acclaimed chef Paolo Parisi at this osteria near Piazza Navona.

📍T3 🏠Via Tor di Millina 📞06-686 4358

$$$

▽ Interactive Tour of Roman Houses Under Palazzo Valentini

Computer technology, light and sound effects, films and projections reconstruct the remains of two grand Roman villas discovered beneath Palazzo Valentini (p98).

△ Family Audio Guide at the Vatican Museums

Explore the collections of the Vatican's museums (p288) by renting the Family Audioguide, which is engagingly narrated by a series of characters ranging from an angel to a grumpy Michelangelo. For a break, head to the museum's pizzeria.

ROME FOR
FAMILIES

With its spectacular ancient ruins, Egyptian obelisks, and theatrical piazzas and fountains, Rome is a city that brings history to life like no other. Peppered with parks, ice cream parlours and take-away pizzerias, it is also a fun city for families, with children made welcome everywhere.

△ Gladiator School

🅦 www.gruppostoricoromano.it
Learn how to fight like a gladiator in a recreated arena at Via Appia Antica 18. Lessons are held by members of a historical re-enactment society.

▽ Cycling the Appia Antica

Ⓦ www.parcoappiaantica.it

Encompassing open countryside, the Parco Regionale dell'Appia Antica makes for a great day trip. The park rents out bikes and toddler seats. Go on a Sunday, when there are often kids' events, including nature trails, insect-spotting and bird-watching.

Did You Know?
—
Kids under the age of 18 who are EU citizens get free entry to national and city museums.

▷ Places to Let Off Steam

Rome's piazzas are great fun to run around in. Head to the huge Piazza Navona, where there is always something going on - from street mime to fire-jugglers to the annual Christmas fair and carnival. It is also home to two of Rome's best toy shops, Berte (no. 107) and Al Sogno (no. 53). For playgrounds, head to Villa Borghese *(p142)*, Parco Adriano *(p286)*, Villa Celimontana *(p233)*, which has pony rides, and the huge Villa Doria Pamphilj *(p325)*.

▽ Technotown

Ⓠ J5 Ⓐ Via Lazaro Spallanzani 1/a

Ⓒ 9:30am–7pm Tue–Sun

Ⓦ technotown.it

Experiment with 3D printers, a camera obscura, photography and film effects at this small science museum. Don't miss the Lego laboratory, where kids (and adults) can create robots.

△ Baths of Caracalla

Experience the biggest baths complex in ancient Rome through virtual reality headsets *(p230)*. The complex is surrounded by grass and umbrella pines - ideal for a picnic and run-around.

Modern Rome

The 20th century opened in Rome with the Art Nouveau fantasies of the Coppodè Quarter (p317), followed by Futuristic – even dystopian – EUR, founded by Mussolini (p323). Watch out too for buildings designed by contemporary international architects, such as Renzo Piano's Auditorium Parco della Musica and Zaha Hadid's MAXXI (p316). See ancient sculptures juxtaposed with the turbines of a former power plant at Centrale Montemartini (p325).

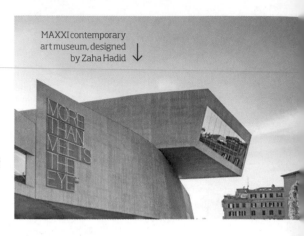

MAXXI contemporary art museum, designed by Zaha Hadid ↓

ROME'S
ARCHITECTURE

Explore Rome on an incredible journey through the history of Western architecture. Ancient Roman relics are strewn throughout the city cheek-by-jowl with medieval basilicas, Renaissance palaces and extravagant Baroque piazzas, churches and fountains.

Ancient Rome

The architects of Imperial Rome combined the Classical styles of ancient Greece with innovative new forms such as the arch, the vault and the dome. Visit the Pantheon to see the world's largest unreinforced concrete dome. Note the three storeys of Doric, Ionic and Corinthian columns on the Colosseum, imitated in façades of palaces and churches throughout the world.

The Colosseum, a ↓ prime example of ancient architecture

Christian Rome

The first places of worship were simply houses belonging to Christians or sites of martyrdoms. Visit San Crisogono *(p263)* to see the excavations of a private home that was used as an early Christian church. The first purpose-built churches were based on the Roman basilica, with three naves and an apse. To see Rome's main basilicas, visit St Peter's *(p284)*, San Giovanni in Laterano *(p214)* and Santa Maria Maggiore *(p202)*. More flamboyant Baroque innovations are Sant'Ivo alla Sapienza *(p127)* and San Carlo alle Quattro Fontane *(p192)*, designed by Borromini, and Bernini's Sant'Andrea al Quirinale *(p191)*.

THE LAYERS OF SAN CLEMENTE

Around 200 AD an aristrocrat built a temple to the fertility god Mithras in the central room of his house. In the 4th century the temple and house were filled in, and a church dedicated to Christian martyr San Clemente was built on top. In the 12th century this was filled with rubble to form the foundation for yet another church.

↑ St Peter's, one of the world's most iconic churches

Secular Rome

Rome is an extravaganza of Baroque piazzas, fountains and stairways, and enticing glimpses of frescoed ceilings through the windows of vast noble palaces. For spectacular views of Rome's buildings and piazzas, take a walk at night to see them lit up in the dark. The interiors of Palazzo Doria Pamphilj *(p114)*, Galleria Borghese *(p144)* and Villa Farnesina *(p272)* give a wonderful taste of glamour.

↑ The ornate Baroque Palazzo Doria Pamphilj

**La Dolce Vita
(Federico Fellini, 1960)**
A paparazzo, played by
Marcello Mastroianni, looks
for love among the decadent
nightlife of Rome in this iconic
Fellini film. In a famous scene,
Anita Ekberg, playing a
Swedish film star, takes a
bath in the Trevi fountain.

→

Anita Ekberg and Marcello
Mastroianni in the Trevi
Fountain in *La Dolce Vita*

ROME FOR
INSPIRATION

Home of the Roman Empire and a major centre of the Renaissance, Rome
has captured the imagination of many great writers and film makers. Trace
the steps of some of the most famous films and books set in Rome.

ON PAGE

Lord Byron
Living in Italy between 1817 and
1823, Byron's experiences in Rome
inspired several episodes in his epic
poem *Childe Harold's Pilgrimage*.
The Tomb of Cecilia Metella inspired
the line: "But who was she, the lady
of the dead, Tomb'd in a palace?"

Edith Wharton
Edith Wharton's short story
Roman Fever, published in 1934, is
set in Rome. The Forum is described
as the "accumulated wreckage of
passion and splendour", acting as a
metaphor for the main characters.

Dan Brown (1964–)
In Dan Brown's best-selling thriller
Angels and Demons, published in
2000, a cardinal is murdered in the
church of Santa Maria della Vittoria
and another is drowned in the
Fontana dei Quattro Fiumi.

Charles Dickens
Charles Dickens visited Rome
in 1844–45, witnessing an
execution, Carnival, an Easter
ceremony in which the Pope
washed the feet of 13 men and
a fireworks display at Castel
Sant' Angelo. He published
an account of his travels in
Pictures from Italy in 1846.

Fireworks at Castel ↑
Sant'Angelo during Sts
Peter and Paul celebrations

Roman Holiday
(William Wyler, 1953)
Starring Audrey Hepburn as a princess and Gregory Peck as an American journalist, *Roman Holiday* gives a sight-seeing tour of Rome, featuring Vespa-riding and romantic scenes at the Colosseum, Trevi Fountain and Spanish Steps.

↓ Audrey Hepburn riding a scooter in *Roman Holiday*

ON FILM

Roma
(Federico Fellini, 1972)
Fellini's surreal and ironic *omage* to his adopted city features a bizarre fashion show in the Vatican with outrageously dressed priests and nuns on the catwalk.

L'Eclisse
(Michelangelo Antonioni, 1962)
Starring Monica Vitti and Alain Delon, this disturbing film about a doomed love affair opens with Vitti splitting up with her lover in the deserted streets of EUR.

The Bicycle Thieves
(Vittorio De Sica, 1948)
This film centres on a desperate father searching the markets of Rome for his stolen bicycle (without which he will be unable to work). Rubbish collectors give him a lift across the Tiber to Porta Portese.

Eat Pray Love
(Ryan Murphy, 2010)
Julia Roberts plays author Elizabeth Gilbert, who comes to Rome to rediscover the joy of eating after the breakup of her marriage. She wanders through the city, indulging in gastronomic delicacies.

Keats
In 1820 Keats rented a house with his friend Joseph Severn at the foot of the Spanish Steps, where he died of consumption the following year, aged only 25. His death inspired Shelley's poem, *Adonaïs*. Visit the house where Keats lived, now a museum containing original letters and other mementoes, including those of fellow romantic poets, notably Percy Bysshe Shelley.

↑ The Keats-Shelley Museum, on Piazza di Spagna

Classical Concerts, Ballet and Theatre

The Auditorium Parco della Musica (p316) is a much-loved focus of Rome's music scene. Many churches also host classical concerts, while Teatro Olimpico on Piazza Gentile da Fabriano 17 is Rome's principal venue for modern dance. Main theatres include Teatro Palladium on Piazza Bartolomeo Romano 8 and Teatro Argentina (p168).

←

Classical music concert at Auditorium Parco della Musica

ROME
AFTER DARK

An after-dark *passeggiata* taking in the lively street life of the historic centre is hard to beat, with bars and cafés galore to choose from. In summer ancient sites, parks and piazzas become outdoor theatres for live music, while throughout the year there is a packed programme of theatre and festivals.

Opera

A highlight of Rome's opera scene is the sheer spectacle of the summer open-air operas at the Baths of Caracalla (p230). The main season runs from November to January at the Teatro dell'Opera, moving outdoors in July and August. Book tickets online at www.operaroma.it.

↓ Verdi's opera *Nabucco* at the Baths of Caracalla

ESTATE ROMANA

Rome's summer-long cultural festival (p53) includes pop-up bars and restaurants along the banks of the Tiber – an atmospheric place to spend an evening.

Outdoor dining after dark on Piazza Navona ↓

Street and Piazza Life

One of the most enjoyable things to do in Rome at night is simply to stroll through the historic centre, around Piazza Navona, Piazza di Spagna, Campo de' Fiori and Trastevere, while people-watching, window-shopping and pausing for a drink in a pavement café. Many shops around Piazza Navona stay open late, while Piazza Navona itself becomes a magnet for mime artists and other street performers.

Rock and Jazz

Jazz, indie rock and world-music artists perform frequently at the Auditorium Parco della Musica, while mainstream mega concerts are staged in sports arenas such as the Palalottamatica on Piazzale Pier Luigi Nervi 1 and Stadio Olimpico on Viale dei Gladiatori.

← Jazz musicians performing in the street in summer

Street Festivals

Rome has a venerable tradition of street celebrations, many with their origins in religious festivals, others born of left-wing politics, notably in the working class San Giovanni area, where the free pop concerts on 1 May and 24 June are a Rome institution. New Year is ushered in with fireworks and free concerts, while Chinese New Year sees stunning fireworks on Piazza del Popolo.

→ New Year fireworks at the Colosseum

ROME FOR
SHOPPERS

In Rome, haute couture and chic boutiques rub shoulders with artisans' studios and small neighbourhood shops. Have fun exploring designer stores, large emporia and crafts workshops. The most interesting shops are in the old centre, so you can combine shopping with sightseeing.

TOP 4 ROME FASHION DESIGNERS

Laura Biagiotti
Rome's queen of classic couture specializes in knitwear and silk.

Silvia Venturini Fendi
The only family member still working at the Fendi fashion house is famous for designing the iconic baguette bag.

Stella Jean
A fusion of Italian style with Caribbean themes reflects Stella Jean's Creole heritage.

Valentino
A high priest of fashion, Valentino is famous for stunning evening wear.

Leather

Gucci (Via dei Condotti 8), Fendi (Largo Goldoni 420) and Ferragamo (Via dei Condotti, 65) have beautiful boutiques in Rome, as do trendy mid-range brands such as Mandarina Duck (Via dei Due Macelli 59). For more artisanal leather goods, try Ibiz (Via dei Chiavari 39) near Campo de' Fiori, La Sella (Via della Cuccagna 16), or have a pair of glamorous, bejewelled Capri-style sandals made to measure at Di Giacomo Sandals (Via Tor di Millina 10/11 off Piazza Navona).

Shelves stacked with leather gloves in a vast array of colours ↑

Designer Fashion

The meccas are Valentino and Fendi, occupying entire palazzi on Piazza di Spagna 35/38 and Largo Goldoni 420, respectively. Queen of cashmere Laura Biagiotti's flagship store is on Via Belsiana 57 near Piazza di Spagna. Via Condotti, Via Frattina and Via Borgognona are lined with other international fashion designer boutiques, all with jaw-dropping window displays.

Famous fashion street Via dei Condotti, with Gucci's flagship store and other major designer boutiques

INSIDER TIP
Shopping Areas

Head to Via del Corso and Via Cola di Rienzo for high-street chains; Via dei Condotti and the pedestrianized streets off Piazza di Spagna for big-name designers; and Monti and Trastevere for vintage, alternative and new designers. COIN (Via Cola di Rienzo) and Rinascente (Via del Tritone) are Rome's main department stores.

Jewellery

Traditional artisan goldsmiths and silversmiths work to order in tiny studios concentrated in the old Jewish Ghetto and around Campo de' Fiori, on Via Giulia and Piazza Monte di Pietà. For classic designer jewellery, visit Rome's oldest jewellery house, Massoni (Via Margutta 54A). For costume jewellery head to Granuzzo on Via dei Coronari 193 or Nicotra di San Giacomo on Via del Governo Vecchio 128.

Window display of fine jewellery at a shop in the centre of Rome

Antiques and Memorabilia

The cream of antiques shops are concentrated in Via dei Coronari, the historic centre of the antiques trade, and Via Margutta and Via del Babuino, known for their fine art galleries. Via Giulia also has high-end antiques shops, while the parallel Via Monserrato and nearby Via dei Banchi Vecchi are worth scouring for more affordable pieces.

↑ Comics Bazaar, crammed full of antiques, at Via dei Banchi Vecchi 127

Foro Italico

Visit the Stadio dei Marmi, the stadium of the Fascist-era Foro Italico, built by Mussolini in the vain hope of securing the 1944 Olympic Games. Equally chilling and kitsch, the stadium is surrounded by 60 colosssal, idealized statues of athletes *(see p324)*.

Stadio dei Marmi, part of the Fascist-era Foro Italico ↑

ROME OFF THE
BEATEN TRACK

There are a host of lesser known sights and neighbourhoods all over Rome that will allow you to experience the city like a local. Get away from the crowds and discover a different, more unusual side of Rome.

EUR

Built by Mussolini in the 1930s as a showcase to the world of the ideal Fascist metropolis, EUR is not merely one of the most Futuristic places of 20th-century Europe, but is also home to the superb Museo della Civiltà Romana (with a vast plaster model of ancient Rome and a Planetarium – *p323*) and an Olympic-sized open-air swimming pool *(p324)*. The stark Palazzo della Civiltà del Lavoro ("Square Colosseum") now houses the headquarters of Fendi.

←

Palazzo della Civiltà del Lavoro, EUR, an icon of Fascist architecture

Gardens on the Aventine Hill

Escape the crowds in the small picturesque gardens on the Aventine Hill, such as the Rose Garden (Roseto Comunale di Roma) and Parco Savello (also known as Giardino degli Aranci), with its orange trees and beautiful views of St Peter's.

→ St Peter's seen from Parco Savello on the Aventine Hill

EAT

Italy's links with its former colony, Eritrea, have led to Rome long having a handful of Ethiopian restaurants.

Enqutatash
Wonderfully seasoned dishes are served with spiced wine.

🏠 Viale della Stazione Prenestina 55
📞 06-273767

$$$

Mesob
Feast on spicy vegetable and pulse dishes with flatbread.

🏠 Via Prenestina 118
🌐 mesob.it

$$$

↓ Unusual, elaborate architecture in the Quartiere Coppedè

💬 INSIDER TIP
CRAFT BEER

World-famous for wine, Italy also produces superb craft beer. Beer aficionados should seek out Open Baladin (Via degli Specchi 6) in the Campo de' Fiori area, which has over 40 craft and 200 bottled beers or Birra Più (Via del Pigneto 105), a bar and shop stocked with craft and vintage Italian beers.

Quartiere Coppedè

To see part of Rome that few people imagine, head to the little cluster of upscale streets between Piazza Buenos Aires and Via Tagliamento, and discover a perfectly preserved quarter of fantastic villas and fairytale palaces created by architect Gino Coppedè in the early 20th century, influenced by Art Nouveau, medieval and Baroque styles *(p317)*.

DISCOUNTED TRAVEL AND PASSES

Organize your time to make the most of public transport passes, which are available for one day, three days and seven days *(p333)*. The **Roma Pass** *(p337)* includes unlimited public transport, entry to two museums of choice and discounted entry to many others. A seven-day ticket, the **Roma Archaeologica Card** includes entry to the Forum, Colosseum, Palatine, Baths of Caracalla, monuments along the Via Appia Antica and all sites of the museums of the Museo Nazionale Romano. It does not include public transport, however.

↓ St Peter's dome and Rome's rooftops seen from above

ROME ON A
SHOESTRING

Rome can be expensive, but its historic centre is compact, meaning that it can mostly be seen on foot. Ancient sites, wonderful piazzas, palace façades and beautiful parks can be enjoyed without spending any money, while the city's churches, which are free to enter, are a treasure trove of art and architecture.

Food and Drink

Rome is full of marvellous delicatessens, bakeries and take-away pizzerias where you can get fabulous food for a fraction of the prices charged in cafés and restaurants. Piazzas, as well as parks, make good locations for picnics. Look out for bars advertising *aperitivo* or "happy hours", where you pay a set price for a drink and can help yourself from an ample buffet. To save money at other times, order and drink at the bar rather than paying extra for table service.

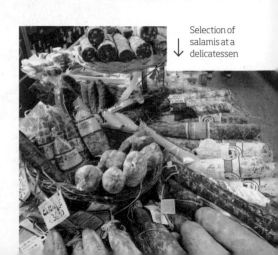

↓ Selection of salamis at a delicatessen

Sights and Views

The Pantheon is the only one of Rome's ancient monuments to which entry is free, thanks to having been converted into a church in the Byzantine era. Many visitors find the Colosseum more impressive from without than within. Entry to the Victor Emmanuel Monument– with some of the best views in Rome – is free, as long as you are prepared to walk to the top instead of taking the lift. There are other great city views from the Pincio Gardens and Janiculum Hill. There is no charge to get close to Trajan's Column – use the zoom on your phone or camera to see details of the marble frieze up close. Access to St Peter's is free, allowing you to see famous works such Michelangelo's *Pietà*, and Bernini's Baldacchino.

INSIDER TIP
Free Entry to Museums

State and city museums are free for EU citizens under 18 and over 65. State museums (including the Vatican) are free for all on the last Sunday of every month.

↑ Mosaics of a blue-and-gold-walled heaven in the apse of Santa Prassede

Art

See Michelangelo's muscle-bound *Moses* matsterpiece for free at San Pietro in Vincoli. Marvel at magnificent Byzantine mosaics in Santa Prassede. Entering the church's tiny Cappella San Zeno is akin to walking into a jewel box. Although entry is charged for exhibitions at MAXXI and MACRO, there are usually free video presentations, and large parts of the buildings, such as MACRO Peroni's roof terrace, can be entered for no charge.

↑ MACRO contemporary art gallery, converted from a former Peroni beer factory

▽ Campo de' Fiori
T4 **7am-1:30pm Mon-Sat**
This market has been held in Campo de' Fiori for centuries. The piazza is transformed by stalls selling fruit and vegetables, meat, poultry and fish, all beautifully displayed. The piazza's excellent delicatessens and bakery complement the market, making it a great place to pick up supplies for a picnic.

ROME'S
MARKETS

Soak up the vibrant atmosphere of Rome's numerous markets, ranging from those on small neighbourhood piazzas designed to serve local residents to the large, famous Testaccio and Porta Portese markets.

△ Porta Portese
F8 **Piazza di Porta Portese** **7am-2pm Sun**
Said to have grown out of the thriving black market of World War II, Porta Portese is where anything and everything seems to be for sale, from vintage and new clothes, shoes, prints and books to chandeliers, household linens and other housewares.

NEIGHBOURHOOD MARKETS

Piazza delle Coppelle
U2 **7am-2pm Mon-Sat**
With its fruit and flower stalls, Piazza delle Coppelle, near the Pantheon, is probably the most delightful of the small food markets scattered around Rome.

Piazza San Cosimato
F7 **6am-1:30pm Mon-Sat**
In the heart of Trastevere, this market has abundant fruit and vegetables and excellent cheeses, hams and salamis.

▽ Circo Massimo Farmer's Market

📍H7 🏛Via di San Teodoro 🕐8am-3pm Sat & Sun

A mecca for foodies, this market attracts niche producers from all over central Italy. It has artisan cheeses, hams, craft breads and beers and unusual pulses, vegetables and fruits.

△ Mercato delle Stampe

📍U1 🏛Largo della Fontanella di Borghese 🕐7am-1pm Mon-Sat

A treasure-trove for lovers of old prints, books, magazines, comics and other printed ephemera, this market is a fabulous place to seek out a special souvenir of Rome, such as a Piranesi reproduction of your favourite vista, ruin or church.

▷ Nuovo Mercato Esquilino

📍M6 🏛Via Principe Amedeo 🕐7am-2pm Mon-Sat

Housed in purpose-built covered premises, this remains the most authentic of Rome's markets - where locals come for kilos of fruit and vegetables at knock-down prices. It is also the best place in Rome to seek out international ingredients and spices, with African and Asian stalls catering to the area's diverse community.

◁ Mercato di Testaccio

📍G9 🏛Via Lorenzo Ghiberti 🕐7am-3:30pm Mon-Sat

A must for anyone who takes food seriously - as well as stalls there are take-away food stands offering anything from tripe sandwiches to gourmet morsels by top chefs.

A YEAR IN
ROME

JANUARY

La Befana (Ephiphany) (6 Jan)
Children's parties and activities throughout the city mark the day when the Christmas witch brings presents.
△ **Chinese New Year** (late Jan or early Feb)
Traditional Chinese parades, martial arts demonstrations and fireworks take place on Via del Corso and Piazza del Popolo.

FEBRUARY

Equilibrio Festival of Dance (mid–late Feb)
The festival showcases contemporary dance at the Auditorium Parco della Musica.
△ **Six Nations Rugby** (mid-Feb)
Matches take place at the Olympic Stadium.

MAY

International Workers' Day (1 May)
A free concert is organized by Italy's main trade union in Piazza San Giovanni in Laterano.
△ **International Horse Show** (early May)
A four-day horse show is held in Villa Borghese.

JUNE

△ **Lungo Il Tevere** (mid-June–end Aug)
Pop-up stalls, cafés and restaurants line the banks of the Tiber River during this summer festival.

SEPTEMBER

△ **Football Season** (early Sep)
September sees the start of the football season.
RomeEuropa (end Sep–early Dec)
This performing arts festival is held in various venues, including Palazzo Farnese.

OCTOBER

International Film Festival (10 days in Oct)
Rome's star-studded International Film Festival held in Auditorium Parco della Musica reflects the city's enduring love of the big screen.
△ **Festival di Musica e Arte Sacra** (Oct/Nov)
Concerts of sacred music are held in various churches throughout Rome during the Festival of Sacred Music and Art, unique in the world.

MARCH

△ **Rome Marathon** (third or fourth Sun)
The annual Rome marathon takes place through the city.

Giornate FAI di Primavera (last weekend)
Throughout Rome many Italian National Trust buildings that are usually off limits can be visited by the public during this Cultural Weekend.

APRIL

△ **Easter Sunday**
The pope holds a Mass and blessing at St Peter's.

Settimana della Cultura (second or third week)
Week of Culture gives free entry to most museums, galleries and archaeological sites for one week.

JULY

△ **Festa de' Noantri** (last two weeks)
Processions and fireworks in Trastevere celebrate the Madonna of Mount Carmel.

Alta Roma Fashion Show (mid–late July)
A fashion show is held on the Spanish Steps.

Estate Romana (Jul/Aug)
This festival of music, theatre and dance includes open-air opera at the Baths of Caracalla

AUGUST

Festa della Madonna della Neve (5 Aug)
A sound-and-light show in front of Santa Maria Maggiore ends in a "snow-storm" of white petals.

Night of San Lorenzo (10 Aug)
Romans flock to the Pincio Gardens to watch the night sky and catch sight of meteor showers.

△ **Ferragosto** (15 Aug)
This national holiday sees free open-air concerts.

NOVEMBER

△ **All Saints' Day** (1 Nov)
Held throughout Italy, this public holiday collectively celebrates all of the Catholic saints. Families get together and many people attend Mass.

RomaEuropa (throughout Nov)
This dance, music and video festival takes place at Teatro Olimpico and Auditorium Parco della Musica.

DECEMBER

△ **Christmas Market** (mid-Dec–6 Jan)
Piazza Navona hosts a daily Christmas market from 10am until 1am.

Christmas Day (25 Dec)
The pope gives a blessing on Piazza San Pietro.

La Festa di Roma (31 Dec)
Fireworks and free concerts take place throughout the city to celebrate New Year's Eve.

A BRIEF
HISTORY

Retaining layers of buildings spanning over two millennia, Rome has been continuously inhabited since it was founded. As the headquarters of the Roman Empire and then of the Catholic Church, the city has played a leading role in history, not just of Europe, but the entire world.

The Beginning

Rome began as an Iron-Age village in the mid-8th century BC, founded according to legend by twin brothers, Romulus and Remus. In 616 BC the Etruscans seized power and dominated the Italian peninsula. In 509 BC the Roman people rebelled and founded a Republic. Over the centuries Rome fought its way south into North Africa; by 146 BC it was the biggest power in the world.

Julius Caesar emerged as a formidable military leader, and, in 44 BC, was declared "dictator of Rome for life". Appalled to see power in the hands of a single individual, a group of Republicans led by Brutus and Cassius assassinated Caesar that same year.

[1] Painting of the Colosseum (c 1842) ↑

[2] The She-Wolf, Capitoline Museums

[3] Illustration of Emperor Augustus riding in procession through the streets of Rome

[4] Mosaic of Emperor Constantine I (c 274–337)

Timeline of events

753 BC
Legendary foundation of Rome by brothers Romulus and Remus

616 BC
Etruscans seize power in Rome

44 BC
Julius Caesar is assassinated on 15 March in the Theatre of Pompey

509 BC
Etruscans expelled and Roman Republic founded

27 BC
Augustus becomes Emperor

2

3

4

The Age of Augustus

The murder of Caesar threw Rome into turmoil. Caesar's deputy, Mark Antony, joined forces with Caesar's adopted son, Octavian, and defeated an army led by Brutus and Cassius. Civil war raged on until 27 BC, when Octavian, now known as Augustus, became Rome's first emperor. Augustus ruled for 40 years, transforming Rome from "a city of brick to a city of marble", creating the first Imperial Forum, and filling the Campus Martius (now the *centro storico*) with temples, theatres and monuments.

The Fall of Rome

After years of prosperity the sheer logistics of keeping such a large empire running was taking its toll. By the 3rd century AD, Rome was falling apart and Christianity was on the rise. Emperor Diocletian had hundreds of Christians killed as he attempted to extinguish the religion. But Christianity flourished, and in AD 313 Emperor Constantine became a Christian himself and shifted the capital of the Empire to Byzantium. In AD 455 and 475 Rome was attacked by Goths and Vandals, the city decayed, the population shrank and disease was rife. The glory days seemed over for ever.

↑ Bronze statue of Emperor Julius Caesar over the Temple of Venus Genetrix

AD 313

Emperor Constantine declares Christianity to be the official religion of the Roman Empire

AD 537

Rome's aqueducts destroyed by Goths. Population drops by 90 percent

AD 608

The Pantheon is converted into a Christian church

AD 64

Fire destroys much of Rome - Emperor Nero is blamed

AD 410

Rome attacked by Goths for the first time

The Rise of the Papacy

In the 7th century Pope Gregory the Great turned Rome's fortunes around, sending out missionaries to spread the word of the Church, and drawing hordes of pilgrims to the city. New churches were built, and the pope and his city became the power centre of the Christian world. When Frankish ruler Charlemagne invaded Italy in AD 800 he was crowned the first Holy Roman Emperor in St Peter's. Over the centuries, however, conflicts between the pope and the Holy Roman Emperor weakened the papacy. The 10th–12th centuries were among the bleakest in Roman history: violent invaders left Rome poverty-stricken and the constantly warring local barons tore apart what remained of the city. Despite this, the first Holy Year was declared in 1300 and thousands of pilgrims arrived in Rome; only nine years later though, the papacy was forced to move to Avignon, leaving Rome to slide into further squalor and strife.

The Renaissance

Pope Nicholas V came to the throne in 1447 determined to make Rome a city fit for the papacy. Among his successors, men like Julius II and Leo X eagerly followed his lead, and the

↑ Portrait of Pope Nicholas V (c 1450), who was pope from 1447 to 1455

Timeline of events

AD 800
Charlemagne is crowned Holy Roman Emperor in St Peter's

1300
Pope Boniface VIII declares the first ever Holy Year and pilgrims flock to Rome

1452
Demolition of old St Peter's basilica begins

1506
Work begins on new St Peter's basilica

1508
Michelangelo begins work on Sistine Chapel ceiling

city's appearance was transformed. The Classical ideals of the Renaissance inspired artists and architects, such as Michelangelo, Bramante and Raphael, to build and decorate churches and palaces, influenced by the styles of recently rediscovered ancient Roman buildings, statues and frescoes. In 1527, however, the continuing power struggle between the Holy Roman Empire and the papacy resulted in the Sack of Rome, when the unruly troops of the Holy Roman Emperor Charles V rampaged throughout the city, burning and looting palaces and churches, leaving behind just a fraction of its former splendour.

The Counter-Reformation and the Baroque

In northern Europe, opposition to the fabulously rich (and famously corrupt) papacy was growing, and people began to embrace the Protestant movement. In response, the Catholic Church burned controversial books, tortured radical thinkers and told artists exactly what they were and were not allowed to paint. As the Church regained confidence – although not political power – popes such as Sixtus V, Urban VIII and Innocent X commissioned the extravagant Baroque piazzas, fountains, palaces and churches that define the city of Rome today.

① Constantine on horseback sculpture by Bernini (1670), St Peter's

② Map of Rome in the Middle Ages

③ Miniature of Pope Gregory the Great (7th century)

④ The sack of Rome by Holy Roman Emperor Charles V, May 1527, attributed to Pieter Brueghel the Elder (16th century)

1527
Troops of Holy Roman Emperor Charles V sack Rome, marking the end of the Roman Renaissance

1585
Rome's streets are replanned by Pope Sixtus V

1626
New St Peter's basilica completed on the site of the old basilica commissioned by Emperor Constantine

1568
Jesuits build the Baroque Gesù church

1651
Bernini designs the Fontana dei Quattro Fiumi on Piazza Navona

1

2

A Capital Again

In the mid-18th century the Italian peninsula was still a collection of city-states and principalities and Rome was but a minor player on the world stage. In 1797 Napoleon conquered the city and briefly united Italy, but in 1815 the pre-Napoleonic patchwork of independent governments was restored. In fact, the brief taste of unification was never forgotten. On 20 September 1870 Italian troops, spearheaded by Giuseppe Mazzini, Count Camillo Cavour and Giuseppe Garibaldi, entered the city and Rome was declared capital of the new Italy, under King Vittorio Emanuele II. New streets – Via Nazionale, Via del Tritone and Via Veneto – were cut through the city centre and a vast area was demolished to make room for the Victor Emmanuel Monument.

The Mussolini Years

After World War I, disillusionment, national debt and social unrest culminated in massive support for the ex-Socialist politician Benito Mussolini. In October 1922, Mussolini marched on Rome with his Blackshirts and, within just three years, was running a Fascist dictatorship. Mussolini constructed an imposing new suburb, EUR, south of Rome.

↑ Portrait of Vittorio Emanuele II, the first king of a united Italy

Timeline of events

1797
Napoleon captures Rome

1861
Kingdom of Italy founded with capital in Turin

1870
Royalist troops take Rome, which becomes capital of unified Italy

1922
Fascists march on Rome; Mussolini becomes Prime Minister

1929
Lateran Treaty creates the Vatican State

1940
Italy enters World War II on the side of Germany

In 1940, Italy joined World War II on the side of Nazi Germany. In September 1943, two months after the Allies had landed in Sicily, the king took power away from Mussolini and Italy switched allegiance to the Allies. Rome was bombed by both sides before being liberated by the Allies on 4 June 1944.

Post-War Rome

In the chaos after the war, Rome was riven by divisions between left- and right-wing parties, and by the 1970s terrorism held the country to ransom. After more than 50 changes of government, the 1990s saw the rise of Silvio Berlusconi, who, despite many scandals, became Italy's longest-serving post-war prime minister until he was made to resign on corruption charges in 2012.

Rome Today

Famous for its past, Rome is embracing the future: much of the historic centre is closed to traffic, and radical new buildings, such as MAXXI (p316), have been erected, while digital technology is transforming museums and ancient sights. The national elections in March 2018 resulted in big gains for populists and far-right parties, reflecting a trend in much of the rest of Europe.

1 Church of Santi Pietro e Paolo in the EUR, a suburb designed by Mussolini

2 Liberation of Rome by the Allies in June 1944

3 Statue of Count Camillo Cavour, a leading figure in the movement towards Italian Unification

4 Pope Francis greeting the faithful

1944
Allied Forces liberate Rome

1946
National Referendum establishes Italy as a Republic; King Umberto II exiled

1978
Premier Aldo Moro kidnapped, then killed, by Red Brigades

2004
A new constitution of the European Union is signed in Rome

2013
Pope Francis elected

2016
Virginia Raggi of the populist 5 Star Movement elected first female mayor of Rome

EXPERIENCE

Interior of St Peter's basilica

CAPITOL

The temple of Jupiter on the Capitol, the
southern summit of the Capitoline Hill, was
the centre of the Roman world. Reached by
a zig-zag path up from the Forum, the temple
was the scene of all the most sacred religious
and political ceremonies. The hill and its temple
came to symbolize Rome's authority as *caput
mundi*, head of the world, and the Capitol gave its
name to the seat of the US Congress. Throughout
the city's history, the Capitol (Campidoglio) has
remained the seat of municipal government.
Today's city council, the Comune di Roma, meets
in the Renaissance splendour of Palazzo Senatorio.
The Capitol also serves as Rome's Registry Office.
Rome's position as a modern capital is forcefully
expressed in the enormous Victor Emmanuel
Monument, which unfortunately blots out the
view of the Capitol from Piazza Venezia. The
present arrangement on the hill dates from
the 16th century, when Michelangelo created
a beautiful piazza reached by a flight of steps,
the Cordonata. Two of the buildings around the
piazza now house the Capitoline Museums.

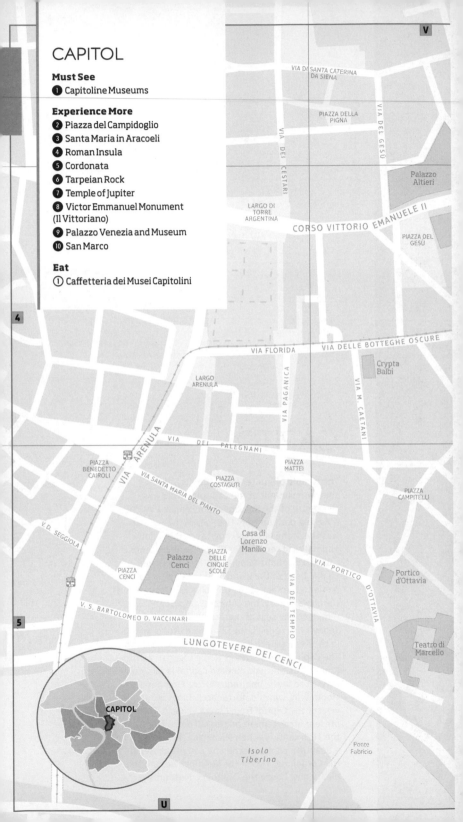

CAPITOL

Must See
❶ Capitoline Museums

Experience More
❷ Piazza del Campidoglio
❸ Santa Maria in Aracoeli
❹ Roman Insula
❺ Cordonata
❻ Tarpeian Rock
❼ Temple of Jupiter
❽ Victor Emmanuel Monument
(Il Vittoriano)
❾ Palazzo Venezia and Museum
❿ San Marco

Eat
① Caffetteria dei Musei Capitolini

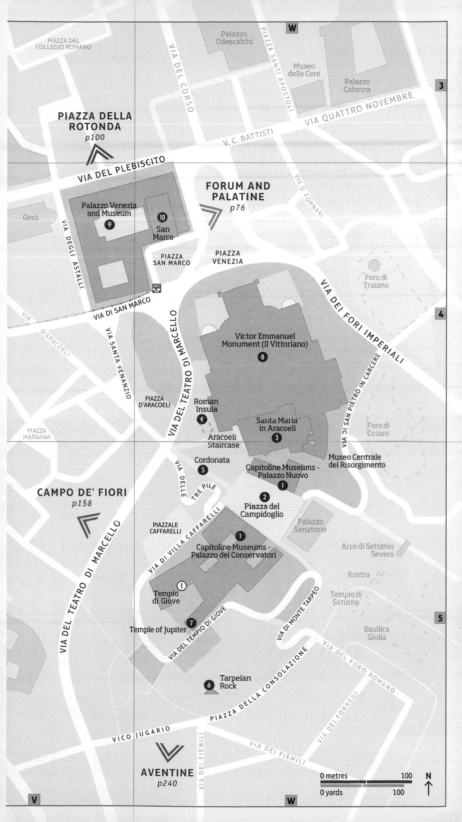

PIAZZA DELLA
ROTONDA
p100

FORUM AND
PALATINE
p76

CAMPO DE' FIORI
p158

AVENTINE
p240

W

3

4

5

V

W

PIAZZA DEL
COLLEGIO ROMANO

VIA DEL CORSO

Palazzo
Odescalchi

PIAZZA SANTI APOSTOLI

Museo
delle Cere

Palazzo
Colonna

VIA QUATTRO NOVEMBRE

V. C. BATTISTI

VIA DEL PLEBISCITO

Gesù

VIA DEGLI ASTALLI

Palazzo Venezia
and Museum
9

10
San
Marco

VIA D. FORNARI

PIAZZA
SAN MARCO

PIAZZA
VENEZIA

VIA DI SAN MARCO

PIAZZA
VENEZIA

VIA DEI FORI IMPERIALI

Foro di
Traiano

VIA
D'ARACOELI

VIA SANTA VENANZIO

VIA DEL TEATRO DI MARCELLO

Victor Emmanuel
Monument (Il Vittoriano)
8

PIAZZA
MARGANA

PIAZZA
D'ARACOELI

Roman
Insula
4

Aracoeli
Staircase

Santa Maria
in Aracoeli
3

Foro di
Cesare

VIA DI SAN PIETRO IN CARCERE

Museo Centrale
del Risorgimento

Cordonata
5

Capitoline Museums -
Palazzo Nuovo
1

VIA DELLE TRE PILE

Piazza del
Campidoglio
2

Palazzo
Senatorio

Arco di Settimio
Severo

PIAZZALE
CAFFARELLI

VIA DI VILLA CAFFARELLI

Capitoline Museums -
Palazzo dei Conservatori
1

Rostra

Tempio di
Saturno

VIA DEL TEATRO DI MARCELLO

Tempio
di Giove
(I)

Temple of Jupiter
7

VIA DEL TEMPIO DI GIOVE

VIA DI MONTE TARPEO

Basilica
Giulia

Tarpeian
Rock
6

PIAZZA DELLA CONSOLAZIONE

VIA DEL FORO ROMANO

VICO JUGARIO

VIA DEI FIENILI

VIA DEI FIENILI

VIA DEI FORAGGI

| 0 metres | | 100 |
| 0 yards | | 100 |

N

1 🚗 🚌 🍴 ☕ 🛍️

CAPITOLINE MUSEUMS

📍 W5 🏛️ Piazza del Campidoglio 1 🚌 63, 70, 75, 81, 87, 160, 170, 204, 628, 716 and other routes to Piazza Venezia 🚊 8 🕐 9:30am-7:30pm daily 🌐 museicapitolini.org

This museum of Classical sculpture is housed in two palaces – Palazzo dei Conservatori and Palazzo Nuovo – either side of Piazza del Campidoglio.

The Capitoline collection began in 1471 when Pope Sixtus IV donated several Classical bronze statues from his personal collection, including the She-Wolf, to the city. The She-Wolf was displayed on the façade of the Palazzo dei Conservatori, and rapidly became the symbol of Rome. Located in two majestic palaces, both with façades designed by Michelangelo, the collection has grown over the centuries to become Rome's finest and most famous assemblage of Classical sculpture. Palazzo dei Conservatori also houses a lovely gallery of Renaissance art. In 1734 Pope Clement XII Corsini decreed that the collection be turned into what is considered to be the world's first public museum.

MUSEUM GUIDE

The main entrance to the two buildings is via Palazzo dei Conservatori. The ground and first floors of this palazzo hold Classical statues, while the second floor is home to a gallery of Renaissance paintings. A tunnel links the Palazzo dei Conservatori with the Palazzo Nuovo, where more Classical sculptures are exhibited on the two main floors.

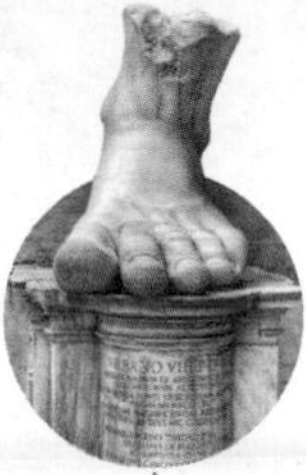

Collection Highlights

c 117–138

▲ Found at Hadrian's Villa in Tivoli, this faun, sculpted in marble the colour of bresaola, is a version of a Greek original. It is an example of Hadrian's fondness for all things Greek.

c 312–315

▲ The foot of a 12 m- (40 ft-) high statue of emperor Constantine I has survived, along with a hand and other body fragments.

c 11th–12th centuries

▲ This bronze portrays the She-Wolf suckling Rome's legendary founders Romulus and Remus. The twins were probably added in the 15th century.

1640s

▲ Bernini's dramatic bust of the mythological Medusa shows her caught in the moment of metamorphosis from human to stone.

↑ Piazza del Campidoglio with the Palazzo Nuovo and a replica of the equestrian statue of Marcus Aurelius

EAT & DRINK

Caffetteria dei Musei Capitolini

The big draw of this café-restaurant on the top floor of the Capitoline Museums is its vast terrace with a panoramic view taking in rooftops and assorted ruins. The vista is especially spectacular at sundown. Opt for superior coffee and cake or an aperitivo and a snack. The café is also open to non-ticket-holders via a separate entrance on Piazzale Caffarelli.

W5 Piazzale Caffarelli 4 museicapitoliniorg/it/oltre_ilmuseo/caffetteria

The frescoed interior ↑
of the Palazzo dei
Conservatori

PALAZZO DEI CONSERVATORI

Dramatically displayed in the centre of a grand glass-roofed gallery at the heart of the palazzo is the gilded bronze equestrian statue of Marcus Aurelius that once stood in Piazza del Campidoglio (where it has been replaced by a replica). Standing at 4 metres (11 feet) high, it is extraordinarily true to life. Among the most significant works in the Palazzo dei Conservatori are the She-Wolf, the ancient Spinario and a wonderfully Baroque snake-haired Medusa by Bernini. The courtyard is home to several marble body parts belonging to a statue of Constantine (p67).

Did You know?

The Marcus Aurelius bronze is much more life-like than other statues of emperors, which were idealized.

PINACOTECA

The Pinacoteca on the second floor holds a small collection of Renaissance art, which includes works by Caravaggio, Tintorotto and Titian. Perhaps the most remarkable is Caravaggio's *Saint John the Baptist*, painted in 1602 for a noble Roman family, the Mattei. The freedom of a private (rather than Church) commission is evident, with John the Baptist represented as a nude adolescent in a posture inspired by the Ignudi of Michelangelo's Sistine Chapel ceiling. The other

↑ Caravaggio's highly
unorthodox painting
of St John the Baptist

Caravaggio shows a gypsy girl reading the palm (and possibly stealing the ring) of a foppish young man. Apparently, spotting the girl on the street, Caravaggio decided to paint her in order to prove the then revolutionary idea that art could be made from life, not simply from copying Classical models.

←
Spinario, a
1st-century AD
bronze of a boy
removing a thorn
from his foot

The Pinacoteca on the second floor holds a small collection of Renaissance art, which includes works by Caravaggio, Tintoretto and Titian.

PALAZZO NUOVO

A tunnel connects the two palazzi. Signs will take you past the gloomy relics of a 2nd-century BC temple dedicated to Veiovis, god of the underworld, to the Tabularium, the ancient city's Public Records Office. Up on the ground floor, don't miss the room just off the courtyard which has a collection of Egyptian statues, including a granite crocodile and two monkeys, found in the streets around Piazza Minerva, where there was once a temple to Egyptian goddess Isis (p111). The main collection is on the first floor. Most of the finest works are Roman copies of Greek masterpieces.

↑ The marble Capitoline Venus dating from around AD 100–150

GREAT VIEW
Tabularium
You can enjoy one of the best views in Rome of the Forum from a window in the ruins of the Tabularium, or ancient Roman Public Records Office, in the basement of the Palazzo Nuovo.

KEY WORKS
Entering the main sculpture galleries of the Palazzo Nuovo is to step into a chandelier-lit world of marble figures. Some are instantly recognizable – the Capitoline Venus emerging from her bath, or the wounded, tousle-haired Dying Gaul – both Roman copies of celebrated Greek works. Others, less famous, are equally compelling. Wander among the statues and see who grabs your attention – a haggard, drunk old Hellenistic woman; a sour-faced Roman matron dressed (or rather undressed) as Venus; Caracalla as a toddler, happily strangling a snake; or the sentimental statue of a little Roman girl playing with a pet dove. Other highlights include the Red Faun, sculpted for Hadrian's Villa in Tivoli (p326); and the Wounded Warrior by 18th-century French sculptor Monnot, in which the twisted torso of a Greek discus-thrower was transformed into a fallen warrior by being tilted on his side and given a shield.

HALLS OF PHILOSPHERS AND EMPERORS
In these two rather intimate, exquisitely decorated halls, the busts of Greek politicians, philosophers, writers and scientists, and Roman emperors, empresses and members of the Imperial family are displayed on elegant marble shelves.

↑ Hall of Emperors and a close-up of a bust

↑ Piazza del Campidoglio, designed in the 16th century by Michelangelo

EXPERIENCE MORE

Piazza del Campidoglio

⊙ W5 🚌 40, 62, 63, 64, 110, 170 🚋 8

When the Holy Roman Emperor Charles V visited Rome in 1536, Pope Paul III Farnese was so embarrassed by the muddy state of the Capitol that he asked Michelangelo to draw up plans for repaving the piazza, and for renovating the façades of the Palazzo dei Conservatori and Palazzo Senatorio.

Michelangelo proposed adding the Palazzo Nuovo to form a piazza in the shape of a trapezium, embellished with Classical sculptures chosen for their relevance to Rome. Building started in 1546 but progressed so slowly that Michelangelo only lived to oversee the double flight of steps at the entrance of Palazzo Senatorio. The piazza was completed in the 17th century, the design remaining largely faithful to

the original. Pilasters two storeys high and balutrades interspersed with statues link the buildings thematically. The piazza faces west towards St Peter's, the Christian equivalent of the Capitol. At its centre stands a replica of a statue of Marcus Aurelius. The original is in the Palazzo dei Conservatori (p66).

3

Santa Maria in Aracoeli

⊙ W4 ⌂ Piazza d'Aracoeli (entrances via Aracoeli Staircase and door behind Palazzo Nuovo) ☎ 06-6976 3839 🚌 40, 62, 63, 64, 110, 170 🚋 8 ⊙ summer: 9am–6:30pm daily; winter: 9am–5:30pm daily

Dating from at least the 6th century, the church of Santa Maria in Aracoeli, or St Mary of the Altar in the Sky, stands on the northern summit of the Capitoline, on the site of the ancient temple to Juno. Its

> **Popular belief has it that all those who climb the steps of Santa Maria in Aracoeli on their knees will win the Italian national lottery.**

22 columns were taken from various ancient buildings; the inscription on the third column to the left tells us that it comes "a cubiculo Augustorum" – from the bedroom of the emperors.

The church of the Roman senators and people, Santa Maria in Aracoeli has been used to celebrate many triumphs over adversity. Its ceiling, with naval motifs, commemorates the Battle of Lepanto (1571), and was built under Pope Gregory XIII Boncompagni, whose family crest, the dragon, can be seen towards the altar end. Many other Roman families and individuals are honoured

SANTO BAMBINO

The 15th-century icon of the Christ child, made from olive wood from Gethsemane, and said to have healing powers, was stolen from Santa Maria in Aracoeli in 1994 and replaced with a replica. People from all over the world still send letters to the statue.

by memorials in the church. To the right of the entrance door, the tombstone of archdeacon Giovanni Crivelli, rather than being set into the floor of the church, stands eternally to attention, partly so that the signature "Donatelli" (by Donatello) can be read at eye-level.

The frescoes in the first chapel on the right, painted by Pinturicchio in the 1480s in the beautifully clear style of the early Renaissance, depict St Bernardino of Siena. On the left wall, the perspective of *The Burial of the Saint* slants to the right, taking into account the position of the viewer just outside the chapel. The church is most famous, however, for an icon with apparently miraculous powers, the Santo Bambino. Its powers are said to include resurrecting the dead, and it is sometimes summoned to the bedsides of the gravely ill. Other than at Christmas when the Christ icon sits in the centre of a crib in the second chapel on the left, it is usually to be found in the sacristy, as is the panel of the *Holy Family* from the workshop of Giulio Romano.

The famed Aracoeli Staircase leading to the church numbers 124 marble steps (122 if you start from the right) and was completed

→

The top of the marble Aracoeli Staircase, with a view across the city

in 1348, some say in thanks for the passing of the Black Death, but probably in view of the Holy Year of 1350.

The 14th-century tribune-turned-tyrant Cola di Rienzo used to harangue the masses from the Aracoeli Staircase; in the 17th century foreigners used to sleep on the steps, until Prince Caffarelli, who lived on the hill, scared them off by rolling barrels filled with stones down them.

Popular belief has it that all those who climb the steps of Santa Maria in Aracoeli on their knees will win the Italian national lottery. From the top there is a good view of Rome, with the domes of Sant'Andrea della Valle and St Peter's slightly to the right.

Roman Insula

📍 W4 🏛 Piazza d'Aracoeli
☎ 06-0608 🚌 40, 62, 63, 64, 110, 170 🚋 8 ⏰ by appt only: call first

Two thousand years ago the urban poor of Rome used to make their homes in *insulae* – apartment blocks. These were often badly maintained by landlords, and expensive to rent in a city where land costs were high. This 2nd-century AD tenement block, of barrel-vault construction, is the only survivor in Rome from that era. The fourth, fifth and part

of the sixth storey remain above current ground level.

In the Middle Ages, a section of these upper storeys was converted into a church; its bell tower and 14th-century Madonna in a niche are visible from the street.

During the Fascist years, the area was cleared, and three lower floors emerged. Some 380 people may have lived in the tenement, in the squalid conditions described by the 1st-century AD satirical writers Martial and Juvenal. The latter mentions that he had to climb 200 steps to reach his garret.

This *insula* may once have had more storeys. The higher you lived, the more dismal the conditions, as the poky spaces of the building's upper levels testify.

Cordonata

📍 W5 🚌 40, 62, 63, 64, 110, 170 🚋 8

From Plazza Venezia, the Capitol is approached by a gently rising, subtly widening ramp – the Cordonata. At the foot is a pair of granite Egyptian lions, and on the left a 19th-century monument to Cola di Rienzo, close to where the dashing 14th-century tyrant was executed. The top of the ramp is guarded by Classical statues of the Dioscuri – Castor and Pollux.

6 Tarpeian Rock

♁ W5 ♦ Via di Monte Caprino and Via del Tempio di Giove 🚌 40, 62, 63, 64, 110, 170 🚋 8

The steep cliff on the southern tip of the Capitoline is called the Tarpeian Rock *(Rupe Tarpea)*, after Tarpeia, the young daughter of Spurius Tarpeius, defender of the Capitol in the 8th-century BC Sabine War.

The Sabines, bent on vengeance for the rape of their women by Romulus and his men, bribed Tarpeia to let them up on to the Capitol. As the Augustan historian Livy records, the Sabines used to wear heavy gold bracelets and jewelled rings on their left hands, and Tarpeia's reward for her treachery was to be given "what they wore on their shield-arms".

The Sabines kept to the letter of the bargain if not to its spirit – they repaid Tarpeia not with their jewellery but by crushing her to death between their shields. Tarpeia was possibly the only casualty of her act of treachery – as the invading warriors met the Roman defenders, the Sabine women leapt between the two opposing armies, forcing a reconciliation. The site was subsequently used as a place of execution: traitors and other condemned criminals were thrown over the sheer face of the rock.

---

7 Temple of Jupiter

♁ W5 ♦ Via del Tempio di Giove 🚌 40, 62, 63, 64, 110, 170 🕐 9:30am-7:30pm daily

The temple of Jupiter, the most important in ancient Rome, was founded in honour of the arch-god around 509 BC on the southern summit of the Capitoline hill. From the few traces that remain, archaeologists have been able to reconstruct the rectangular, Greek appearance of the temple as it once stood. In places it is possible to see remnants of its particularly Roman feature, the podium. Most of this lies beneath the Museo Nuovo wing of the Palazzo dei Conservatori *(p66)*.

By walking around the site, from the podium's southwestern corner in Via del Tempio di Giove to its southeastern corner in Piazzale Caffarelli, you can see that the temple was about the same size as the Pantheon.

---

8 Victor Emmanuel Monument

♁ W4 ♦ Piazza Venezia 📞 06-678 3587 🚌 40, 62, 63, 64, 110, 170 🚋 8 🕐 Summer: 9:30am-5:30pm daily; winter: 9:30am-4:30pm daily (last adm: 30 mins before closing)

Known as Il Vittoriano, this monument was begun in 1885 and inaugurated in 1911 in honour of Victor Emmanuel II of Savoy, the first king of a unified Italy. The king is depicted here in a gilt bronze equestrian statue, oversized like the monument itself – the statue is 12 m (39 ft) long.

The edifice also contains a museum of the Risorgimento, the events that led to unification *(p58)*. Built in white Brescian marble, the "wedding cake" (just one of its many nicknames) can be seen from almost every part of Rome and will never mellow into the ochre tones of surrounding buildings. It is widely held to be the epitome of self-important, insensitive

The view of Rome from the top of the Victor Emmanuel Monument is spectacular at dusk, especially between late autumn and early spring when it offers an incredible vantage point for watching the murmurations of millions of starlings.

↑ *The Immaculate Conception* by Pier Francesco Mola (1612-66) in the San Marco basilica

architecture, though the views it offers are spectacular. A glass lift at the back of the building takes visitors to the very top.

Palazzo Venezia and Museum

📍V4 🏠Via del Plebiscito 118 📞06-6999 4388 🚌40, 62, 63, 64, 110, 170 🚊8 🕐8:30am-7:30pm Tue-Sun (last adm: 1 hr before closing) 🚫1 Jan, 1 May, 25 Dec

The arched windows and doors of this Renaissance civic building are so harmonious that the façade was once attributed to the great Humanist architect Leon Battista Alberti (1404–72). It was more probably built by Giuliano da Maiano, who is known to have carved the fine doorway on to the piazza.

Palazzo Venezia was built in 1455–64 for the Venetian cardinal Pietro Barbo, who later became Pope Paul II. It was at times a papal residence, but it also served as the Venetian Embassy to Rome before passing into French hands in 1797. Since 1916 it has belonged to the

The huge, white marble Victor Emmanuel Monument in Rome's Piazza Venezia

state; in the Fascist era, Mussolini used Palazzo Venezia as his headquarters and addressed crowds from the central balcony.

The interior is best seen by visiting the Museo del Palazzo Venezia, Rome's most under-rated museum. It holds first-class collections of early Renaissance painting; painted wood sculptures and Renaissance chests from Italy; tapestries from all over Europe; majolica; silver; Neapolitan ceramic figurines; Renaissance bronzes; arms and armour; Baroque terracotta sculptures by Bernini, Algardi and others; and 17th- and 18th-century Italian painting. There is a marble screen from the Aracoeli convent, destroyed to make way for the Victor Emmanuel Monument, and a bust of Paul II, showing him to rank with Martin V and Leo X among the fattest-ever popes. The building also hosts major temporary exhibitions.

San Marco

📍W4 🏠Piazza San Marco 48 📞06-679 5205 🚌40, 62, 63, 64, 110, 170 🚊8 🕐10am-1pm & 4-6pm Tue-Sun (Sat & Sun: to 8pm)

The basilica of San Marco was founded in 336 by Pope Mark, in honour of St Mark the Evangelist. The Pope's relics lie under the altar. The church was restored by Pope Gregory IV in the 9th century.

Further major rebuilding took place in 1455–71, when Pope Paul II Barbo made San Marco the church of the Venetian community in Rome. The blue and gold coffered ceiling is decorated with Pope Paul's heraldic crest, the lion rampant, recalling the lion of St Mark. The appearance of the rest of the interior, with its colonnades of Sicilian jasper, was largely the creation of Filippo Barigioni in the 1740s.

A SHORT WALK
THE CAPITOL AND PIAZZA VENEZIA

Distance 1 km (0.6 mile) **Nearest bus** 40, 62, 63, 64, 110, 170 **Time** 20 minutes

The absence of cars on the Capitol makes the hill a welcome retreat for a short stroll. Climb up the broad flight of steps (the Cordonata) to Michelangelo's spectacular Piazza del Campidoglio. This is flanked by the Palazzo Nuovo and Palazzo dei Conservatori, housing the Capitoline Museums with their fine collections of sculptures and paintings. It's worth braving the traffic on the piazza to visit Palazzo Venezia and its museum.

The huge white marble Victor Emmanuel monument to Italy's first king was completed in 1911.

PIAZZA VENEZIA

PIAZZA VENEZIA

PIAZZA VENEZIA

START

San Marco, the church for Venetian ex-patriates in Rome, has a fine 9th-century apse mosaic (p73).

The Palazzo Venezia museum's finest exhibits date from the late Middle Ages (p73).

VIA DEL TE

0 metres 100 N
0 yards 100

The Roman Insula is a ruined apartment block dating from Imperial Rome (p71).

← *The Aracoeli staircase leading to Santa Maria in Aracoeli*

The treasures hidden behind the church of Santa Maria Aracoeli's brick façade include a 15th-century fresco of the Funeral of St Bernardino by Pinturicchio (p70).

The Palazzo Nuovo, part of the Capitoline Museums, houses many fine Classical sculptures (p69).

Palazzo Senatorio was used by the Roman Senate from about the 12th century. It now houses the offices of the mayor.

Michelangelo designed both the geometric paving and the façades of the buildings on Piazza del Campidoglio (p70).

When it was built in 1348, the Aracoeli staircase became a centre for political debate (p71).

Palazzo dei Conservatori, part of the Capitoline Museums, displays a fine series of reliefs from the Temple of Hadrian in the courtyard (p66).

Michelangelo's great Cordonata staircase changed the orientation of the Capitol towards the west (p71).

Ruins of the Temple of Jupiter, the most important temple in ancient Rome (p72)

In ancient Rome traitors were thrown to their death from the Tarpeian Rock on the Capitol (p72).

VIA DI SAN PIETRO IN CARCERE

FINISH

MARCELLO

VIA DEL TEMPIO DI GIOVE

CAPITOL

Locator Map
For more detail see pp64–5

FORUM AND PALATINE

Although the relics of ancient Rome are strewn throughout the city, the most concentrated and fully excavated cluster lie on the flat, once marshy area between the Capitoline, Esquiline and Palatine hills, home to the original Roman Forum, the Colosseum and the Imperial Fora. The Roman Forum was the official heart of the ancient city, the centre of political, commercial and judicial life, and according to the playwright Plautus, teemed with "lawyers and litigants, bankers and brokers, shopkeepers and strumpets, good-for-nothings waiting for a tip from the rich". Nearby, the Colosseum was the centre of entertainment. As Rome's population boomed, the original Forum became too small, and in 46 BC Julius Caesar built a new one, setting a precedent followed by emperors from Augustus to Trajan. Looking down on all this, the Palatine Hill was the most desirable residential area in Rome, home to some of the city's most famous inhabitants. The great orator Cicero had a house here, as did the lyric poet Catullus. Augustus was born on the hill and continued to live here in very modest circumstances even when he became emperor.

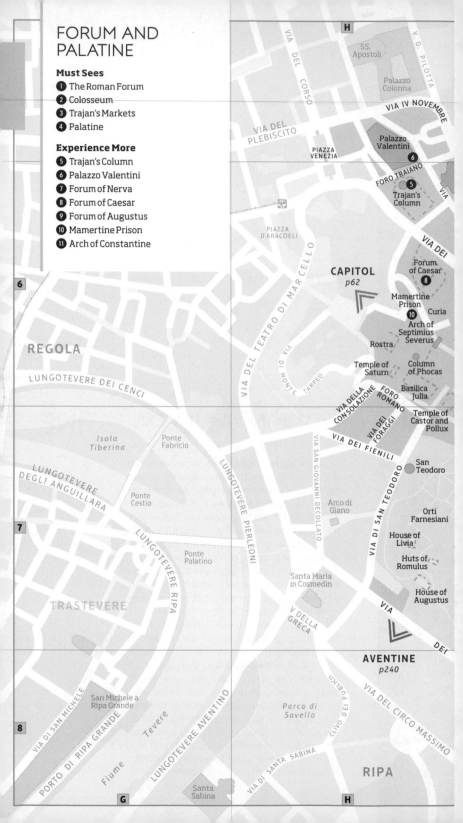

FORUM AND PALATINE

Must Sees
1. The Roman Forum
2. Colosseum
3. Trajan's Markets
4. Palatine

Experience More
5. Trajan's Column
6. Palazzo Valentini
7. Forum of Nerva
8. Forum of Caesar
9. Forum of Augustus
10. Mamertine Prison
11. Arch of Constantine

SS. Apostoli

Palazzo Colonna

VIA DEL CORSO

VIA IV NOVEMBRE

V. D. PILOTTA

VIA DEL PLEBISCITO

PIAZZA VENEZIA

Palazzo Valentini

6

FORO TRAIANO

5

Trajan's Column

VIA DEI

PIAZZA D'ARACOELI

VIA DEL TEATRO DI MARCELLO

CAPITOL
p62

Forum of Caesar

8

Mamertine Prison

10

Curia

Arch of Septimius Severus

Rostra

Temple of Saturn

Column of Phocas

REGOLA

LUNGOTEVERE DEI CENCI

VIA DI MONTE TARPEO

VIA DELLA CONSOLAZIONE

FORO ROMANO

VIA DEI FORAGGI

Basilica Julia

Temple of Castor and Pollux

VIA DEI FIENILI

San Teodoro

Isola Tiberina

Ponte Fabricio

LUNGOTEVERE DEGLI ANGUILLARA

Ponte Cestio

LUNGOTEVERE PIERLEONI

VIA SAN GIOVANNI DECOLLATO

Arco di Giano

VIA DI SAN TEODORO

Orti Farnesiani

House of Livia

Huts of Romulus

Ponte Palatino

LUNGOTEVERE RIPA

TRASTEVERE

Santa Maria in Cosmedin

V. DELLA GRECA

House of Augustus

VIA DEI

AVENTINE
p240

San Michele a Ripa Grande

VIA DI SAN MICHELE

PORTO DI RIPA GRANDE

Fiume Tevere

LUNGOTEVERE AVENTINO

Parco di Savello

CLIVO DEI PUBLICII

VIA DEL CIRCO MASSIMO

VIA DI SANTA SABINA

Santa Sabina

RIPA

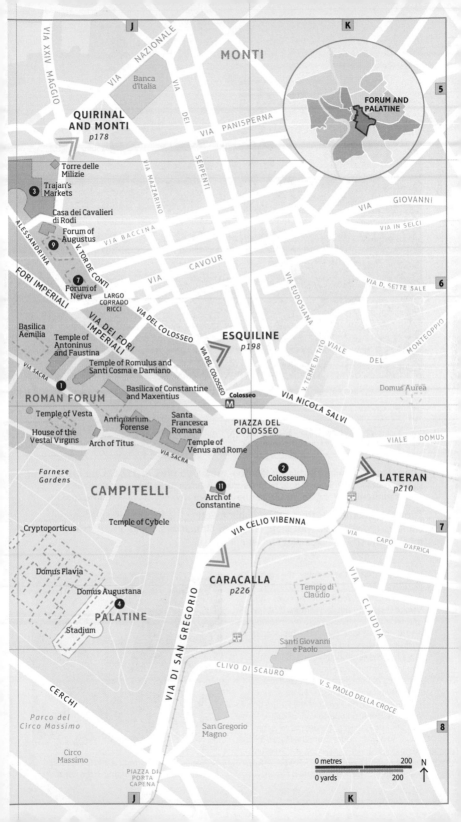

VIA XXIV

MAGGIO

VIA NAZIONALE

VIA DEI

VIA MAZZARINO

VIA SERPENTI

MONTI

VIA PANISPERNA

FORUM AND
PALATINE

Banca
d'Italia

QUIRINAL
AND MONTI
p178

◆ Torre delle
Milizie

③ Trajan's
Markets

Casa dei Cavalieri
di Rodi

⑨ Forum of
Augustus

V. TOR DE CONTI

VIA BACCINA

VIA CAVOUR

VIA GIOVANNI

VIA IN SELCI

ALESSANDRINA

FORI IMPERIALI

⑦ Forum of
Nerva

LARGO
CORRADO
RICCI

VIA DEI FORI IMPERIALI

VIA DEL COLOSSEO

ESQUILINE
p198

VIA EUDOSIANA

VIA D. SETTE SALE

VIALE

DEL

MONTEOPPIO

Basilica
Aemilia

Temple of
Antoninus
and Faustina

Temple of Romulus and
Santi Cosma e Damiano

Basilica of Constantine
and Maxentius

VIA SACRA

① ROMAN FORUM

VIA DEL COLOSSEO

Colosseo
Ⓜ

V. TERME DI TITO VIALE

Domus Aurea

VIA NICOLA SALVI

Temple of Vesta

Antiquarium
Forense

House of the
Vestal Virgins

Arch of Titus

VIA SACRA

Santa
Francesca
Romana

Temple of
Venus and Rome

PIAZZA DEL
COLOSSEO

VIALE DOMUS

Farnese
Gardens

CAMPITELLI

Temple of Cybele

⑪ Arch of
Constantine

② Colosseum

LATERAN
p210

Cryptoporticus

VIA CELIO VIBENNA

VIA CAPO D'AFRICA

VIA CLAUDIA

Domus Flavia

Domus Augustana

④ PALATINE

Stadium

VIA DI SAN GREGORIO

CARACALLA
p226

Tempio di
Claudio

Santi Giovanni
e Paolo

CLIVO DI SCAURO

V. S. PAOLO DELLA CROCE

CERCHI

Parco del
Circo Massimo

San Gregorio
Magno

Circo
Massimo

PIAZZA DI
PORTA
CAPENA

0 metres   200
0 yards   200

N ↑

1 ✏️ Ⓜ️ 🛍️

THE ROMAN FORUM

📍J6 🏛️Via della Salara Vecchia 5/6 📞Tel 06-39 96 7700 🚌85, 87, 117, 175, 186, 810
🚊3 Ⓜ️Colosseo ⏰8:30am–1 hour before sunset. Admission includes entry to the
Colosseum and the Palatine. Tickets can be bought in advance at www.coopculture.it

The Roman Forum was the scene of public meetings, law courts and gladiatorial combats and was lined with shops and open-air markets. It was also the site of many of the city's key temples and monuments.

In the early days of the Republic, the Forum was like a large piazza – a hive of social activity – containing shops, food stalls, temples and the Senate House. By the 2nd century BC it was decided that Rome required a more salubrious centre, and the food stalls were replaced by business centres and law courts. The Forum remained the ceremonial centre of the city under the Empire. Emperors repeatedly renovated old buildings and erected new temples and monuments.

To appreciate the layout of the Forum before visiting its confusing patchwork of ruined temples and basilicas, it is best to view the whole area from above, from the Piazza di Campidoglio (p63). Excavation of the Forum continues, and the ruins uncovered date from many different periods of Roman history.

↑ Basilica of Constantine and Maxentius, once the largest building in the Forum

INSIDER TIPS
Tips for Visiting

The quietest times to visit the Roman Forum are early morning or late afternoon. Holders of a Roma Pass *(p337)* enter the Forum via a special, faster queue. Hire an audio guide (€5), which can be purchased with your ticket, or check out the various apps online. For a quieter experience, the Palatine *(p94)* is invariably much less crowded.

←

Temple of Saturn (right) and the Temple of Castor and Pollux (left)

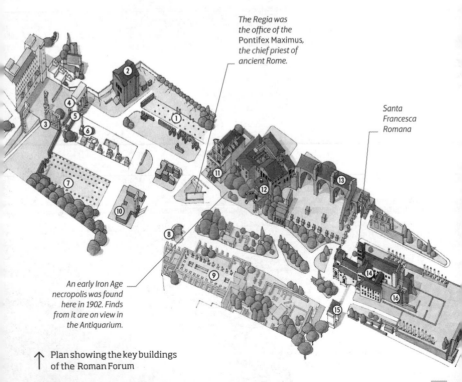

The Regia was the office of the Pontifex Maximus, the chief priest of ancient Rome.

Santa Francesca Romana

An early Iron Age necropolis was found here in 1902. Finds from it are on view in the Antiquarium.

↑ Plan showing the key buildings of the Roman Forum

Basilica Aemilia

This building was once a rectangular colonnaded hall, with a multicoloured marble floor and a bronze-tiled roof. It was built by the consuls Marcus Aemilius Lepidus and Marcus Fulvius Nobilor in 179 BC. The two consuls, who were elected annually, exercised supreme power over the Republic.

Basilicas in ancient Rome served no religious purpose; they were meeting halls for politicians, moneylenders and *publicani* (businessmen contracted by the state to collect taxes). A consortium agreed to hand over a specified sum to the state, but its members were allowed to collect as much as they could and keep the difference. This is why tax-collectors in the Bible were so loathed.

The basilica was rebuilt many times; it was finally burned down when the Visigoths sacked Rome in AD 410.

Curia

A modern restoration now stands over the ruins of the hall where Rome's Senate (chief council of state) used to meet. The first Curia stood on the site now occupied by the church of Santi Luca e Martina, but after the building was destroyed by fire in 52 BC, Julius Caesar built a new Curia at the edge of the Forum. This was restored by Domitian in AD 94 and, after another fire, rebuilt by Diocletian in the 3rd century. The current building is a 1937 restoration of Diocletian's Curia. Inside are two relief panels commissioned by Trajan to decorate the Rostra.

→

The Curia, or the Court of Rome, rebuilt by Diocletian in the 3rd century

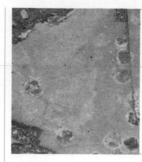

MELTED COINS

Business seems to have carried on until the last minute at the Basilica Aemilia. You can still spot Roman coins melted into its pavement from the 5th century AD when the Visigoths invaded and set it on fire.

Rostra

Speeches were delivered from this dais, the most famous (thanks to Shakespeare) being Mark Antony's "Friends, Romans, Countrymen" oration after the assassination of Julius Caesar in 44 BC. Caesar himself had just reorganized the Forum and this speech was made from the newly sited Rostra, where the ruins now stand. In the following year the head and hands of Cicero were put on show here after he was put to death by the second Triumvirate (Augustus, Mark Antony and Marcus Lepidus). Fulvia, Mark Antony's wife, stabbed the great orator's tongue with a hairpin.

The dais took its name from the ships' prows *(rostra)* with which it was decorated. Sheathed in iron (for ramming enemy vessels), these came from ships captured at the Battle of Antium in 338 BC.

 (4)

Arch of Septimius Severus

This triumphal arch was built in AD 203 to celebrate the tenth anniversary of the accession of Septimius Severus. The relief panels – largely eroded – celebrate the emperor's victories in Parthia (modern-day Iraq and Iran) and Arabia. Originally, the inscription along the top of the arch was to Septimius and his two sons, Caracalla and Geta, but after Septimius died Caracalla murdered Geta, and had his brother's name removed. Even so, the holes into which the letters of his name were pegged are still visible.

 (5)

Temple of Saturn

The most prominent of the ruins in the fenced-off area between the Forum and the Capitoline Hill is the Temple of Saturn. It consists of a high platform, eight columns and a section of entablature. There was a temple dedicated to Saturn here as early as 497 BC, but it had to be rebuilt many times and the current remains date only from 42 BC.

Saturn was the mythical god-king of Italy, said to have presided over a prosperous and peaceful Golden Age from which slavery, private property, crime and war were absent. As such, he appealed particularly to the lower and slave classes. Every year, between 17 December and 23 December, Saturn's reign was remembered in a week of sacrifices and feasting, known as the Saturnalia. As long as the revels lasted, the normal social order was turned upside down. Slaves were permitted to drink and dine with (and sometimes even be served by) their masters. Senators and other high-ranking Romans would abandon the aristocratic togas that they usually wore to distinguish themselves from the lower classes and wear more democratic, loose-fitting gowns. During the holidays, all the courts of law and schools in the city were closed. No prisoner could be punished, and no war could be declared. People also celebrated the Saturnalia

↑ The Arch of Septimius Severus, one of the best-preserved ruins

in their own homes: they exchanged gifts and played light-hearted gambling games, the stakes usually being nuts, a symbol of fruit-fulness. Much of the spirit and many of the rituals of the Saturnalia have been preserved in the Christian celebration of Christmas.

 (6)

Column of Phocas

This column is one of the few to have remained upright since the day it was put up. It is the youngest of the Forum's monuments, erected in AD 608 in honour of the Byzantine emperor, Phocas, who had just paid a visit to Rome. The column may have been placed here as a mark of gratitude to Phocas for giving the Pantheon to the pope (pp104–5).

> **Much of the spirit and many of the rituals of the Saturnalia have been preserved in the Christian celebration of Christmas.**

⑦
Basilica Julia

This immense basilica was begun by Julius Caesar in 54 BC and completed after his death by his great-nephew Augustus. It was damaged by fire almost immediately afterwards in 9 BC, but was subsequently repaired. After numerous sackings only the steps, pavement and column stumps remain. The basilica had a central hall, surrounded by a double portico. The hall was on three floors, while the outer portico had only two.

The Basilica Julia was the seat of the *centumviri*, a body of 180 magistrates who tried civil law cases. They were split into four chambers of 45 men, and unless a case was very complicated they would all sit separately. The four courts were divided only by screens or curtains. Lawyers hired crowds of spectators, who applauded every time the lawyer who was paying them made a point and jeered at his opponents. Scratched into the steps are chequerboards where the clappers and booers played dice and other gambling games to while away the time between cases.

⑧
Temple of Vesta

The Forum's most elegant temple, a circular building originally surrounded by a ring of 20 fine fluted columns, dates from the 4th century AD, though there had been a temple on the site for far longer. It was partially reconstructed in 1930.

⑨
House of the Vestal Virgins

As soon as a girl became a Vestal she came to live in the House of the Vestal Virgins. This was once an enormous complex with about 50 rooms on three storeys. The only remains today are some of the rooms around the central courtyard. This space is perhaps the most evocative part of the Forum. Overlooking ponds of water lilies and goldfish is a row of eroded, and mostly headless, statues of senior Vestals, dating from the 3rd and 4th centuries AD. The better-preserved examples are in the Palazzo Massimo alle Terme *(p186)*.

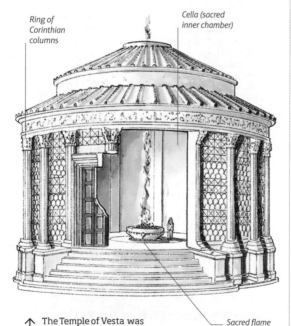

Ring of Corinthian columns

Cella (sacred inner chamber)

Sacred flame

↑ The Temple of Vesta was circular in shape and had 20 Corinthian columns

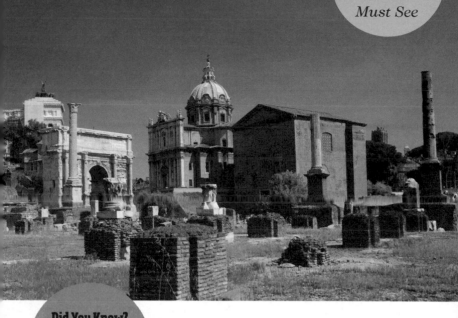

 ⑩

Temple of Castor and Pollux

The three slender fluted columns of this temple form one of the Forum's most beautiful ruins. The first temple here was probably dedicated in 484 BC in honour of the mythical twins and patrons of horsemanship, Castor and Pollux. During the battle of Lake Regillus (499 BC) against the ousted Tarquin kings, the Roman dictator Postumius promised to build a temple to the twins if the Romans were victorious. Some said the twins appeared on the battlefield, helped the Romans to victory and then materialized in the Forum – the temple marks the spot – to announce the news. The three surviving columns date from the last occasion on which the temple was rebuilt – by the Emperor Tiberius after a fire in AD 6.

 ⑪

Temple of Antoninus and Faustina

One of the Forum's oddest sights is the Baroque façade of the church of San Lorenzo in Miranda rising above the porch of a Roman temple. First dedicated in AD 141 by Emperor Antoninus Pius to his late wife Faustina, the temple was rededicated to them both on the death of the emperor. In the 11th century it was converted into a church because it was believed that San Lorenzo had been condemned to death there. The current church dates from 1601.

↑ Remains of the Basilica Julia, a Roman court of civil law

THE VESTAL VIRGINS

The cult of Vesta, the goddess of fire, dates back to at least the 8th century BC. Six virgins kept the sacred flame of Vesta burning in her circular temple. The girls, who came from noble families, were selected when they were between 6 and 10 years old, and served for 30 years. They had high status and financial security, but were buried alive if they lost their virginity and whipped by the high priest if the sacred flame died out. Although they were permitted to marry after finishing their service, few did so.

Temple of Romulus and Santi Cosma e Damiano

No one is exactly sure to whom the Temple of Romulus was dedicated, but it was probably to the son of Emperor Maxentius, and not to Rome's founder.

The temple is a circular brick building, topped by a cupola, with two rectangular side rooms and a concave porch. The heavy, dull bronze doors are original.

Since the 6th century the temple has acted as a vestibule to the church of Santi Cosma e Damiano, which itself occupies an ancient building – a hall in Vespasian's Forum of Peace. The entrance to the church is on Via dei Fori Imperiali. The beautiful carved figures of its 18th-century Neapolitan *presepio* (crib or Nativity scene) are on view, and the church has a vivid Byzantine apse mosaic with Christ pictured against orange clouds.

Basilica of Constantine and Maxentius

The basilica's three vast, coffered barrel vaults are powerful relics of what was the largest building in the Forum. Work began in AD 308 under Emperor Maxentius. When he was deposed by Constantine after the Battle of the Milvian Bridge in AD 312, work on the massive project continued under the new regime. The building, which, like other Roman basilicas, was used for the administration of justice and for carrying on business, is often referred to simply as the Basilica of Constantine. The area covered by the basilica was roughly 100 m by 65 m (330 ft by 215 ft). It was originally designed to have a long nave and aisles running from east to west, but Constantine switched the axis around to create three short broad aisles with the main entrance in the centre of the long south wall. The height of the bulding was 35 m (115 ft). In the apse at the western end, where it could be seen

Did You Know?

It was not until the 18th century that excavations of the Roman Forum began, revealing what can be seen today.

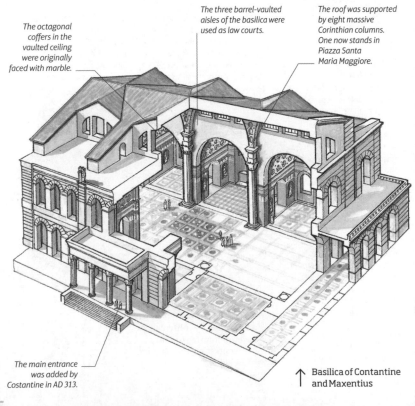

The octagonal coffers in the vaulted ceiling were originally faced with marble.

The three barrel-vaulted aisles of the basilica were used as law courts.

The roof was supported by eight massive Corinthian columns. One now stands in Piazza Santa Maria Maggiore.

The main entrance was added by Costantine in AD 313.

↑ Basilica of Contantine and Maxentius

from all over the building, stood a 12 m- (39 ft-) statue of the emperor, made partly of wood and partly of marble. The giant head, hand and foot are on display in the courtyard of the Palazzo dei Conservatori (see p67). The roof of the basilica glittered with gilded tiles until the 7th century when they were stripped off to cover the roof of the old St Peter's.

Antiquarium Forense

The former convent of Santa Francesca Romana is now occupied by the offices in charge of the excavations of the Forum and a small museum. The museum contains Iron Age burial urns, graves and their skeletal occupants along with some ancient bric-a-brac exhumed from the Forum's drains. There are also fragments of statues, capitals, friezes and other architectural decoration taken from the Forum's buildings.

Arch of Titus

This triumphal arch was erected in AD 81 by the Emperor Domitian in honour of the victories of his brother Titus and his father Vespasian

↑ Detail of a relief from the Basilica Aemilia in the Antiquarium Forense

↑ Temple of Venus and Rome, designed by Emperor Hadrian and inaugurated in 121 AD

in Judaea. In AD 66 the Jews, weary of being exploited by unscrupulous Roman officials, rebelled. A bitter war broke out which ended four years later in the sacking of Solomon's temple in Jerusalem, the fall of Jerusalem and the Jewish Diaspora.

Although the reliefs inside the arch are badly eroded, you can make out a triumphant procession of Roman soldiers carrying off spoils from the Temple of Jerusalem. The booty includes the altar, silver trumpets and a golden seven-branched candelabrum.

Temple of Venus and Rome

The Emperor Hadrian designed this temple himself. The temple, thought to have been the largest and most splendid in ancient Rome, was dedicated to Roma, the personification of the city, and to Venus Felix, ancestor of the Roman people. Each goddess had her own *cella* (shrine). When the architect Apollodorus pointed out that the seated statues in the niches were too big (had

they tried to "stand" their heads would have hit the vaults), Hadrian had him put to death. The temple has had extensive restoration, and a number of the columns have been re-erected. There are excellent views of the Colosseum from here.

SANTA FRANCESCA ROMANA

Santa Francesca Romana was a 14th-century housewife, who became convinced of the constant presence of a guardian angel lighting the road before her whenever she travelled. For this reason, in 1925, she was made the patron saint of motorists. On her feast day, 9 March, the city's trams and buses are blessed, and the road outside her church next to the Temple of Venus and Rome is packed with cars whose drivers are seeking her blessing.

COLOSSEUM

📍 K7 🏛 Piazza del Colosseo 1 📞 06-3996 7700 🚌 75, 81, 85, 87, 117, 673, 810
🚋 3 to Piazza del Colosseo Ⓜ Colosseo ⏰ 8:30am–approx 1 hour before sunset
daily (last admission 1 hour before closing). Admission includes Palatine and
Forum (additional fees for upper tier and guided tours of underground areas).
Tickets can be bought in advance at www.coopculture.it

**Rome's greatest amphitheatre was commissioned by Emperor Vespasian
in AD 72. This magnificent structure was where the Imperial passion for
bloody spectacle reached its peak of excess.**

Built by Jewish slaves on the marshy site of a lake in the
grounds of Nero's palace, the Domus Aurea (p206), the
Colosseum was the arena where deadly gladiatorial combats
and wild animal fights were staged by the emperor and
wealthy citizens for public viewing, free of charge. The
Colosseum was built to a practical design, with its 80 arched
entrances allowing easy access to 55,000 spectators, but it is
also a building of great beauty. It was one of several similar
amphitheatres built in the Roman Empire – other surviving
examples are at El Djem in North Africa, Nîmes and Arles in
France, and Verona in northern Italy. Despite being damaged
over the years by neglect and theft, the Roman Colosseum
remains a majestic sight.

INSIDER TIP
Roma Pass

Holders of a Roma Pass (see
p337) gain direct entry via
a special turnstile. The
quietest time to visit is early
morning – aim to arrive at
least 30 minutes before the
scheduled opening time.
Beware "gladiators" who
charge tourists for photos.

Timeline

80
Vespasian's son,
Titus, stages
inaugural festival in
the amphitheatre
lasting 100 days

404
▽ Gladiatorial
combats
banned

442
Building
damaged
in an
earthquake

72
△ Emperor
Vespasian
begins work on
the Colosseum

81–96
Amphitheatre
completed in
reign of
Domitian

523
△ Wild animal
fights banned

1200s
Frangipane
family turns
Colosseum into
a fortress

The Colosseum at sunset; internal corridors (inset)

1312
△ Emperor Henry VII gives Colosseum to the Senate and people of Rome

15th–16th centuries
Ruins used as quarry; travertine blocks recycled by popes

1870
All vegetation removed

1893–6
▽ Structure below arena revealed

The Colosseum amphitheatre seen from above

How Fights were Staged in the Arena

The emperors held shows here, which often began with animals performing circus tricks. Then on came the gladiators, who fought each other to the death. When one was killed, attendants dressed as Charon, the mythical ferryman of the dead, carried his body off on a stretcher, and sand was raked over the blood ready for the next bout. A badly wounded gladiator would surrender his fate to the crowd. The "thumbs up" sign from the emperor meant he could live, "thumbs down" that he die, and the victor became an instant hero. Roman gladiators were usually slaves, prisoners of war or condemned criminals. Most were men, but there were a few female gladiators.

The velarium was a huge awning which shaded spectators from the sun.

The outer walls are made of travertine. Stone plundered from the façade during the Renaissance was used to build several palaces, bridges and parts of St Peter's.

Did You Know?

The founder of the Colosseum, Vespasian, was a professional soldier.

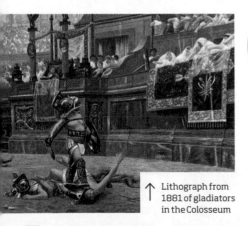

↑ Lithograph from 1881 of gladiators in the Colosseum

→ Drawing of the Colosseum showing how it looked at the time of its opening in AD 80

←

Inside view of the Colosseum showing remains of the underground rooms where animals were kept

Animals were brought here from as far away as North Africa and the Middle East. The games held in AD 248 to mark the 1,000th anniversary of Rome's founding saw the death of a host of lions, elephants, hippos, zebras and elks in wild-animal hunting spectacles.

A complex of rooms, passages and lifts over several floors lies underneath the arena. Metal fencing kept animals penned in, while archers stood by just in case any escaped. A winch brought the animal cages up to arena level when they were due to fight. A ramp and trap door enabled the animal to reach the arena after walking along a corridor.

SEA BATTLES IN THE ARENA

Historian Dion Cassius, writing in the 4th century AD, relates how, 150 years earlier, the Colosseum's arena was flooded to stage a mock sea battle. Scholars now believe that the spectacle probably took place in the Naumachia of Augustus, a water-filled arena across the Tiber in Trastevere.

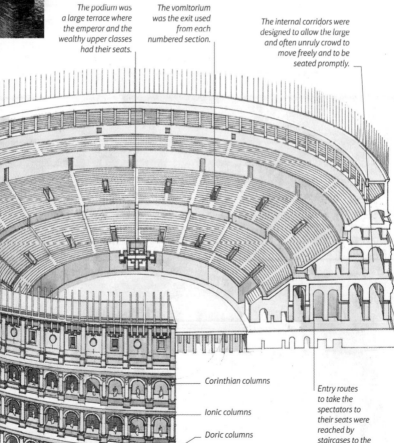

The podium was a large terrace where the emperor and the wealthy upper classes had their seats.

The vomitorium was the exit used from each numbered section.

The internal corridors were designed to allow the large and often unruly crowd to move freely and to be seated promptly.

Corinthian columns

Ionic columns

Doric columns

Arched entrances (80 in total) were numbered to speed up the entry of the vast crowds.

Entry routes to take the spectators to their seats were reached by staircases to the various levels.

3 🔨 🛍️

TRAJAN'S MARKETS

📍J6 🏠 Via IV Novembre 94 📞06-0608 🚌64, 70, 170
and routes to Piazza Venezia ⏰9:30am–7:30pm daily
(last admission 1 hour before closing)

Originally considered among the wonders of the
Classical world, this visionary complex of 150 shops
and offices was built by Emperor Trajan and architect
Apollodorus of Damascus in the 2nd century AD.

The ancient Roman equivalent of the modern shopping mall,
Trajan's Markets was a complex of shops on five levels, selling
everything from silks and spices imported from the Middle East
to fresh fish, fruit, flowers, wine, oil and fabrics. The top tier
was occupied by welfare offices that administered the free corn
ration to Roman men and boys. Via Biberatica, the main street
that ran through the market, is named after the drinking inns
that once lined it. The two large halls on the lowest level were
used for concerts. The Torre delle Milizie, the large tower above
the Markets, was built in the middle ages.

↑ Bronze statue of
Emperor Trajan, a
benevolent ruler

MARKET SHOPPING

Shops opened early and closed at about noon. The most upmarket stores were decorated with mosaics of the goods they sold. Almost all the shopping was done by men, although women visited dressmakers and cobblers. The traders were also almost all male. In employment records for the period AD 117–193, the only female shopkeepers mentioned are three wool-sellers, two jewellers, a greengrocer and a fishwife.

Remnants of the Forum of Trajan, built in front of the markets in AD 107–113 ↑

EAT

Terre e Domus della Provincia di Roma

Right by Trajan's Markets, this small modern restaurant serves Roman cuisine made with the freshest local ingredients. The *cacio e pepe* pasta is especially good, and there's a very strong wine list.

📍 H5 🏠 Largo di Foro di Traiano 83
🌐 palazzovalentini.it/terre-domus

€€€

←
The red-brick Trajan's Markets complex, the world's first shopping mall

4 ⊘ ⊗

PALATINE

📍 J7 🏛 Via di San Gregorio 30 📞 Tel 06 39 96 77 00 🚌 75, 80, 81, 175, 673, 850 🚋 3
Ⓜ Colosseo 🕐 8:30am–1 hour before sunset. Admission includes entry to the Forum, Colosseum and Palatine Museum. Tickets can be bought in advance at www.coopculture.it

The Palatine, once the residence of emperors and aristocrats, is the most pleasant of Rome's ancient sites. The ruins range from the simple house in which Augustus is thought to have lived, to the Domus Flavia and Domus Augustana, the public and private wings of a luxurious palace built by Domitian.

The remains of elaborate fountains, colourful marble floors, fine stone carvings, columns, stuccoes and frescoes can be seen within the magnificent walls of the Imperial palaces. The Palatine Hill is a green haven, shaded by pines, with wild flowers growing among the ancient ruins. The hill offers fantastic views of the Roman Forum, the Colosseum, the Capitoline Hill and the Circus Maximus. In the 16th century the first private botanical gardens in Europe were built by the Farnese family on the Palatine – the area was dug up during excavations and re-landscaped.

↑ The Palatine Hill viewed through an arch of the neighbouring Colosseum

A History of the Palatine Hill

The Founding

According to legend, the twins Romulus and Remus were brought up on the Palatine by a wolf. Romulus, having killed his brother, is said to have founded the village that was destined to become Rome. Traces of mud huts dating back to the 8th century BC have been found on the hill, lending archaeological support to the legend.

The Republic

By the 1st century BC the Palatine was the most desirable address in Rome and home to the leading citizens of the Republic. Its aristocractic residents were notoriously indulgent and their villas were magnificent dwellings with doors of ivory, floors of bronze and frescoed walls.

The Empire

The first emperor, Augustus, was born on the Palatine in 63 BC and lived here in a modest house. Domitian's house, the Domus Flavia and its private quarters, Domus Augustana, remained the official residence of future emperors (who were referred to as "Augustus") for over 300 years.

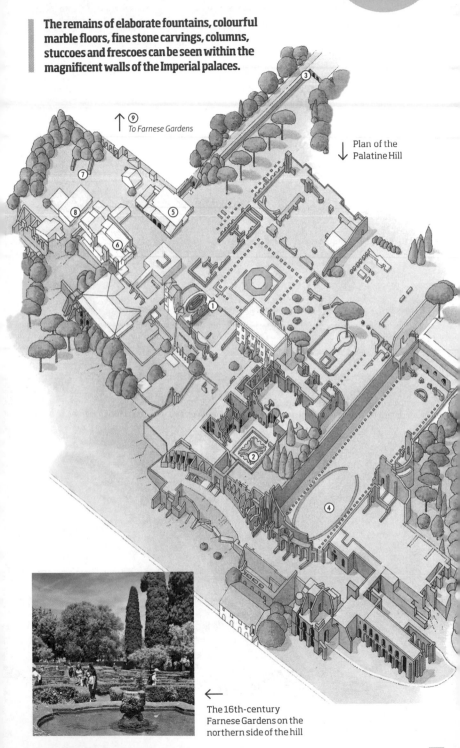

↑ ⑨
To Farnese Gardens

↓ Plan of the
Palatine Hill

The 16th-century Farnese Gardens on the northern side of the hill

① Domus Flavia

In AD 81 Domitian, the third of the Flavian dynasty of emperors, decided to build a splendid new palace on the Palatine Hill. The palace had an official wing (Domus Flavia) and a private house (Domus Augustana). It was the main Imperial palace for 300 years.

At the front of the Domus Flavia, the surviving fragments of columns and walls trace the shapes of three adjoining rooms. The Basilica was where the emperor presided over legal cases. The central Aula Regia was a throne room decorated with 12 black basalt statues. The Lararium (now covered with corrugated plastic) contained a shrine for the household gods known as Lares (usually the owner's ancestors). It may have been used for official ceremonies or by the palace guards.

Fearing assassination, Domitian had the walls of the courtyard covered with shiny marble slabs designed to act as mirrors so that he could see anyone lurking behind him. In the event, he was assassinated in his bedroom, possibly on the orders of his wife, Domitia. The courtyard is now a pleasant place; the flower beds follow the maze pattern of a sunken fountain pool.

② Domus Augustana

This part of Domitian's palace was called the Domus Augustana because it was the private residence of the "august" emperors. On the upper level a high brick wall remains, and you can make out the shape of its two courtyards. The far lower level is closed to the public, though you can look down on its sunken courtyard with the geometric foundations of a fountain in its centre. Sadly, you cannot see the stairs linking the two levels (once lit by sunlight falling on a mirror-paved pool), nor the surrounding rooms, paved with coloured marble.

③ Cryptoporticus

The Cryptoporticus, a series of underground corridors, was built by Nero to connect his Domus Aurea (p206) with the palaces of earlier emperors on the Palatine. Its vaults are decorated with delicate stucco reliefs – copies of originals now kept in the Palatine's museum.

↓ The Domus Flavia, the official wing of what was once a vast emperor's palace

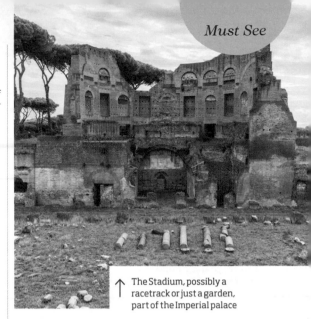

Must See

Stadium

The Stadium was laid out at the same time as the Palace of Domitian. It is unclear whether it was a public stadium, a private track for exercising horses, or simply a large garden. The alcove in the eastern wall looks as though it may have held a box from which the emperor could have watched races. It is, however, known that the Stadium was used for foot races by the Ostrogothic king, Theodoric, in the 6th century – he added the oval-shaped enclosure at the southern end of the site.

↑ The Stadium, possibly a racetrack or just a garden, part of the Imperial palace

House of Livia

Dating from the 1st century BC, this was probably the house in which the Emperor Augustus and his wife Livia lived and is one of the best preserved houses on the Palatine. In comparison with later Imperial palaces, it is a relatively modest home. According to Suetonius, the biographer of Rome's early emperors, Augustus slept in the same small bedroom for 40 years on a low bed.

A flight of steps leads down to a mosaic-paved corridor into a courtyard off which are three small reception rooms. The frescoes in the central one include a faded scene of Hermes rescuing Zeus's beloved Io, who is guarded by Argos. In the left-hand room are frescoed griffins and other beasts, while the decor in the right-hand room includes both landscapes and cityscapes.

29

is the number of European languages whose word for "palace" derives from the Palatine.

House of Augustus

Painted in about 30 BC, the frescoes in the House of Augustus are among the most impressive existing examples of Roman wall paintings, similar in quality to those found in Pompeii and Herculaneum. In vivid shades of red, blue and ochre, they include *trompe l'oeil* effects, such as a room whose walls are painted to resemble a stage with side doors, and a garden vista.

Although the frescoes are impressive, the house itself is modest. This is where Augustus (or Octavian, as he was then known) lived before assuming supreme power as Rome's first emperor.

Temple of Cybele

Other than a platform with a few column stumps and capitals, there is little to see of the Temple of Cybele, a popular fertility goddess imported to Rome from Asia. The priests of the cult castrated themselves in the belief that if they sacrificed

their own fertility it would guarantee that of the natural world. The annual festival of Cybele, in early spring, culminated with eunuch-priests slashing their bodies to offer up their blood to the goddess, and the ceremonial castration of novice priests.

Huts of Romulus

According to legend, after killing his brother Remus, Romulus founded a village on the Palatine. In the 1940s a series of holes was found, and archaeologists deduced that these must originally have held the supporting poles of three Iron-Age huts – the first foundations of Rome.

Farnese Gardens

Tree-lined avenues, rose gardens and elegant pavilions grace part of what was once an extensive pleasure-garden, designed by the noted architect Vignola and built in the 16th century for Cardinal Alessandro Farnese over the ruins of Tiberius's palace.

EXPERIENCE MORE

5

Trajan's Column

 H6 Via dei Fori Imperiali 🚌 64, 70, 170 and routes to Piazza Venezia

This elegant marble column was inaugurated by Trajan in AD 113, and celebrates his two campaigns in Dacia (Romania) in AD 101–3 and AD 107–8. The column, base and pedestal are 40 m (131 ft) tall – precisely the same height as the spur of Quirinal Hill excavated to make room for Trajan's Forum.

Spiralling up the column are minutely detailed scenes from the campaigns. The column is pierced with small windows to illuminate its internal spiral staircase (closed to the public).

When Trajan died in AD 117 his ashes were placed in a golden urn in the hollow base of the column. The column's survival was largely due to the intervention of Pope Gregory the Great (reigned 590–604). He was so moved by a relief of Trajan helping a woman whose son had been killed that he begged God to release the emperor's soul from hell. God duly appeared to the pope to say that Trajan had been rescued, but asked him not to pray for the souls of any more pagans. Legend has it that when Trajan's ashes were exhumed his skull and tongue were not only intact, but his tongue told of his release from hell. The land around the column was then declared sacred and the column was

← Trajan's Column topped with a statue of St Peter

💬 INSIDER TIP
Trajan's Column

At Palazzo Valentini there are screenings of a brilliant animation of the bas-reliefs of Trajan's Column. Be sure to book in advance.

spared. In 1587, the statue of Trajan atop the column was replaced with one of St Peter.

6

Palazzo Valentini

 H5 Via IV Novembre 119/a ⏰ 9:30am-6:30pm Wed-Mon; visits by guided tour only 🌐 palazzo valentini.it

During maintenance work in the basement of Palazzo Valentini in 2005, the remains of two houses belonging to a leading patrician family of Imperial ancient Rome were discovered. Elegant living rooms, courtyards, a kitchen and a private baths complex were revealed, complete with traces of their elaborate original decorations – mosaics, frescoes and coloured marbles.

Using digital technology, light and sound effects, film and projections, the houses have been "reconstructed", creating a virtual-reality museum. There are tours in English and Italian.

7

Forum of Nerva

 J6 Piazza del Grillo 1 (via the Forum of Augustus) 📞 06-0608 🚌 85, 87, 186, 810 🔒 to the public but viewable from above

The Forum of Nerva was begun by his predecessor, Domitian, and completed in

↑ The remains of the Forum of Caesar, the first of Rome's Imperial fora

AD 97. Little more than a long corridor with a colonnade along the sides and a Temple of Minerva at one end, it was also known as the Forum Transitorium because it lay between the Forum of Peace, built by Vespasian in AD 70, and the Forum of Augustus. Vespasian's forum is almost completely covered by Via dei Fori Imperiali, as is much of the Forum of Nerva. Excavations have unearthed shops and taverns, but only part of the forum can be seen.

8

Forum of Caesar

 H6 Via del Carcere Tulliano 📞 06-0608 🚌 85, 87, 186, 810, 850 ⏰ by appt only.

The first of Rome's Imperial fora was built by Julius Caesar. He spent a fortune buying up

and demolishing houses on the site. Pride of place went to a temple dedicated in 46 BC to the goddess Venus Genetrix, from whom Caesar claimed descent. The temple contained statues of Caesar and Cleopatra as well as of Venus. All that remains is a platform and three Corinthian columns. The forum was enclosed by a double colonnade sheltering a row of shops, but this burned down in AD 80 and was rebuilt by Domitian and Trajan.

Some parts are visible from above in Via dei Fori Imperiali.

 9

Forum of Augustus

📍J6 🏛Piazza del Grillo 1 📞06-0608 🚌64, 70, 170 and routes to Piazza Venezia 🕐to the public but viewable from above

The Forum of Augustus was built to celebrate Augustus's victory over Julius Caesar's assassins, Brutus and Cassius, at the Battle of Philippi in 41 BC. The temple in its centre was dedicated to Mars the Avenger. The forum stretched from a high wall at the foot of the sleazy Suburra quarter to the edge of the Forum of Caesar. At least half of it is now concealed below Mussolini's Via dei Fori Imperiali. The temple is easily identified, with its cracked steps and four Corinthian columns. Originally it had a statue of Mars which looked very like Augustus.

10

Mamertine Prison

📍H6 🏛Clivo Argentario 1 📞06-698 961 🚌85, 87, 186, 810 🕐8:30am–4:30pm daily (guided tours by appt only; call for details)

Below the 16th-century church of San Giuseppe dei Falegnami (St Joseph of the Carpenters) is a dank dungeon in which, according to Christian legend, St Peter was imprisoned. He is said to have caused a spring to bubble up into the cell, using the water to baptize his guards.

The prison was in an old cistern with access to the city's main sewer (the Cloaca Maxima). The lower cell was used for executions and bodies were thrown into the sewer. The Gaulish leader Vercingetorix, defeated by Julius Caesar in 52 BC, was executed here.

 11

Arch of Constantine

📍J7 🏛Between Via di San Gregorio and Piazza del Colosseo 🚌75, 85, 87, 673, 810 🚊3 Ⓜ Colosseo

This arch was dedicated in AD 315 to mark Constantine's victory three years before over his co-emperor, Maxentius. Constantine claimed he owed his victory to a vision of Christ, but there is nothing Christian about the arch – most of the medallions, reliefs and statues were scavenged from earlier monuments. Inside the arch are reliefs of Trajan's victory over the Dacians, probably by the same artist who worked on Trajan's Column.

PIAZZA DELLA ROTONDA

The Pantheon, one of the great buildings in the history of European architecture, has stood at the heart of Rome for nearly 2,000 years. The historic area around it has seen uninterrupted economic and political activity throughout that time. Palazzo di Montecitorio, built for Pope Innocent XII as a papal tribunal in 1694, is now the Italian parliament and many nearby buildings are government offices. This is also the main financial district of Rome, housing banking headquarters and the stock exchange. Not many people live in the area, but in the evenings, Romans stroll in the narrow streets and fill the bustling restaurants and cafés that make this a focus for the city's social life.

PIAZZA DELLA ROTONDA

Must Sees
1 Pantheon
2 Gesù

Experience More
3 Temple of Hadrian
4 Piazza di Sant'Ignazio
5 Sant'Ignazio di Loyola
6 Palazzo del Collegio Romano
7 Palazzo Baldassini
8 La Maddalena
9 Sant'Eustachio
10 Santa Maria sopra Minerva
11 Pie' di Marmo
12 Palazzo di Montecitorio
13 Obelisk of Montecitorio
14 Palazzo Borghese
15 Santa Maria in Campo Marzio
16 Column of Marcus Aurelius
17 Palazzo Doria Pamphilj
18 Via della Gatta
19 Palazzo Capranica
20 San Lorenzo in Lucina
21 Fontanella del Facchino
22 Palazzo Altieri

Eat
1 Armando al Pantheon
2 Osteria dell'Ingegno

Drink
3 Caffè Sant'Eustachio
4 Tazza d'Oro

Gelaterie
5 Della Palma
6 Giolitti
7 Grom
8 Punto Gelato

PIAZZA DELLA ROTONDA

0 metres 150
0 yards 150

N

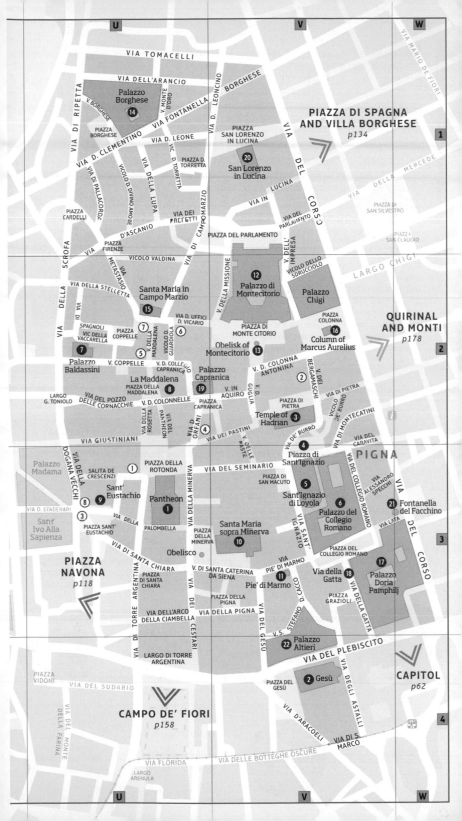

PANTHEON

📍U3 🏛️Piazza della Rotonda 🚌116 and routes along Via del Corso, Corso Vittorio Emanuele II & Corso del Rinascimento 🕐9am-7:30pm Mon-Sat, 9am-6pm Sun, 9am-1pm public hols 🌐pantheonroma.com

With its awe-inspiring domed interior, the Pantheon – the Roman temple of "all the gods" – is the best-preserved ancient building in Rome. Unlike many other Roman structures that fell into disrepair, it became a church in the 7th century, ensuring its continued use and conservation.

Inside the Pantheon

The interior of the church is dominated by the vast hemispherical dome, which has both a height and diameter of 43.3 m (142 ft). The hole at the top of the dome, the oculus, provides the only light; we owe this marvel of engineering to the Emperor Hadrian, who designed the structure (AD 118–125) to replace an earlier temple built by Marcus Agrippa, son-in-law of Augustus. The shrines that line the wall of the Pantheon range from the Tomb of Raphael to those of the kings of Italy.

↑ The immense portico, built on the foundations of Agrippa's temple

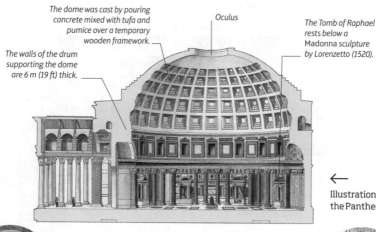

The dome was cast by pouring concrete mixed with tufa and pumice over a temporary wooden framework.

The walls of the drum supporting the dome are 6 m (19 ft) thick.

Oculus

The Tomb of Raphael rests below a Madonna sculpture by Lorenzetto (1520).

← Illustration of the Pantheon

Timeline

118–25
Hadrian builds new Pantheon

27–25 BC
▲ Marcus Agrippa builds first Pantheon

609
▼ Pope Boniface IV consecrates Pantheon as church of Santa Maria ad Martyres

663
Byzantine Emperor Constans II strips gilded tiles from the roof

1309–77
While the papal seat is in Avignon, Pantheon is used as a poultry market

1632
▲ Urban VIII melts bronze from portico for the baldacchino in St Peter's

Did You Know?

The Pantheon's dome remains the largest unreinforced concrete dome in the world.

Oculus and coffered interior of the Pantheon's dome ↑

②

GESÙ

**⑨V4 ⌂Piazza del Gesù ☎06-697 001 🚌H, 46, 62, 64,
70, 81, 87, 186, 492, 628, 810 and other routes 🚋8
🕐7am–12:30pm & 4-7:45pm daily**

Dating from between 1568 and 1584, the Gesù was
the first Jesuit church to be built in Rome. Its design
has been much imitated throughout the Catholic world.

Epitomizing Counter-Reformation Baroque architecture, the
layout proclaims the church's two major functions: a large nave
with side pulpits for preaching to crowds, and a main altar as the
centrepiece for the celebration of the Mass. By providing people
with prayer books and filling the nave with enough light for
people to read, the Jesuits hoped to increase the popularity of
Catholicism during the Thirty Years' War when Catholics were
losing followers to the Protestants. The illusionistic decoration
by Il Baciccia in the nave and dome was added after the war in
the late 17th century. Its message is clear and triumphant: faithful Catholic worshippers will be joyfully uplifted into the heavens
while Protestants and other heretics are flung into hell's fires.

← The façade of the Gesù
church, designed by
Giacomo della Porta

→ Stuccoes by Antonio Raggi,
designed by Il Baciccia to
complement the figures on
his own nave frescoes

Timeline

1540
▲ Founding
of the Society
of Jesus (the
Jesuits)

1568–71
▲ Vignola builds the
church, under the
patronage of Cardinal
Alessandro Farnese

1571
Giacomo della
Porta's design
chosen for the
façade

1584
Church's
consecration

1622
▼ Ignatius of Loyola
is canonized

1773
Pope Clement
XIV orders the
suppression of
the Jesuit
order

ST IGNATIUS AND THE JESUIT ORDER

Spanish soldier Ignatius of Loyola (1491-1556) joined the Church after being wounded in battle in 1521. He came to Rome in 1537 and founded the Jesuits, sending missionaries and teachers all over the world to win souls for Catholicism.

↑ The splendid, highly ornate main nave and altar inside the Gesù

EXPERIENCE MORE

❸

Temple of Hadrian

⑨ V2 ⑧ La Borsa, Piazza di Pietra ➡117, 119, 492 and routes along Via del Corso or stopping at Piazza San Silvestro ⑨ for exhibitions

This temple honours the emperor Hadrian as a god and was dedicated by his son and successor, Antoninus Pius in AD 145. The remains of the temple are visible on the southern side of Piazza di Pietra, incorporated in a 17th-century building. This was originally a papal customs house, completed by Carlo

Fontana and his son in the 1690s. Today the building houses the Roman stock exchange (La Borsa).

Eleven marble Corinthian columns 15 m (49 ft) high stand on a base of *peperino*, a volcanic rock quarried from the Alban hills, to the south of Rome. The columns decorated the northern flank of the temple enclosing its inner shrine, the *cella*. The *peperino* wall of the *cella* is still visible behind the columns, as is part of the coffered portico ceiling.

A number of reliefs from the temple, representing conquered Roman provinces, are now in the courtyard of

the Palazzo dei Conservatori (*p66*). They reflect the mostly peaceful foreign policy of emperor Hadrian's reign.

---

❹

Piazza di Sant'Ignazio

⑨ V2 & 3 ➡117, 119, 492 and routes along Via del Corso or stopping at Piazza San Silvestro

One of the major works of the Roman Rococo, Piazza di Sant'Ignazio (1727–8) is Filippo Raguzzini's master-piece. It offsets the imposing façade of the church of Sant'Ignazio with the intimacy of the houses belonging to the bourgeoisie. The theatrical setting, the curvilinear design and the playful forms of its windows, balconies and balusters mark the piazza as

> **Built in Baroque style, Sant'Ignazio di Loyola's vast interior, lined with precious stones, marble, stucco and gilt, creates a sense of theatre.**

↑ The exuberant frescoed ceiling of Sant'Ignazio di Loyola

EAT

Armando al Pantheon

Just steps away from the Pantheon, this wood-panelled trattoria has been going strong since 1961, never straying from its menu of Roman dishes cooked to perfection – from *spaghetti all'amatriciana* to *coda alla vaccinara* (oxtail stew). It's deservedly popular, so book ahead.

🅚 U3 🅐 Salita de' Crescenzi 31 armandoal pantheon.it

€€€

Osteria dell'Ingegno

In a picture-perfect little piazza, this buzzing restaurant has a menu of traditional dishes with a modern twist, such as duck with mandarin and endive, and pasta with lamb and juniper sauce. The arty interior and jazz soundtrack add to the appeal.

🅚 V2 🅐 Piazza di Pietra 45 osteriadellingegno.com

€€€

one of a highly distinct group of structures. Along with Palazzo Doria Pamphilj (1731), the façade of La Maddalena (1735) and the aristocratic Spanish Steps (1723), it belongs to the moment when Rome's opulent Rococo triumphed over conservative Classicism.

Sant'Ignazio di Loyola

🅚 V3 🅐 Piazza di Sant'Ignazio ☎ 06-679 4406 🚍 117, 119, 492 and routes along Via del Corso ⏰ 7:30am-7pm Mon-Sat, 9am-7pm Sun

The church was built by Pope Gregory XV in 1626 in honour of St Ignatius of Loyola, founder of the Society of Jesus and the man who most embodied the zeal of the Counter-Reformation.

Together with the Gesù (p106), Sant'Ignazio forms the centre of the Jesuit area in Rome. Built in Baroque style, Sant'Ignazio di Loyola's vast interior, lined with precious stones, marble, stucco and gilt, creates a sense of theatre. The church has a Latin-cross plan, with an apse and many side chapels. A cupola was planned but never built, so the space it would have filled was covered by a vast fake perspective painting by Andrea Pozzo. The stunning *trompe l'oeil* frescoes give the illusion of a cupola open to a bright sky on the nave ceiling.

Palazzo del Collegio Romano

🅚 V3 🅐 Piazza del Collegio Romano 🚍 117, 119, 492 and routes along Via del Corso or stopping at Piazza Venezia 🚫 to the public

On the same block as the church of Sant'Ignazio is the majestic palazzo used by Jesuits as a college where many future bishops, cardinals and popes studied. The college was confiscated in 1870 and turned into an ordinary school. The façade is adorned with a bell, a clock and two sundials. On the right is a tower built in 1787 as a meteorological observatory. Until 1925 its time signal regulated all the clocks within the city.

⑦ Palazzo Baldassini

⑨U2 ⌂Via delle Coppelle 35 ☎06-684 0421 🚌116 and many routes along Via del Corso and Corso Rinascimento ⊙by reservation only (call the number above)

Melchiorre Baldassini commissioned Antonio da Sangallo the Younger to build his home in Florentine Renaissance style in 1514–20. With its cornices marking the different floors and wrought-iron window grilles, this is one of the best examples of an early 16th-century Roman palazzo. It stands in the part of Rome still known as the Renaissance Quarter, which flourished around the long, straight streets such as Via di Ripetta and Via della Scrofa, built at the time of Pope Leo X (reigned 1513–21).

⑧ La Maddalena

⑨U2 ⌂Piazza della Maddalena ☎06-899 281 🚌116 and many routes along Via del Corso and Corso Vittorio Emanuele II ⊙8:30-11:30am & 5-6:30pm daily (9-11:30am Sat)

Situated in a small piazza near the Pantheon, the Maddalena, built in 1735, has a Rococo façade that epitomizes the love of light and movement of the late Baroque. Its curves are reminiscent of Borromini's San Carlo alle Quattro Fontane *(p192)*. The façade has been lovingly restored, although die-hard Neo-Classicists dismiss its painted stucco as icing sugar.

The small size of the Maddalena did not deter the 17th- and 18th-century decorators who filled the interior with ornaments from the floor to the top of the elegant cupola. The organ loft

↑ The church of Sant'Eustachio seen from Via della Palombella, which links Piazza della Minerva with Piazza Sant'Eustachio

and choir are particularly powerful examples of the Baroque's desire to fire the imagination of the faithful.

Many of the paintings and sculptures found within the Maddalena adopt the Christian imagery of the Counter-Reformation. In the niches of the nave, the statues are personifications of virtues such as Humility and Simplicity. There are also scenes from the life of St Camillus de Lellis, who died in the adjacent convent in 1614. The church belonged to his followers, the Camillians, a preaching order active in Rome's hospitals. Like the Jesuits, they commissioned powerful works of art to convey the force of their religious message.

⑨ Sant'Eustachio

⑨U3 ⌂Piazza Sant'Eustachio ☎06-686 5334 🚌116 and routes along Corso Vittorio Emanuele II ⊙9am-noon & 4-7:30pm daily

The origins of this church date back to early Christian times, when it offered relief to the poor. In the medieval period, many charitable brother-hoods elected St Eustace as their patron. The church's Romanesque bell tower is one of the few surviving remains of the medieval church, which was completely redecorated in the 17th and 18th centuries.

Nearby is the excellent Caffè Sant'Eustachio *(p113)*.

Santa Maria sopra Minerva

📍 V3 🏠 Piazza della Minerva 42 📞 06-679 3926 🚌 116 and routes along Via del Corso, Via del Plebiscito and Corso Vittorio Emanuele II ⏰ 10:30am-12:30pm & 3-7pm daily; Cloister: ⏰ call in advance for details

Few other churches display such a complete and impressive record of Italian art. Dating from the 13th century, the Minerva is one of the few examples of Gothic architecture in Rome. It was the traditional stronghold of the Dominicans, whose anti-heretical zeal earned them the nickname of *Domini Canes* (the hounds of the Lord).

Built on ancient ruins, supposed to have been the Temple of Minerva, the simple T-shaped vaulted building acquired rich chapels and works of art by which its many patrons wished to be remembered. Note the Cosmatesque 13th-century tombs and the exquisite works of 15th-century Tuscan and Venetian artists. Local talent of the period can be admired in Antoniazzo Romano's *Annunciation*, featuring Cardinal Juan de Torquemada, uncle of the infamous Spanish Inquisitor.

The more monumental style of the Roman Renaissance is well represented in the tombs of the 16th-century Medici popes, Leo X and his cousin Clement VII, and in the richly decorated Aldobrandini Chapel. Near the steps of the choir is the celebrated sculpture of the *Risen Christ*, started by Michelangelo but completed by Raffaello da Montelupo in 1521. There are also splendid works of art from the Baroque period, including a tomb and a bust by Bernini.

The church also contains the tombs of many famous Italians: St Catherine of Siena, who died here in 1380; the Venetian sculptor Andrea Bregno (died 1506); the Humanist Cardinal Pietro Bembo (died 1547); and Fra Angelico, the Dominican friar and painter, who died in Rome in 1455.

Originally meant to decorate Palazzo Barberini as a joke, the elephant and obelisk sculpture in front of the church is typical of Bernini's inexhaustible imagination. (The elephant was actually sculpted by Ercole Ferrata to Bernini's design.) When the ancient obelisk was found in the garden of the monastery of Santa Maria sopra Minerva, the friars wanted the monument erected in their piazza. Despite opposition from Bernini, the elephant was provided with a cube underneath it (partly covered by an enormous saddle-cloth) at the insistance of a friar, who was Bernini's rival. The friar claimed that the gap under the animal's abdomen would undermine its stability. Bernini knew better, however: you need only look at the Fontana dei Quattro Fiumi in Piazza Navona *(p122)* to appreciate his use of empty space.

Pie' di Marmo

📍 V3 🏠 Via Santo Stefano del Cacco. 🚌 62, 63, 64, 70, 81, 87, 116, 186, 492 and other routes along Via del Corso, Via del Plebiscito and Corso Vittorio Emanuele II.

Bronze and marble statues filled the streets of ancient Rome. Fragments of these giants, usually gods or emperors, are still scattered over the city. This piece, a huge sandalled marble foot *(pie' di marmo)* in a small side-street, comes from an area dedicated to the Egyptian gods Isis and Serapis and was probably part of a temple statue. In ancient times statues were painted and covered with jewels and clothes given by the faithful – a great fire risk with unattended burning tapers.

12

Palazzo di Montecitorio

V2 **Piazza di Monte Citorio** 116 and all routes along Via del Corso or stopping at Piazza San Silvestro usually 1st Sun each month (except Jul & Aug); times vary (see website); pick up tickets in advance from info point on Via Uffici del Vicario. **camera.it**

The palazzo's first architect, Bernini, got the job after he presented a silver model of his design to the wife of his patron, Prince Ludovisi. The building was completed in 1694 by Carlo Fontana and became the Papal Tribunal of Justice. In 1871 it was chosen to be Italy's new Chamber of Deputies, and by 1927 it had doubled in size, with a second grand façade. The 630 members of the Italian parliament are elected by a majority system with proportional representation.

13

Obelisk of Montecitorio

V2 **Piazza di Monte Citorio 33** 116 and routes along Via del Corso or to Piazza San Silvestro

The measurement of time in ancient Rome was always a hit-and-miss affair: for many years the Romans relied on an imported, inaccurate sundial, a trophy from the conquest of Sicily. In 10 BC the Emperor Augustus laid out an enormous sundial in the Campus Martius. The shadow was cast by a huge granite obelisk that he had brought back from Heliopolis in Egypt. Unfortunately, this sundial, too, became inaccurate after only 50 years, possibly owing to subsidence.

The obelisk was still in the piazza in the 9th century, but then disappeared until it was rediscovered lying under medieval houses in the reign of Pope Julius II (1503–13). However, it was only under Pope Benedict XIV (reigned 1740–58) that the obelisk

was finally unearthed. It was erected in its present location in 1792 by Pope Pius VI.

14

Palazzo Borghese

U1 **Largo della Fontanella di Borghese** 81, 117, 492, 628 to the public

The palazzo was acquired in about 1605 by Cardinal Camillo Borghese, just before he became Pope Paul V. Flaminio Ponzio was hired to enlarge the building and give it the grandeur appropriate to the pope's family. He added a wing overlooking Piazza Borghese and the delightful porticoed courtyard inside. Subsequent enlargements included the building and decoration of a great *nymphaeum* known as the Bath of Venus. For more than two centuries this palazzo housed the Borghese family's famed collection of paintings, which was bought by the Italian state in 1902 and transferred to the Galleria Borghese (*p144*).

→ The façade of Palazzo Montecitorio, the Italian Chamber of Deputies

DRINK

Caffè Sant'Eustachio

Many Romans believe that Sant'Eustachio serves the city's best coffee – hence the hordes of locals that throng this tiny bar from morning till late. There's also a tempting selection of coffee flavoured cakes.

 U3 Piazza di Sant'Eustachio 82 santeustachioil caffe.com

Tazza d'Oro

Right next to the Pantheon, this historic bar has a fabulously retro interior and serves excellent coffee and pastries, as well as *granita di caffè* – a cooling treat on a hot day.

U2 Via degli Orfani 84 tazzadoro coffeeshop.com

15

Santa Maria in Campo Marzio

U2 Piazza di Campo Marzio 45 116 and routes on Via del Corso and Corso Rinascimento to the public

It is not possible to access the interior of this church, but it is still worth visiting to see the courtyard by Baroque architect Giovanni Antonio de Rossi, who used an archi-tectural illusion to make it look wider than it actually is. Around the courtyard there are fascinating remnants of medieval houses. The church itself was rebuilt in 1685 by De Rossi, using a square Greek-cross plan with a cupola.

The Column of Marcus Aurelius celebrating his victories and (right) a detail of the carving

16

Column of Marcus Aurelius

V2 Piazza Colonna 116 and routes along Via del Corso or to Piazza San Silvestro

Clearly an imitation of the column of Trajan (p98), this monument was erected after the death of Marcus Aurelius in AD 180 to commemorate his victories over the barbarian tribes of the Danube. The 80-year lapse between the two works produced a great artistic change: the wars of Marcus Aurelius are rendered with simplified pictures in stronger relief for clarity and immediacy. The spirit of the work is more akin to the 4th-century Arch of Constantine (p99) than to Trajan's monument. A new emphasis on the supernatural points to the end of the Hellenistic tradition and the beginning of Christianity.

Composed of 28 drums of marble, the column was restored in 1588 by Domenico Fontana on the orders of Pope Sixtus V. The emperor's statue on the summit was replaced by a bronze of St Paul. The 20 spirals of the low relief detail the German war (AD 172–3), and the Sarmatic war (AD 174–5). The column is nearly 30 m (100 ft) high and 3.7 m (12 ft) in diameter, with an internal spiral staircase. The easiest way to appreciate the sculp-tural work is to study casts of the reliefs at the Museo della Civiltà Romana at EUR (p323).

17 Palazzo Doria Pamphilj

📍 V3 🏛 Via del Corso 305
🚌 64, 81, 85, 117, 119, 492
and many other routes
🕐 9am-7pm daily 🚫 1 Jan,
Easter Sun, 25 Dec
🌐 doriapamphilj.it

Palazzo Doria Pamphilj is a great island of stone in the heart of Rome, the oldest parts dating from 1435. Through the Corso entrance you can see the 16th-century porticoed courtyard with the coat of arms of the della Rovere family. The Aldobrandini were the next owners. Between 1601 and 1647 the mansion acquired a second courtyard and flanking wings at the expense of a public bath that stood nearby.

When the Pamphilj family took over, they completed the Piazza del Collegio Romano façade and the Via della Gatta wing, a splendid chapel and a theatre inaugurated by Queen Christina of Sweden in 1684.

In the first half of the 1700s, Gabriele Valvassori created the gallery above the courtyard and a new façade along the Corso, using the highly decorative style of the Rococo period, which now dominates the building. The stairways and salons, the Mirror Gallery and the picture gallery all give a sense of light and space.

The family collection in the Doria Pamphilj gallery has over 400 paintings dating

↑ Palazzo Capranica, a typical example of early Renaissance architecture

from the 15th to the 18th century, including the famous portrait of Pope Innocent X Pamphilj by Velázquez. There are also works by Titian, Caravaggio, Lorenzo Lotto and Guercino. The rooms in the private apartment have many of their original furnishings, including splendid Brussels and Gobelin tapestries.

18 Via della Gatta

📍 V3 🚌 62, 63, 64, 70, 81,
87, 186, 492 & and routes
along Via del Plebiscito and
Corso Vittorio Emanuele II

This narrow street runs between the Palazzo Doria Pamphilj and the smaller Palazzo Grazioli. The ancient marble sculpture of a cat (gatta) that gives the street its name is on the first cornice on the corner of Palazzo Grazioli.

19 Palazzo Capranica

📍 U2 🏛 Piazza Capranica
101 🚌 116 and routes
along Via del Corso or to
Piazza San Silvestro
🚫 to the public

One of Rome's small number of surviving 15th-century buildings, the palazzo was commissioned by Cardinal Domenico Capranica both as his family residence and as a college for higher education. Its fortress-like appearance is a patchwork of subsequent additions, not unusual in the late 15th century, when Rome was still hovering between medieval and Renaissance

EAT

A generous scoop of gelato artigianale (artisanal ice cream) is a must. Do as the Romans do, and top with panna (whipped cream).

Della Palma
📍 U2 🏛 Via della Maddalena 19
📞 06-6880 6752

Giolitti
📍 U2 🏛 Via degli Uffici del Vicario 40
🌐 giolitti.it

Grom
📍 U2 🏛 Via della Maddalena 31A
🌐 grom.it

Punto Gelato
📍 U3 🏛 Piazza di Sant'Eustachio 47
🌐 gunthergelato italiano.com

← The ancient marble cat sculpture from which Via della Gatta takes its name

↑ The main altar in the ancient Roman basilica of San Lorenzo in Lucina

taste. The Gothic-looking windows on the right of the building show the cardinal's coat of arms, and the date 1451 is inscribed on the doorway underneath. The palazzo now houses a conference centre.

 20

San Lorenzo in Lucina

📍V1 🏛Via in Lucina 16A
📞06-687 1494 🚌81, 117, 492, 628 🕐8am-8pm daily

The church is one of Rome's oldest Christian places of worship, and was probably built on a well sacred to Juno, protectress of women. It was rebuilt during the 12th century, and today's external appearance is quite typical of the period, featuring a portico with reused Roman columns crowned by medieval capitals, a plain triangular pediment and a Romanesque bell tower with coloured marble inlay.

The interior was totally rebuilt in 1856–8. The old basilica plan was destroyed and the two side naves were replaced by Baroque chapels. Do not miss the fine busts in the Fonseca Chapel, designed by Bernini, or the *Crucifixion* by Guido Reni above the main altar. There is also a 19th-century monument honouring French painter Nicolas Poussin, who died in Rome in 1655 and was buried in the church.

 21

Fontanella del Facchino

📍V3 🏛Via Lata 🚌64, 81, 85, 117, 119, 492 and many other routes

Il Facchino (the Porter), once in the Corso, now set in the wall of the Banco di Roma, was one of Rome's "talking statues" like Pasquino (*p126*). Created around 1590, the fountain may have been based on a drawing by painter Jacopino del Conte. The statue of a man holding a barrel most likely represents a member of the Università degli Acquaroli (Fraternity of Water-carriers), though it is also said to be of Martin Luther, or of the porter Abbondio Rizzio, who died carrying a barrel.

 22

Palazzo Altieri

📍V4 🏛Via del Gesù 49
🚌46, 62, 63, 64, 70, 81, 87, 186, 492 and routes along Via del Plebiscito and Corso Vittorio Emanuele II 🚊8 ⊘to the public

The Altieri family first appears in Rome's history in the 9th century. This palazzo was built by the last male heirs, the brothers Cardinal Giambattista di Lorenzo Altieri and Cardinal Emilio Altieri, who later became Pope Clement X (reigned 1670–76). Many surrounding houses were demolished, but an old woman called Berta refused to leave, so her hovel was incorporated into the palazzo. Its windows are still visible on the west end of the building.

A SHORT WALK
PIAZZA DELLA ROTONDA

Distance 0.7 km (0.4 mile) **Nearest bus** 116 and other routes along Corso del Rinascimento **Time** 15 minutes

If you wander through this area, sooner or later you will emerge into Piazza della Rotonda with its jumble of open-air café tables in front of the Pantheon. The refreshing splash of the fountain makes it a welcome resting place. In this warren of narrow streets, it can be hard to realize just how close you are to some of Rome's finest sights. The magnificent art collection of Palazzo Doria Pamphilj and the Baroque splendour of the Gesù are just a few minutes' walk from the Pantheon. At night there is always a lively buzz of activity, as people dine in style or enjoy the coffee and ice cream for which the area is famous.

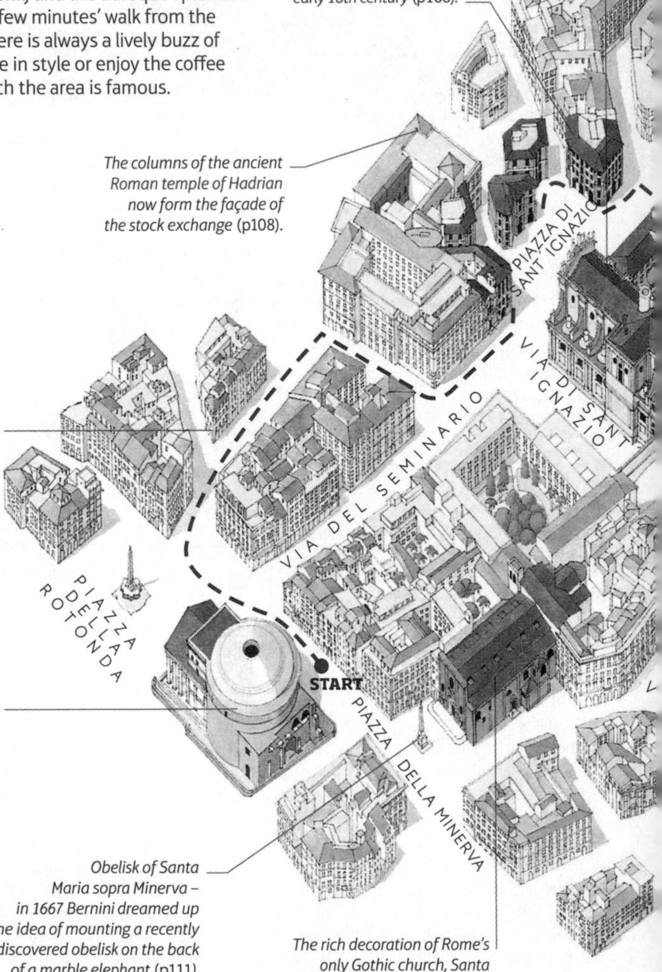

Andrea Pozzo painted the glorious Baroque ceiling in Sant'Ignazio di Loyola in 1685 to celebrate St Ignatius and the Jesuit order (p109).

Piazza di Sant'Ignazio is a rare example of stylish domestic architecture from the early 18th century (p108).

The columns of the ancient Roman temple of Hadrian now form the façade of the stock exchange (p108).

La Tazza d'Oro enjoys a reputation for the potent coffee consumed on its premises as well as for its freshly ground coffee to take away.

PIAZZA DI SANT'IGNAZIO

VIA DI SANT'IGNAZIO

VIA DEL SEMINARIO

PIAZZA DELLA ROTONDA

START

PIAZZA DELLA MINERVA

The awe-inspiring interior of Rome's best-preserved ancient temple, the Pantheon, is only hinted at from the outside (p104).

Obelisk of Santa Maria sopra Minerva – in 1667 Bernini dreamed up the idea of mounting a recently discovered obelisk on the back of a marble elephant (p111).

The rich decoration of Rome's only Gothic church, Santa Maria Sopra Minerva, was added in the 19th century.

↑ The Pantheon and the Obeslisk of Santa
Maria sopra Minerva on Piazza della Rotonda

Did You Know?

If you visit the
Pantheon when it's
raining you can see
rain falling through
the dome's oculus.

The water in the
small 16th-century
Fontanella del
Facchino fountain
spurts from a
barrel held by
a porter.

Up until 1870, the college
in the Palazzo del Collegio
Romano educated many
leading figures in the
Catholic Church (p109).

Among the masterpieces in the
art gallery of the magnificent
Palazzo Doria Pamphilj (p114)
is a portrait of Pope Innocent X
by Velázquez (1650).

FINISH

The Via della Gatta
is named after the
statue of a cat (p114).

This enormous 17th-
century Palazzo Altieri is
decorated with the arms
of Pope Clement X (p115).

The design of the first-ever
Jesuit church, the Gesù, had
a great impact on religious
architecture (p106).

The Pie' di Marmo, a marble
foot, is a stray fragment from
a gigantic Roman statue (p111).

| 0 metres | 75 |
| 0 yards | 75 |

N

PIAZZA NAVONA

The foundations of the buildings surrounding the elongated oval of Piazza Navona were the ruined grandstands of the vast ancient Stadium of Domitian. The piazza still provides a dramatic spectacle today, with the obelisk of the Fontana dei Quattro Fiumi in front of the church of Sant'Agnese in Agone as its focal point. The predominant style of the area is Baroque, many of its finest buildings dating from the reign of Innocent X Pamphilj (1644–55), patron of Bernini and Borromini. Of special interest is the complex of the Chiesa Nuova, headquarters of the Filippini, the order founded by San Filippo Neri, the 16th-century "Apostle of Rome".

PIAZZA NAVONA

Must See

① Piazza Navona

Experience More

② Santa Maria della Pace
③ Palazzo Madama
④ San Luigi dei Francesi
⑤ Sant'Agostino
⑥ Palazzo Pamphilj
⑦ Palazzo Massimo alle Colonne
⑧ Pasquino
⑨ Sant'Ivo alla Sapienza
⑩ Palazzo Braschi
⑪ Sant'Andrea della Valle
⑫ Via del Governo Vecchio
⑬ Chiesa Nuova
⑭ Oratorio dei Filippini
⑮ Torre dell'Orologio

⑯ Palazzo del Banco di Santo Spirito
⑰ San Salvatore in Lauro
⑱ Museo Napoleonico
⑲ Via dei Coronari
⑳ Palazzo Altemps

Eat

① Tre Scalini
② Lo Zozzone
③ Osteria del Pegno
④ Casa Bleve
⑤ Hostaria dell'Orso

Stay

⑥ Hotel Raphael

Shop

⑦ Antica Libreria Cascianelli
⑧ Delfina Delettrez

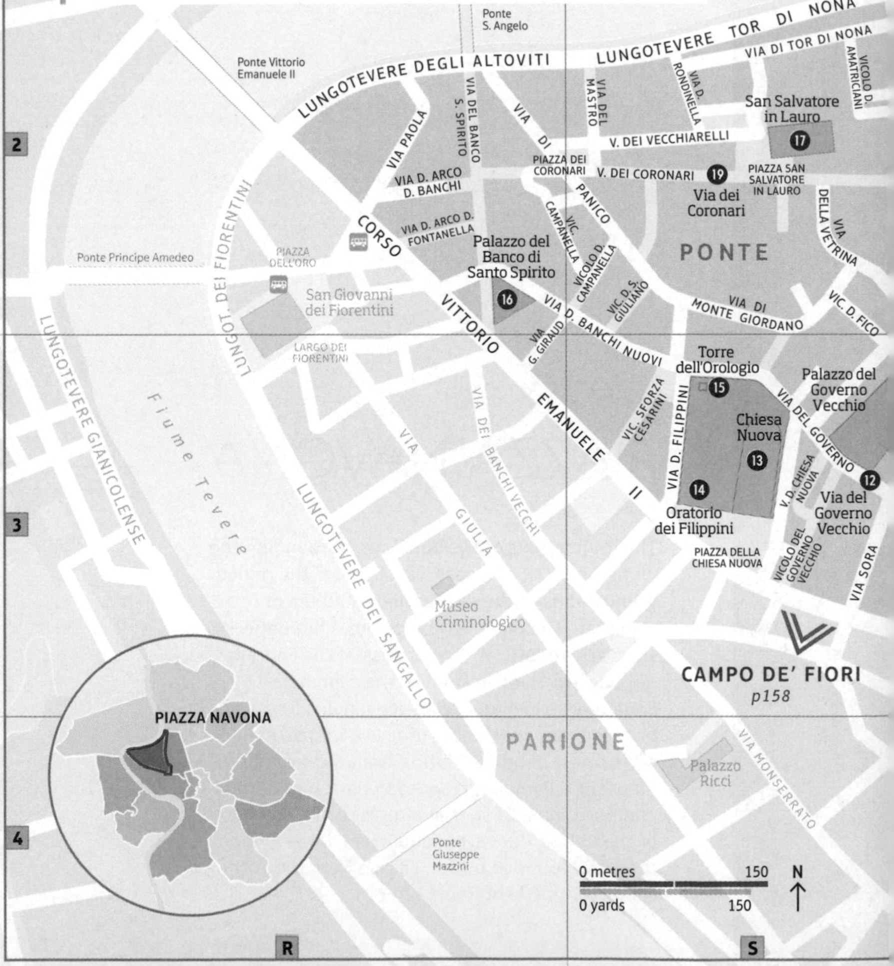

CAMPO DE' FIORI p158

PIAZZA NAVONA

0 metres 150
0 yards 150

N ↑

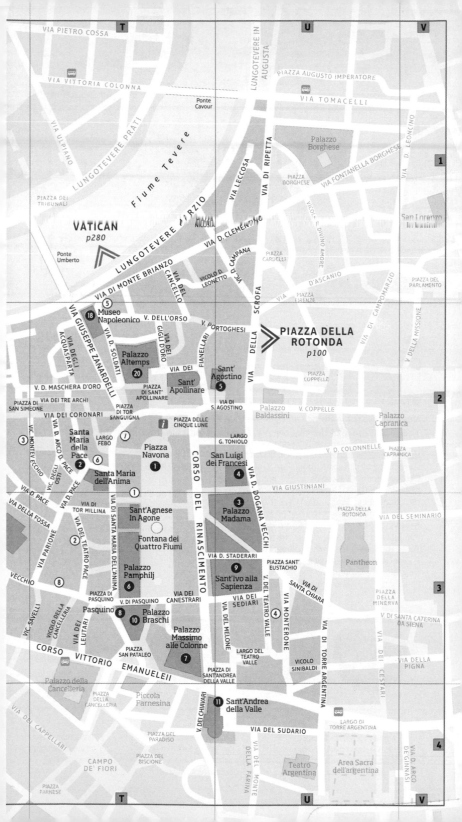

① PIAZZA NAVONA

📍 T2 🚌 46, 62, 64, 70, 81, 87, 116, 492, 628

No other piazza in Rome can rival the theatricality of Piazza Navona. The social centre of the city, the piazza buzzes with life day and night.

Rome's most famous and theatrical piazza is surrounded by cafés and dominated by the Egyptian obelisk, cascading waters and gleaming marble statues of Bernini's Fontana dei Quattro Fiumi. Located on the site of an ancient Roman stadium, the oval piazza has long been a lively part of Rome. In the Renaissance years there was a market here. Today the square is equally bustling, and is especially spectacular at night when the fountains are flood-lit and the café-terraces illuminated with flame-throwing lamps.

DOMITIAN'S STADIUM

◎ 📍 T2 🏠 Via di Tor Sanguigna 3
📞 06-68 80 5311 🕐 10am-7pm Sun-Fri, 10am-8pm Sat 🌐 stadiodomiziano.com

A section of the massive underground brickwork ruins of Domitian's Stadium can be seen at this museum. Video reconstructions in 3D and an audio guide bring the story of the stadium to life.

Timeline

1500–1600
Rome's city market is transferred from the Campidoglio to Piazza Navona.

1655–1866
Every August, the fountain outlets are plugged and the piazza flooded. The lower classes swim in the square while aristocrats look on.

1–100 AD
△ A stadium is built for athletic contests (agones), chariot races and other sports. Piazza Navona will follow the shape of this stadium.

1644–1655
△ Pope Innocent X commissions a new church, palace and fountain for the square.

1869
Rome's city market moves to the nearby Campo de' Fiori.

EAT

Tre Scalini
This terrace café is famous for its *tartufo* - dense dark chocolate ice cream made from 13 varieties of Swiss chocolate studded with shards of bitter chocolate and served with a wafer and smear of whipped cream.

◉T2 ⌂Piazza Navona 28 ☏06-6880 1996

↑ Piazza Navona, with the Fontana del Moro in the foreground

Fountains

Work on Bernini's Fontana dei Quattro Fiumi in the centre of the square started in 1648, and was financed by a tax levied on bread, even though there was a famine at the time. The fountain is thought to symbolize the power of the papacy over the entire world, represented by the four rivers (Plate, Ganges, Nile and Danube). The obelisk originally stood on the Appian Way, and sits on a sculpted rock, decorated with the dove and olive branch emblems from Pope Innocent X's coat of arms.

Featuring a Moor wrestling with a dolphin, the Fontana del Moro at the southern end was originally designed by Giacomo della Porta and consisted simply of the dolphin and four Tritons. In 1653, Bernini embellished it by designing the statue of a Moor to straddle the dolphin. In 1874, the original was moved to the Galleria Borghese and replaced with a copy.

At the northern end of the square, the Fontana del Nettuno began as a public drinking and washing fountain, with a basin designed by Giacomo della Porta. In the late 19th century Romans no longer depended on public fountains for their water supplies, and the fountain became a purely decorative one.

↑ The square's centrepiece, Fontana dei Quattro Fiumi, designed by Bernini

Sant'Agnese in Agone

This Baroque church, on the left-hand side of the square, has a concave façade designed by Borromini in 1657. It stands on the site where, according to legend, in 304 AD Agnese, a 13-year-old girl from an early Christian family, was exposed naked to the spectators in Domitian's Stadium for refusing to marry and renounce her faith. Story has it that her hair grew miraculously, cascading over her body and concealing it from the crowds. Agnese was then condemned to death and martyred.

Statues of Neptune and the Nereids in the Fontana del Nettuno

EXPERIENCE MORE

② Santa Maria della Pace

📍T2 🏛Vicolo dell'
Arco della Pace 5 🚌46, 62,
64, 70, 81, 87, 116, 492, 628
🕐8:30am–8:25pm daily

A drunken soldier allegedly pierced the breast of a painted Madonna on this site, causing it to bleed. Pope Sixtus IV della Rovere (reigned 1471–84) placated the Virgin by ordering Baccio Pontelli to build her a church if she would bring the war with Turkey to an end. Peace was restored and the church was named Santa Maria della Pace (St Mary of Peace).

The cloister was added by Bramante in 1504. As in his famous round chapel, the Tempietto (p275), he scrupulously followed Classical rules of proportion and achieved a monumental effect in a relatively small space. Pietro da Cortona may have had Bramante's Tempietto in mind when he added the church's charming semicircular portico in 1656. The interior, a short nave ending under an octagonal cupola, houses Raphael's famous frescoes of four Sybils, and four Prophets by his pupil Timoteo Viti, painted for the banker Agostino Chigi in 1514. Baldassarre Peruzzi

also did some work in the church (he painted the fresco in the first chapel on the left), as did the architect Antonio da Sangallo the Younger, who designed the second chapel on the right.

---

③ Palazzo Madama

📍U3 🏛Corso del
Rinascimento ☎06-67061
🚌70, 81, 87, 116, 186,
492, 628 🕐10am–6pm
generally first Sat of month
(exc Aug); tickets available
from 8:30am on day of visit
🌐senato.it

This 16th-century palazzo was built for the Medici family. It was the residence of Medici cousins Giovanni and Giuliano, both of whom became popes: Giovanni as Leo X and Giuliano as Clement VII. Caterina de' Medici, Clement VII's niece, also lived here before she was married to Henri, son of King François I of France, in 1533.

The palazzo takes its name from Madama Margherita of Austria, illegitimate daughter of Emperor Charles V, who married Alessandro de' Medici and, after his death, Ottavio Farnese. Thus, part of the art collection of the Florentine Medici family was inherited by the Roman Farnese family.

The spectacular façade was built in the mid-17th century by Cigoli and Paolo Maruccelli. The latter gave it an ornate cornice and whimsical decorative details on the roof. Since 1871 the palazzo has been the seat of the upper house of the Italian parliament.

←
Detail of Raphael's fresco depicting four Sybils (c.1514), in the Chigi Chapel of Santa Maria della Pace

> All three Caravaggios in San Luigi dei Francesi display very disquieting realism and a highly dramatic use of light.

San Luigi dei Francesi

📍U2 🏛Piazza di San Luigi dei Francesi 5 📞06-688 271 🚌70, 81, 87, 116, 186, 492, 628 🕐9:30am-12:45pm & 2:30-6:30pm daily (Sun: from 11:30am; Thu: am only)

The French national church was founded in 1518, but it took until 1589 to complete. It holds the tombs of many illustrious French people, including Chateaubriand's lover Pauline de Beaumont, who died in Rome in 1805.

Three Caravaggio masterpieces hang in the fifth chapel on the left, all dedicated to St Matthew. Painted between 1597 and 1602, these were Caravaggio's first great religious works: the *Calling of St Matthew*, the *Martyrdom of St Matthew* and *St Matthew and the Angel*. The first version of this last painting was rejected because of its vivid realism; never before had a saint been shown as a tired old man with dirty feet. All three Caravaggios in San Luigi dei Francesi display very disquieting realism and a highly dramatic use of light.

↑ The Baroque decoration on the ceiling and columns inside the church of San Luigi dei Francesi

Sant'Agostino

📍U2 🏛Piazza di Sant' Agostino 80 🚌70, 81, 87, 116, 186, 492, 628 🕐7:30am-noon & 4-7:30pm daily

One of the earliest of Rome's Renaissance churches – and with a façade made of travertine taken from the Colosseum – Sant'Agostino is associated with mothers, thanks to a statue of the Madonna del Parto (Pregnant Madonna) by Jacopo Sansovino that is believed to have the power to help pregnant women. The Virgin's Classical features and heavy drapery suggest she may have been inspired by a statue of Juno Lucina, the Roman goddess of childbirth. Don't miss the extraordinary *Madonna di Loreto* by Caravaggio. Depicting a peasant-like Madonna standing in a doorway welcoming two pilgrims, it is remarkably – and, at the time, controversially – realistic. The soles of the pilgrims' feet are filthy, and even the Madonna has dirty toenails.

Palazzo Pamphilj

📍T3 🏛Piazza Navona 14 🚌46, 62, 64, 70, 81, 87, 116, 492, 628 🕐 for guided tours only 🌐ambascia tadelbrasile.it

In 1644 Giovanni Battista Pamphilj became Pope Innocent X. During his ten-year reign, he heaped riches on his own family, especially his domineering sister-in-law, Olimpia Maidalchini. The "talking statue" Pasquino *(p126)* gave her the nickname "Olim-Pia", Latin for "formerly virtuous". She lived in the grand Palazzo Pamphilj, which has wonderful 17th-century frescoes by Pietro da Cortona depicting scenes from the life of Aeneas and a gallery by Borromini. The building now houses the Brazilian embassy and cultural centre.

COURTESANS AT SANT'AGOSTINO

Sant'Agostino was a notoriously popular church with 16th-century courtesans, for whom going to a "society" church, dressed in all their finery, was a crucial publicity exercise. The women looked magnificent, dripping with jewellery and dressed in the latest, most ostentatious styles, with their hair bleached blonde and elaborately curled. Crowds of young men would gather outside the church, waiting for them to arrive. A priest from Sant'Agostino would hear their confessions. "Just think, Your Excellency, what a lot of fine things he must have heard…," wrote one courtesan, Beatrice Ferrarese, to her lover Lorenzo de' Medici.

→ The courtyard of the 16th-century Palazzo Massimo alle Colonne, designed by Baldassare Peruzzi

EAT

Lo Zozzone

A Roman institution, this cosy place serves delicious *pizza bianca* with an array of fillings from mozzarella to artichoke, plus tasty pasta dishes and crisp Roman-style pizza.

 T3 Via del Teatro Pace 32
06-6880 8575

€€€

Osteria del Pegno

This romantic little restaurant with low lighting can be found on the ground floor of a 15th-century palazzo and offers a menu of perfectly executed Italian dishes. Complimentary limoncello and homemade biscuits round off a meal nicely.

 S2 Vicolo Montevecchio 8
06-6880 7025

€€€

Casa Bleve

Set in a grand vaulted dining room, this enoteca-restaurant has an impressive wine list and a menu of gourmet offerings such as braised beef cheek served in Nebbiolo wine.

U3 Via del Teatro Valle 48
casableve.com

€€€

❼

Palazzo Massimo alle Colonne

 T3 Corso Vittorio Emanuele II 141 40, 46, 62, 64, 70, 81, 87, 116, 186, 492, 628

During the last two years of his life, Baldassarre Peruzzi built this palazzo for the Massimo family, whose home had been destroyed in the 1527 Sack of Rome. Peruzzi displayed great ingenuity in dealing with an awkwardly shaped site. The previous building had stood on the ruined Theatre of Domitian, which created a curve in the great processional Via Papalis. Peruzzi's convex colonnaded façade follows the line of the street. His originality is also evident in the small square upper windows, the courtyard and the stuccoed vestibule. A single column from the theatre has been set up in the piazza.

The Massimo family traced its origins to Quintus Fabius Maximus, conqueror of Hannibal in the 3rd century BC, and their coat of arms is borne by an infant Hercules. Over the years this family dynasty produced many great Humanists, and in the 19th century, it was a Massimo who negotiated peace with Napoleon. On 16 March each year the family chapel opens to the public for a few hours (7am–1pm) to commemorate young Paolo Massimo's resurrection from the dead by San Filippo Neri in 1538.

---

❽

Pasquino

 T3 Piazza di Pasquino 40, 46, 62, 64, 70, 81, 87, 116, 492, 628

This rough chunk of marble is all that now remains of a Hellenistic group, probably representing the incident in Homer's *Iliad* in which Menelaus shields the body of the slain Patroclus. For years it lay as a stepping stone in a muddy medieval street until it was erected on this corner in 1501, near the shop of an

Sant'Ivo alla Sapienza

U3 **Corso del Rinascimento 40** **06-0608** **40, 46, 64, 70, 81, 87, 116, 186, 492, 628** **9am-noon Sun**

The church's lantern is crowned with a cross on top of a twisted spiral – a highly distinctive landmark from Rome's roof terraces. No other Baroque church is quite like this one, made by Borromini, based on a design of astonishing geometrical complexity. The church stands in the courtyard of the Palazzo della Sapienza, seat of the old University of Rome from the 1400s until 1935.

Palazzo Braschi

T3 **Piazza San Pantaleo 10** **06-6710 8303** **40, 46, 62, 64, 70, 81, 87, 116, 186, 492, 628** **10am-7pm Tue-Sun (ticket office closes at 6pm)**

The last Roman palazzo to be built for the family of a pope, Palazzo Braschi was erected in the late 18th century for Pope Pius VI Braschi's nephews. Architect Cosimo Morelli gave the building its imposing façade overlooking the piazza.

The palazzo now houses the municipal Museo di Roma, with exhibits illustrating life in Rome from medieval times to the 19th century.

Sant'Andrea della Valle

U4 **Piazza Sant'Andrea della Valle** **06-686 1339** **H, 40, 46, 62, 64, 70, 81, 87, 116, 186, 492, 628** **8** **7:30am-12:30pm & 4:30-7:30pm daily**

The church is the scene of the first act of Puccini's opera *Tosca*. Opera fans will not find the Attavanti Chapel a mere poetic invention. The real church still has much to recommend it – the impressive façade shows the flamboyant Baroque style at its best. Inside, a golden light filters through high windows, showing off the gilded interior. Here lie the two popes of the Sienese Piccolomini family: on the left of the central nave is the tomb of Pius II, the first Humanist pope (reigned 1458–64); Pope Pius III lies opposite – he reigned for less than a month in 1503.

The church is famous for its beautiful dome, which is the largest in Rome after St Peter's. It was built by Carlo Maderno in 1622–5 and was painted with splendid frescoes by Domenichino and Giovanni Lanfranco. The latter's extravagant style, to be seen in the dome fresco *Glory of Paradise*, won him most of the commission, and the jealous Domenichino is said to have tried to kill his colleague. He failed, but Domenichino's jealousy was unnecessary, as shown by his two beautiful paintings of scenes from the life of St Andrew around the apse and altar. In the Strozzi Chapel, built in the style of Michelangelo, the altar has copies of the *Leah* and *Rachel* by Michelangelo in San Pietro in Vincoli (*p205*).

Did You Know?

Pasquino is the origin of the word "pasquinade", or "lampoon," posted in a public place.

outspoken cobbler named Pasquino. Freedom of speech was not encouraged in papal Rome, so the cobbler wrote out his satirical comments on current events and attached them to the statue.

Other Romans followed suit, hanging their maxims and verses on the statue by night to escape punishment. Despite the wrath of the authorities, the sayings of the "talking statue" (renamed Pasquino) were part of popular culture up until the 19th century. Anonymous political maxims were hung on other statues, too. Sometimes satirical poems are still stuck onto the Pasquino statue.

↑ The coat of arms of Pope Francis on the portal of Sant'Andrea della Valle

Madonna and Angels (1606–8), by Peter Paul Rubens, which hangs above the altar in the Chiesa Nuova

EAT

Hostaria dell'Orso

Formerly an ancient inn, this restaurant is housed in a palazzo with a 15th-century portico and loggia built with columns from Roman ruins. Dine outside on the terrace on delicious European dishes. Past illustrious visitors have included the 16th-century French writers Rabelais and Montaigne.

📍T1 🏛Via dei Soldati 25 📞06-6830 1192 🕐Only for dinner

€€€

⑫ Via del Governo Vecchio

📍S3 🚌40, 46, 62, 64

The street takes its name from Palazzo del Governo Vecchio, which was the seat of papal government in the 17th and 18th centuries. Once part of the Via Papalis, which led from the Lateran to St Peter's, the street is lined with 15th- and 16th-century houses and small workshops. Particularly interesting are those at No. 104 and No. 106. The small palazzo at No. 123 was once thought to have been the home of the architect Bramante.

Opposite is Palazzo del Governo Vecchio. It is also known as Palazzo Nardini, from the name of its founder, which is inscribed, aalong with the date 1477, on the first-floor windows.

⑬ Chiesa Nuova

📍S3 🏛Piazza della Chiesa Nuova 📞06-687 5289 🚌40, 46, 62, 64 🕐7:30am-noon & 4:30-7pm daily

San Filippo Neri (St Philip Neri) is the most appealing of the Counter-Reformation saints. An unconventional reformer, he required his noble Roman followers to humble themselves in public – for example by setting noblemen to work as labourers on building his church. With the help of Pope Gregory XIII, his church was constructed in place of an old medieval church and it has been known ever since as the Chiesa Nuova (new church).

Begun in 1575 by Matteo da Città di Castello and continued by Martino Longhi the Elder, it was consecrated in 1599 (but the façade, by Fausto Rughesi, was only finished in 1606). Against San Filippo's wishes, the interior was decorated after his death; Pietro da Cortona frescoed the nave, dome and apse, taking nearly 20 years. There are also three paintings by Rubens: Madonna and Angels; Saints Domitilla, Nereus and Achilleus; and Saints Gregory, Maurus and Papias. San Filippo is buried in his own chapel, to the left of the altar.

Statue of librettist Pietro Metastasio in Piazza della Chiesa Nuova

STAY

Hotel Raphael
This magnificent vine-covered hotel offers modern luxe rooms designed by architect Richard Meier, as well as more traditional options. There is a good vegetarian restaurant, too, and a stunning rooftop bar.

T2 Largo Febo 2
raphaelhotel.com

€€€

14
Oratorio dei Filippini

S3 Piazza della Chiesa Nuova 06-6710 8100
46, 62, 64 to the public

With the adjoining church and convent, the Oratory formed the centre of Filippo Neri's religious order, founded in 1575. Its members are known as Filippini. The musical term "oratorio" (a religious text sung by solo voices and chorus)

---

derives from the services that were held here. Filippo Neri came to Rome aged 18 to work as a tutor at a time of religious strife, an economic slump and an outbreak of the plague after the Sack of Rome in 1527. Newcomers like Neri and Ignazio di Loyola set out to revive the spiritual life of the city.

Neri formed a brotherhood of laymen who helped pilgrims and the sick (see *Santissima Trinità dei Pellegrini p161*). He founded the Oratory as a centre for religious discourse. Its conspicuous curving brick façade was built by Borromini.

15
Torre dell'Orologio

S3 Piazza dell'Orologio
40, 46, 62, 64

Borromini built this clock tower to decorate one corner of the Convent of the Oratorians of San Filippo Neri in 1647–9. Its front and rear are concave and the sides convex. The mosaic of the Madonna under the clock is by Pietro da Cortona, while on the corner of the building is a small tabernacle to the Madonna flanked by angels in the style of Bernini.

16
Palazzo del Banco di Santo Spirito

R2 Via del Banco di Santo Spirito 40, 46, 62, 64 normal banking hours

Formerly the mint of papal Rome, this palazzo is often referred to as the Antica Zecca (old mint). The upper storeys of the façade, built by Antonio da Sangallo the Younger in the 1520s, are in the shape of a Roman triumphal arch. Above it stand two Baroque statues symbolizing Charity and Thrift, and in the centre of the arch above the main entrance an inscription records the founding of the Banco di Santo Spirito by Pope Paul V Borghese in 1605.

Pope Paul was a very shrewd financier and he encouraged Romans to deposit their money at the bank by offering the vast estates of the Hospital of Santo Spirito (*p298*) as security. The building still houses a modern bank.

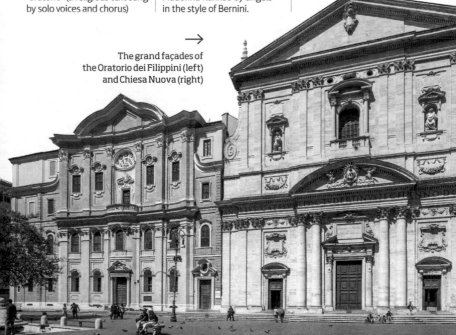

→
The grand façades of the Oratorio dei Filippini (left) and Chiesa Nuova (right)

San Salvatore in Lauro

📍S2 🏛Piazza San Salvatore in Lauro 15 ☎06-687 5187 🚌70, 81, 87, 116, 186, 280, 492 🕐9am–noon & 3-7pm daily

Named "in Lauro" after the laurel grove that grew here in ancient times, this church was built at the end of the 1500s by Ottaviano Mascherino. The bell tower and sacristy were 18th-century additions by Nicola Salvi, famous for the Trevi Fountain *(p182)*.

The church contains the first great altarpiece by the 17th-century artist Pietro da Cortona, *The Birth of Jesus*, in the first chapel to the right.

The adjacent convent of San Giorgio includes a frescoed refectory and the monument to Pope Eugenius IV (reigned 1431–47), moved here when the old St Peter's was pulled down. An extravagant Venetian, Eugenius would willingly spend thousands of ducats on his gold tiara, but requested a "simple, lowly burial place" near his predecessor Pope Eugenius III.

In 1669 San Salvatore in Lauro became the seat of a

pious association, the Confraternity of the Piceni, who were inhabitants of the Marche region. Fanatically loyal to the pope, the Piceni were employed as papal soldiers and tax collectors.

Museo Napoleonico

📍T2 🏛Piazza di Ponte Umberto 1 🚌70, 81, 87, 116, 186, 280, 492 🕐10am–6pm Tue–Sun 🚫1 Jan, 1 May, 25 Dec 🌐museonapoleonico.it

This museum is dedicated to Napoleon Bonaparte and his family. Items that belonged to Napoleon himself include an Indian shawl he wore during his exile on St Helena.

After Napoleon's death in 1821 the pope allowed many of the Bonaparte family to settle in Rome, including his sister Pauline who married the Roman Prince Camillo Borghese. The museum has a cast of her right breast, made by Canova in 1805 as a study for his statue of her as a reclining Venus, now in the Museo Borghese *(p142)*. Portraits and personal effects of other members of the family are on display, including uniforms, court dresses, and a penny-farthing bicycle that belonged to Prince Eugène, the son of Emperor Napoleon III.

The collection was assembled in 1927 by the Counts Primoli, the sons of Napoleon Charles's sister, Carlotta.

The palace next door, in Via Zanardelli, houses the Racolta Praz, a huge selection of over one thousand *objets d'art*, paintings and furniture. Dating from the 17th and 18th centuries, they were collected by the art historian and literary critic Mario Praz.

← A bust of Napoleon on display in the Museo Napoleonico

↑ A bustling street corner at the top of the historic Via dei Coronari

Via dei Coronari

📍S2 🚌40, 46, 62, 64, 70, 81, 87, 116, 186, 280, 492

Large numbers of medieval pilgrims making their way to St Peter's walked along this street to cross over the Tiber at Ponte Sant'Angelo. Of the businesses that sprang up, the most enduring was the selling of rosaries. The street is still named after the rosary sellers *(coronari)* who had their shops along it in medieval times. It followed the course of the ancient Roman Via Recta (straight street), which ran from today's Piazza Colonna to the Tiber.

Making one's way through the vast throng of people in Via dei Coronari could be extremely hazardous. In the Holy Year of 1450, some 200 pilgrims died, crushed by the crowds or drowned in the Tiber. Although the rosary sellers have been replaced by antiques dealers, the street still has many original

The street is still named after the rosary sellers *(coronari)* who had their shops along it in medieval times.

buildings from the 15th and 16th centuries. One of the earliest, at Nos. 156–7, is known as the House of Fiammetta, the mistress of Cesare Borgia.

Palazzo Altemps

🅟 T2 🏠 Via di Sant' Apollinare 46 ☎ 06-3996 7700 🚌 70, 81, 87, 116, 280, 492, 628 🕐 9am-7:45pm Tue-Sun (last adm: 1 hour before closing) 🚫 1 Jan, 25 Dec

An extraordinary collection of Classical sculpture is housed in this branch of the Museo Nazionale Romano. The palazzo was originally built for Girolamo Riario, nephew of Pope Sixtus IV, in 1480 and was restored as a museum in the 1990s. The Riario coat of arms can still be seen in the janitor's room. In the popular uprising that followed the pope's death in 1484, the building was sacked and Girolamo fled the city.

In 1568 the palazzo was bought by Cardinal Marco Sittico Altemps, and it was renovated by Martino Longhi the Elder in the 1570s. He added the great belvedere, crowned with obelisks and a marble unicorn.

The Altemps family were ostentatious collectors; the courtyard and its staircase are lined with ancient sculptures. These form part of the museum's collection, together with the Ludovisi collection of ancient sculptures, which were previously housed in the Museo Nazionale Romano in the Baths of Diocletian (p187). On the first floor, at the far end of the courtyard, visitors can admire the Painted Loggia, dating from 1595. The Ludovisi throne, a Greek original carved in the 5th century BC, is on the same floor. In the Salone del Camino is the powerful statue *Galatian's Suicide*, a marble Roman replica of a group originally made in bronze in ancient Greece. Nearby is the Ludovisi Sarcophagus, dating from the 3rd century AD.

SHOP

Antica Libreria Cascianelli

This wonderful old shop (founded in 1837) is an Aladdin's cave stuffed full of antiquarian books, vintage posters, postcards and maps, as well as antiques – a delightful and rewarding place for a browse.

🅟 T2 🏠 Largo Febo 14 ☎ 328-785 0288

Delfina Delettrez

A scion of the Fendi dynasty, Delettrez is a jeweller whose bold and distinctive designs are beautifully arrayed in this sparkling little boutique, which is designed to resemble a jewellery box.

🅟 T3 🏠 Via del Governo Vecchio 67 🌐 delfinadelettrez.com

A SHORT WALK
PIAZZA NAVONA

Distance 0.8 km (0.5 mile) **Nearest bus** 46, 62, 64, 70, 81, 87, 116, 492, 628 **Time** 20 minutes

To discover an older Rome, walk along Via del Governo Vecchio to admire the façades of its Renaissance buildings and browse in the fascinating antiques shops. No other piazza in Rome can rival the theatricality of Piazza Navona. Day and night there is always something going on in the pedestrian area around its three flamboyant fountains. The Baroque is also represented in many of the area's churches.

The musical term *oratorio* comes from the Oratorio di Filippini, a place of informal worship (p129).

The Chiesa Nuova was rebuilt in the late 16th century for the order founded by San Filippo Neri (p128).

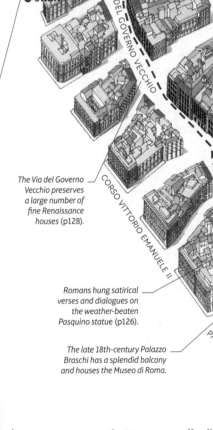

The Torre dell' Orologio clock tower by Borromini (1648) is part of the Convent of the Filippini (p129).

START

VIA DEL CORALLO

VIA DEL GOVERNO VECCHIO

The Via del Governo Vecchio preserves a large number of fine Renaissance houses (p128).

CORSO VITTORIO EMANUELE II

PIAZZ DI PASQUI

Romans hung satirical verses and dialogues on the weather-beaten Pasquino statue (p126).

PIAZ DI SA PANTALE

The late 18th-century Palazzo Braschi has a splendid balcony and houses the Museo di Roma.

← The Fontana del Nettuono and Sant'Agnese in Agone on Piazza Navona

| 0 metres | 50 |
| 0 yards | 50 |

N ↗

Locator Map
For more detail see pp120–21

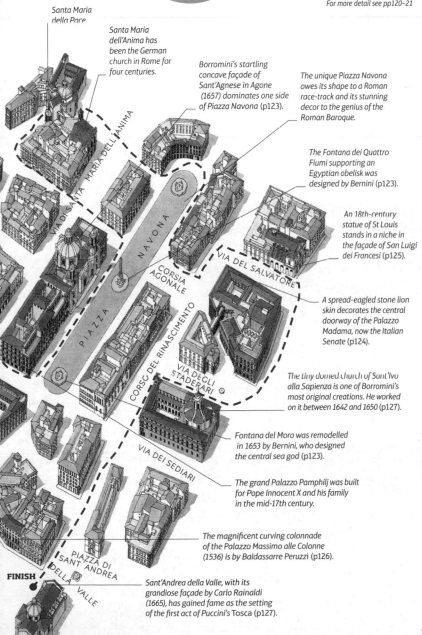

Santa Maria della Pace

Santa Maria dell'Anima has been the German church in Rome for four centuries.

Borromini's startling concave façade of Sant'Agnese in Agone (1657) dominates one side of Piazza Navona (p123).

The unique Piazza Navona owes its shape to a Roman race-track and its stunning decor to the genius of the Roman Baroque.

The Fontana dei Quattro Fiumi supporting an Egyptian obelisk was designed by Bernini (p123).

An 18th-century statue of St Louis stands in a niche in the façade of San Luigi dei Francesi (p125).

A spread-eagled stone lion skin decorates the central doorway of the Palazzo Madama, now the Italian Senate (p124).

The tiny domed church of Sant'Ivo alla Sapienza is one of Borromini's most original creations. He worked on it between 1642 and 1650 (p127).

Fontana del Moro was remodelled in 1653 by Bernini, who designed the central sea god (p123).

The grand Palazzo Pamphilj was built for Pope Innocent X and his family in the mid-17th century.

The magnificent curving colonnade of the Palazzo Massimo alle Colonne (1536) is by Baldassarre Peruzzi (p126).

Sant'Andrea della Valle, with its grandiose façade by Carlo Rainaldi (1665), has gained fame as the setting of the first act of Puccini's Tosca (p127).

FINISH

PIAZZA DI SPAGNA AND VILLA BORGHESE

By the 16th century, the increase in the numbers of visiting pilgrims and ecclesiasts was making life in Rome's already congested medieval centre unbearable. A new triangle of roads was built, still in place today, designed to channel pilgrims as swiftly as possible from the city's north gate, Porta del Popolo, to the Vatican. By the 18th century hotels had sprung up all over the district. With Piazza di Spagna at its heart, this area remains busy day and night, the target of visitors from all over the world. Beyond the still visible traces of the old city walls lie the extensive grounds of Villa Borghese, now Rome's most popular public park. The villa and gardens were designed in the early 17th century by Cardinal Scipione Borghese as a recreational retreat at the edge of Rome and to house his private art collection. The present gardens were redeveloped in the early 19th century and have a boating lake, a replica of Shakespeare's Globe Theatre, a zoo, a few cafés and several of Rome's finest museums.

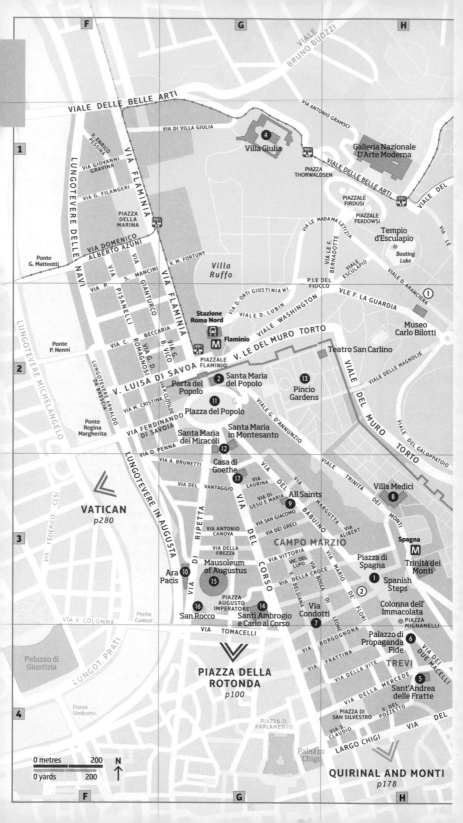

VIALE BRUNO BUOZZI

VIALE DELLE BELLE ARTI

VIA DI VILLA GIULIA

VIA ANTONIO GRAMSCI

V. ENRICO PESSINA

VIA GIOVANNI GRAVINA

VIA G. FILANGERI

1

Villa Giulia **4**

Galleria Nazionale D'Arte Moderna

VIALE DELLE BELLE ARTI

PIAZZA THORWALDSEN

PIAZZALE FIRDUSI

PIAZZALE FERDOWSI

VIA LE MADAMA LETIZIA

Tempio d'Esculapio

VIA LE

VIA LE E BERNADOTTE

VIA LE F. BERNADOTTE

VIALE ESCULAPIO

Boating Lake

VIA D'ARANCIERA

PIAZZA DELLA MARINA

VIA DOMENICO ALBERTO AZUNI

V. M. FORTUNY

Villa Ruffo

VIA D. ORTI GIUSTINIANI

P.LE DEL FIOCCO

VLE F. LA GUARDIA

①

VIA S. MANCINI

VIA GIANTURCO

VIA FLAMINIA

Ponte G. Matteotti

LUNGOTEVERE DELLE NAVI

VIA P. PISANELLI

BECCARIA

VIALE D. LUBIN

VIALE WASHINGTON

Museo Carlo Bilotti

Ponte P. Nenni

LUNGOTEVERE MICHELANGELO

LUNGOTEVERE ARNALDO DA BRESCIA

VIA C. ROMAGNOSI

VIA G. B. VICO

VIA G. D.

Stazione Roma Nord

Ⓜ Flaminio

PIAZZALE FLAMINIO

V. LE DEL MURO TORTO

Teatro San Carlino

VIALE DELLE MAGNOLIE

2

VIA M. CRISTINA

V. LUISA DI SAVOA

Porta del Popolo **2**

Santa Maria del Popolo

Pincio Gardens **13**

VIA DEL MURO TORTO

Ponte Regina Margherita

VIA FERDINANDO DI SAVOIA

Piazza del Popolo **11**

VIALE G. D'ANNUNZIO

VIALE DEL GALOPPATOIO

VIA D. PENNA

Santa Maria dei Miracoli

Santa Maria in Montesanto

12

VIALE TRINITÀ DEI MONTI

Villa Medici **8**

VIA A. BRUNETTI

Casa di Goethe **17**

VIA DEL VANTAGGIO

VIA LAURINA

VIA DI GESÙ E MARIA

VATICAN
p280

VIA FEDERICO CESI

3

VIA DEL BABUINO

VIA MARGUTTA

All Saints **9**

VIA SAN GIACOMO

VIA DEI GRECI

VIA ALIBERT

VIA ANTONIO CANOVA

CAMPO MARZIO

Spagna **Ⓜ**

LUNGOTEVERE IN AUGUSTA

VIA DELLA FREZZA

VIA VITTORIA

VIC. DEL LUPO

VIA MARIO DE' FIORI

Piazza di Spagna **1**

Trinità dei Monti

VIA DI RIPETTA

Ara Pacis **10**

Mausoleum of Augustus **15**

VIA DELLA CROCE

VIA BELSIANA

VIA DELLA BOCCA DI LEONE

Spanish Steps **2**

Colonna dell' Immacolata

PIAZZA AUGUSTO IMPERATORE

San Rocco **16**

Santi Ambrogio e Carlo al Corso **14**

Via Condotti **7**

PIAZZA MIGNANELLI

Palazzo di Propaganda Fide **6**

VIA DEI DUE MACELLI

VIA TOMACELLI

VIA V. COLONNA

Ponte Cavour

Palazzo di Giustizia

VIA DEL CORSO

VIA BORGOGNONA

VIA FRATTINA

VIA DELLA VITE

TREVI

Sant'Andrea delle Fratte **5**

LUNGOT. PRATI

Ponte Umberto

PIAZZA D. PARLAMENTO

PIAZZA DI SAN SILVESTRO

VIA DELLA MERCEDE

V. DEL POZZETTO

VIA S. CLAUDIO

4

0 metres 200

0 yards 200

N ↑

Palazzo Chigi

LARGO CHIGI

VIA DEL

PIAZZA DELLA ROTONDA
p100

QUIRINAL AND MONTI
p178

PIAZZA DI SPAGNA AND VILLA BORGHESE

Must Sees
1. Piazza di Spagna
2. Santa Maria del Popolo
3. Villa Borghese
4. Villa Giulia

Experience More
5. Sant'Andrea delle Fratte
6. Palazzo di Propaganda Fide
7. Via Condotti
8. Villa Medici
9. All Saints
10. Ara Pacis
11. Piazza del Popolo
12. Santa Maria dei Miracoli and Santa Maria in Montesanto
13. Pincio Gardens
14. Santi Ambrogio e Carlo al Corso
15. Mausoleum of Augustus
16. San Rocco
17. Casa di Goethe

Eat & Drink
1. Casina del Lago Café
2. Antico Caffè Greco

PIAZZA DI SPAGNA

📍 H3 🚌 116, 117, 119 Ⓜ Spagna

Shaped like a crooked bow tie and surrounded by tall, shuttered houses painted in muted shades of ochre, pink and cream, Piazza di Spagna is the most famous square in Rome.

The square was long the haunt of expatriates and foreign visitors. In the 17th century the Spanish embassy was here, and the area around it was deemed to be Spanish territory – anyone who unwittingly trespassed was in danger of being dragooned into the Spanish army. In the 18th and 19th centuries the square stood at the heart of the main hotel district, attracting visitors from all over the world. Today the piazza is thronged with people all day and, in summer, most of the night. The church at the top of the steps, Trinità dei Monti, founded by the French in 1485, is famous for its breathtaking views.

Fontana della Barcaccia

Designed either by Gian Lorenzo Bernini or his father, Pietro, this fountain was an ingenious solution to the fact that the

water pressure on the square was so low that spectacular cascades were not possible. Instead, the fountain represents a sinking boat, lying half submerged in a shallow pool. Pope Urban VIII Barberini commissioned the fountain in 1627.

←

Fontana della Barcaccia, the least showy of Rome's Baroque fountains

KEATS-SHELLEY MEMORIAL HOUSE

♿ 📍 H3 🏛 Piazza di Spagna 26
🕐 10am-1pm & 2-6pm Mon-Sat
🌐 keats-shelley-house.org

This is where the poet John Keats stayed with his friend, the painter Joseph Severn, in 1820. Suffering from consumption, Keats had been sent to Rome by his doctor, in the hope that it would help him recuperate. Depressed because of scathing criticism of his poetry, and unrequited love, Keats died a few months later aged 25. His death inspired poet Percy Bysshe Shelley to write the poem *Mourn not for Adonaïs*. Shelley died the following year in a boating accident; both poets are buried in the Protestant cemetery *(p248)*. The house is now a museum dedicated to the Romantic poets.

↑ The Spanish Steps with azaleas in full bloom and the church of Trinità dei Monti

SANTA MARIA DEL POPOLO

Q G2 **A** Piazza del Popolo 12 **🚌** 117, 119, 490, 495, 926 **🚋** 2 **Ⓜ** Flaminio **🕐** 7:30am–12:30pm & 4–7pm Sun-Thu, 7:30am-7pm Fri & Sat **W** santamariadelpopolo.it

Occupying the site where, according to legend, Nero was buried, this early Renaissance church was commissioned by Pope Sixtus IV della Rovere in 1472. It is one of Rome's greatest stores of artistic treasures.

Among the artists who worked on the building were Andrea Bregno and Pinturicchio. Later additions were made by Bramante and Bernini. Many illustrious families have chapels here, all decorated with appropriate splendour. The Della Rovere Chapel has delightful frescoes by Pinturicchio, the Cerasi Chapel has two Caravaggio masterpieces, but the finest of all is the Chigi Chapel designed by Raphael in 1513–16 for his patron, the banker Agostino Chigi. The most striking of the church's many Renaissance tombs are the two by Andrea Sansovino behind the main altar.

↑ One of two Caravaggios in the Cerasi Chapel, *The Crucifixion of St Peter* uses dramatic foreshortening to highlight the sheer effort involved in turning the saint's crucifix upside down.

↑ Behind the altar, the stained-glass windows by the French artist Guillaume de Marcillat were the first in Rome.

1213–27
▼ Chapel enlarged under Gregory IX

1485–9
▼ Della Rovere Chapel painted by Pinturicchio

Timeline

1099
▲ Paschal II builds chapel over tombs of the Domitia family (which included Nero) in honour of the Madonna

1472–8
▲ Sixtus IV builds church (one of the first Renaissance churches in Rome)

↑ The dome of Raphael's Chigi Chapel, with mosaics showing God as creator of the seven heavenly bodies

Rowing on the lake in the Villa Borghese gardens ↓

3

VILLA BORGHESE

📍 G2 🏠 Entrances at Piazzale Flaminio, Porta Pinciana & Pincio Gardens 🚌 52, 53, 88, 116, 490, 495 🚊 3, 19

One of Rome's largest parks, Villa Borghese was laid out in the early 17th century by Cardinal Scipione Borghese, the pleasure-loving nephew of Pope Paul V.

A keen art collector, Scipione Borghese amassed one of Europe's finest collections of paintings, sculptures and antiquities. The young Bernini created many of his loveliest sculptures for Scipione, many of which are still displayed in the Museo e Galleria Borghese (formerly called Casino Borghese), created specifically to house the collection. Borghese was also a patron of Caravaggio. The park was redesigned in the 18th century by Scottish landscape artist Jacob More, with artificial lakes and Neo-Classical temples. In 1903 the park became the property of the Italian state and was opened to the general public. A replica of Shakespeare's Globe Theatre was added in 2003.

EAT

Casina del Lago café
This charming little café has great outdoor seating on a terrace (heated in winter), overlooking the lake. It offers simple pasta and rice dishes, salads and sandwiches, along with coffees, wine, cakes and pastries. Enjoy a ten percent discount with an entrance ticket to the Carlo Bilotti museum.

📍 H2 🏠 Viale dell'Aranciera 2
📞 06-8535 2623
🕐 Mon in winter

€€€

Villa Borghese

Casina di Raffaello

📍 J2 🏛 Piazza di Siena ⏰ 9am-6pm Tue-Sun (till 3:30pm in winter), 10am-7pm Sat, Sun & hols (till 6pm in winter) 🌐 casinadi raffaello.it

This diminutive house – said to have once been owned by the painter Raphael – is now dedicated to young children between the ages of three and ten. It has indoor and outdoor play areas, a reading corner, wooden toys and a fun-packed programme of activities for children and all the family.

② Museo Carlo Bilotti

📍 H2 🏛 Viale Fiorello La Guardia 📞 06-0608 🚌 116 Ⓜ Flaminio-Piazza del Popolo (Line A) ⏰ 1-7pm Tue-Fri (winter: 10am-4pm), 10am-7pm Sat & Sun 🌐 museocarlo bilotti.it

Housing the art collection of perfume baron and art collector Carlo Bilotti, this bijou's museum has a permanent collection of 22 works by Giorgio de Chirico, along with a portrait of Bilotti's wife and daughter by Andy Warhol. It hosts contemporary art and photography exhibitions (there is an entry fee only for special exhibitions).

③ Bioparco

📍 J1 🏛 Piazzale Giardino Zoologico 📞 06-360 8211 🚌 3, 52, 53, 217, 360, 910 & 926 🚋 3, 19 Ⓜ Flaminio-Piazza del Popolo & Spagna (Line A) ⏰ Late Oct-late Mar: 9:30am-5pm daily; late Mar-late Oct: 9:30am-6pm daily (till 7pm Sat & Sun in Apr-Sep)

Rome's zoo is devoted to research, the preservation of animals in danger of extinction and the education of the public. It houses more than 1,300 animals, ranging from lions, hippos and elephants to snakes and crocodiles, and has excellent information boards.

A BAROQUE THEME PARK

The gardens were the Baroque equivalent of a theme park, with joke fountains - designed to squirt unwitting passersby - exotic birds, a grotto with artificial rain and a mechanical talking satyr. Scipione originally opened the park to the public, but after a visitor was outraged by the erotic paintings in a summerhouse, Paul V decided it would be more circumspect to keep it private.

Globe Theatre

📍 J1 🏛 Largo Aqua Felix
🕐 Jul & Aug: 7:30pm Sat & Sun; book tickets for performances at www.greenticket.it and tour tickets by calling 0-0608
🌐 globetheatre roma.com

London's Globe Theatre was reconstructed here in just three months. Every summer the theatre showcases Shakespeare's plays with a mixture of productions in Italian and English. Tickets for performances include a tour of the theatre.

GNAM (Galleria Nazionale d'Arte Moderna)

📍 H1 🏛 Viale delle Belli Arti 131 📞 06-3229 8221
🚌 3 🚊 19 🕐 8:30am–7:15pm Tue–Sun 🌐 lagallerianazionale.com

Rome's museum of 19th- and 20th-century art makes its first impact with a stunning cracked-mirror floor designed by the contemporary Italian artist Alfredo Pirri. The collections are spread over two floors. On the ground floor is a section called "Excuse me, is this art?". It includes several pieces by French artist Marcel Duchamp along with slashed and pierced canvasses created by Lucio Fontana in the 1950s. The second floor displays works by Italian Futurists such as Gino Severini, Mario Sironi and Giacomo Balla, as well as Giorgio de Chirico and Sicilian artist Renato Guttoso. Other highlights include works by Cy Twombly, Jean Arp, Alberto Giacometti and Henry Moore.

→

Villa Borghese, built by architect Flaminio Ponzio to designs by Scipione Borghese

Museo e Galleria Borghese

📍 K1 🏛 Piazzale del Museo Borghese 5 🚌 52, 53, 116, 910 to Via Pinciana 🚊 3, 19 to Viale delle Belle Arti 🕐 9am–7pm Tue–Sun 🌐 galleria borghese.beni culturali.it

Cardinal Scipione Borghese built Villa Borghese in the 17th century as a country villa for elaborate parties, its three wings embracing the surrounding gardens. Scipione Borghese was an extravagant patron of the arts and filled the villa with exotic antique statues and virtuoso sculptures. The museum is divided into two sections: the sculpture collection (Museo Borghese) occupies the ground floor, and the picture gallery (Galleria Borghese) is on the upper floor.

> Scipione Borghese was an extravagant patron of the arts and filled the villa with exotic antique statues and virtuoso sculptures.

Museo Borghese

The highlights of the sculpture collection that form the Museo Borghese are the superb pieces by Bernini inspired by Greek mythology. The sculpture of *David* shows him with brows furrowed, lips gripped and catapult held taut, about to swing the full weight of his body to launch a stone to kill the giant Goliath. The virtuoso *Apollo and Daphne* shows Daphne in the process of metamorphosizing into a laurel tree to escape the sun god Apollo.

Galleria Borghese

The gallery's fine art collection includes Titian's evocation of the difference between chaste and sexual love, *Sacred and Profane Love*, as well as several works by Caravaggio – notably the *Madonna del Palafranieri*, removed from St Peter's because it was felt to be inappropriately realistic, a feverish *Self-Portrait of the Artist as Bacchus*, reputedly painted while the artist was ill, and the decadent *Boy with a Basket of Fruit* in which flecked vine leaves and over-ripe fruit exude a decaying fecundity. Another major work is Raphael's *Deposition* (1507), which was commissioned by Perugian matriarch Atalanta Baglioni to honour her assassinated son, who is depicted as a red-shirted pall-bearer.

↑ *Sacred and Profane Love* (1514) by Titian

↑ The mighty *David* (1624) by Bernini – the face was modelled on the artist's own

4 (icons)

VILLA GIULIA

G1 ⌂ Piazzale di Villa Giulia 9 **☎** 06-322 6571 🚌 52, 926 to Viale Bruno Buozzi; 88, 490, 495 to Viale Washington 🚋 3, 19 to Piazza Thorvaldsen 🕐 9am–8pm Tue–Sun (last adm: 6:30pm)

Since 1889 Villa Giulia has housed the Museo Nazionale Etrusco, with its outstanding collection of pre-Roman antiquities from central Italy. It holds the most important collection of Etruscan art in Italy.

Built as a country retreat for Pope Julius III in the 16th century, Villa Giulia was designed by exceptional architects: Vignola (designer of the Gesù), Vasari and the sculptor Ammannati. Michelangelo also contributed. The villa's main features are its façade, the courtyard and garden and the *nymphaeum*.

↑ Euphronius Vase (room 13a), a 6th-century BC Greek vase, depicting Hypnos, god of sleep, and Thanatos, god of death

Etruscan Finds

Etruria was not a nation, but a federation of politically and economically independent cities in central Italy. The Etruscans were energetic traders – their wealth was based on prodigious natural resources of metals. If the finds from the tombs of the wealthy are any indication, they had a voracious appetite for the beautiful artifacts produced by their Greek and Phoenician trading partners. Tomb finds include the elaborately decorated chalices, wine jugs and kraters that may have graced Etruscan banqueting tables; mirrors and jewellery; and some extra-ordinary home accessories including a lion-foot candelabra.

Artifacts on display come from most of the major excavations in Tuscany and Lazio. Rooms 1–13b and 30–40 are arranged by site and include Vulci, Todi, Veio and Cerveteri, while the remaining rooms are devoted to important objects that have been returned after being illegally excavated and sold, as well as private collections that have been donated to the museum.

VILLA PONIATOWSKI

G1 ⌂ Piazzale di Villa Giulia 3 **☎** 06-4423 9949 🕐 9am–1:45pm Tue–Sat (advance booking required)

The museum's additional collections are at the nearby Villa Poniatowski, which has beautifully restored frescoed rooms. Exhibits include fine gold jewellery, a tomb carved from a tree trunk and decorated make-up containers.

← Façade of the Renaissance Villa Giulia, designed by several leading architects

← Sarcophagus of the Spouses (room 12), a 6th-century BC terracotta masterpiece from Cerveteri, showing a dead couple at the eternal banquet

↑ The beautiful portico of Villa Giulia with fresoces by Pietro Venale, leading to the courtyard

EXPERIENCE MORE

 5

Sant'Andrea delle Fratte

📍H4 🏠Via Sant'Andrea delle Fratte 1 📞06-679 3191 🚌116, 117 Ⓜ️Spagna 🕐summer: 6:30am-12:30pm & 4:30-8pm; winter: 6:15am-1pm & 4-7pm

When Sant'Andrea delle Fratte was built in the 1100s, this was the northernmost edge of Rome. Though the church is now firmly within the city, its name (*fratte* means "thickets") recalls its original setting.

The church was completely rebuilt in the 17th century, partly by Borromini. His bell tower and dome are notable for the complex concave and convex surfaces. The bell tower is particularly fanciful, with angel caryatids, flaming torches, and exaggerated scrolls like semi-folded hearts supporting a spiky crown.

In 1842, the Virgin Mary appeared in the church to a Jewish banker, who promptly converted to Christianity and became a missionary. Inside, the chapel of the Miraculous Madonna is the first thing you notice. The church is better known, however, for the angels that Borromini's rival, Bernini, carved for the Ponte Sant' Angelo. Pope Clement IX declared they were too lovely to be exposed to the weather, so they remained with Bernini's family until 1729, when they were moved to the church.

 6

Palazzo di Propaganda Fide

📍H4 🏠Via di Propaganda 1 📞06-6988 0266 🚌116, 117 Ⓜ️Spagna

The Jesuit Congregation for the Propagation of the Faith was founded in 1622. Though Bernini had originally been commissioned to create their headquarters, Innocent X, who became pope in 1644, preferred the style of Borromini, who was asked to continue. His extraordinary west façade, completed in 1662, is striped with broad pilasters, between which the first-floor windows bend in and the central bay bulges. A rigid band divides its floors, and the cornice above the convex central bay swerves inwards. The more you look at it, the more restless it seems; a sign perhaps of the increasing unhappiness of the architect who committed suicide in 1667.

 7

Via Condotti

📍G3 & 4 🚌81, 116, 117, 119, 492 and many routes along via del Corso or stopping at Piazza San Silvestro Ⓜ️Spagna

Named after the conduits that carried water to the Baths of Agrippa near the Pantheon, Via Condotti is now home to the most traditional of Rome's

Via Condotti, the famous shopping street leading to the Spanish Steps

Medici bought it in 1576. From the terrace you can look across the city to Castel Sant'Angelo, from where Queen Christina of Sweden is said to have fired the large cannon ball which now sits in the basin of the fountain. The villa's most famous resident was Galileo, who was imprisoned here for falling foul of the Inquisition in 1630–33.

The villa is home to the French Academy, which was founded by Louis XIV in 1666 with the aim of giving a few select painters the chance to study in Rome. Nicolas Poussin was one of the first advisers to the Academy, Ingres was a director, and former students include Jean-Honoré Fragonard and François Boucher.

It is now used for concerts and exhibitions. Guided tours take in the landscaped gardens and frescoed rooms. A highlight is the Stanza degli Uccelli.

 9

All Saints

📍 J2 🏛 Via del Babuino 153B 📞 06-3600 1881 🚌 117, 119 🕒 8:30am–7pm daily

In 1816 the pope gave English residents and visitors the right to hold Anglican services in

designer clothes shops. Stores selling shoes and other leather goods are also well represented. The street is popular for early evening strolls, when elegant Italians mingle with casually dressed tourists.

The street is home to Gucci, Louis Vuitton, Dolce e Gabbana, Bulgari, Salvatore Ferragamo, Burberry, Prada and Trussardi, among other designer boutiques.

 8

Villa Medici

📍 G3 🏛 Accademia di Francia a Roma, Viale Trinità dei Monti 1 🚌 117, 119 Ⓜ Spagna 🕒 9:30am–6:30pm Tue-Sun for guided visits 🌐 villamedici.it

Superbly positioned on the Pincio hill above Piazza di Spagna, this 16th-century villa has kept the name it assumed when Cardinal Ferdinando de'

→

A stained-glass window featuring English text at the All Saints church

←

→

EAT & DRINK

Antico Caffè Greco

Founded in 1760, this café was once a meeting point for artists and intellectuals, including Keats and Byron, and it retains the feel of a refined salon. Coffee and cake here is a (pricey) treat.

📍 H3 🏛 Via dei Condotti 86 🌐 anticocaffegreco.eu

Rome, but it was not until the early 1880s that they acquired a site to build their own church. The architect was G E Street, who is best known in Britain for his Neo-Gothic churches and the London Law Courts. The style of All Saints is also Victorian Neo-Gothic, and although the interior is splendidly decorated with different coloured Italian marbles, it has a very English air. Street also designed St-Paul's-within-the-Walls in Via Nazionale, whose interior is a jewel of British Pre-Raphaelite art.

The street on which All Saints stands got its name from the Fontana del Sileno, notorious for its ugliness, and nicknamed "baboon".

10
Ara Pacis

G3 ⌂Lungotevere in Augusta 🚌70, 81, 117, 119, 186, 628 🕒9:30am-7:30pm daily (last adm: 6:30pm). 🚫1 Jan, 1 May, 25 Dec 🌐arapacis.it

Reconstructed at considerable expense over the course of many years, the Ara Pacis (Altar of Peace) is one of the most significant monuments of ancient Rome. It celebrates the peace created throughout the Mediterranean area by Emperor Augustus following his victorious campaigns in Gaul and Spain. The monument was commissioned by the Senate in 13 BC and completed four years later. It was positioned in such a way that the shadow of the huge obelisk sundial on Campus Martius *(p112)* would fall upon it on Augustus's birthday.

Forming a square enclosure on a low platform with the altar in the centre, the Ara Pacis is decorated with magnificent friezes and reliefs carved in Carrara marble. The reliefs on the north and south walls depict a procession that took place on 4 July 13 BC, in which the members of the emperor's family can be identified, ranked by their position in the succession. At the time, the heir apparent was Marcus Agrippa, husband of Augustus's daughter Julia. All the portraits in the relief are carved with extraordinary realism, even the innocent toddler clinging to his mother's skirts.

Owing to expansion of the river the Ara Pacis had been submerged in mud. The tale of its rediscovery dates back to the 16th century, when the first panels were unearthed. One of the sections ended up in Paris, while another found its way to Florence. Further discoveries were made in the late 19th century, when archaeologists finally realized just what they had found. The monument as it appears today has all been pieced together since 1938, with some parts original and other parts reproductions. In 1999 the American architect Richard Meier designed a dedicated building to house the entire structure.

↓ The Ara Pacis monument and (right) a detail of one of the many intricate reliefs

11
Piazza del Popolo

G2 🚌117, 119, 490, 495, 926 🚋2 Ⓜ Flaminio

A vast cobbled oval standing at the apex of the triangle of roads known as the Trident, Piazza del Popolo forms a grand symmetrical ante-chamber to the heart of Rome. Twin Neo-Classical façades stand on either side of the Porta del Popolo; an Egyptian obelisk rises in the centre; and the matching domes and porticoes of Santa Maria dei Miracoli and Santa Maria in Montesanto flank the beginning of Via del Corso.

Although it is now one of the most unified squares in Rome, Piazza del Popolo evolved gradually over the centuries. In 1589 the great town-planning pope, Sixtus V, had the obelisk erected in the centre by Domenico Fontana. Over 3,000 years old, the obelisk in

Piazza del Popolo, with Santa Maria dei Miracoli, Santa Maria in Montesanto and the Egyptian obelisk

Piazza del Popolo was originally brought to Rome by Augustus to adorn the Circus Maximus after the conquest of Egypt. Almost a century later Pope Alexander VII commissioned Carlo Rainaldi to build the twin Santa Marias.

In the 19th century the piazza was turned into a grandiose oval by Giuseppe Valadier, the designer of the Pincio Gardens. He encased Santa Maria del Popolo in a Neo-Classical shell to make its south façade match the overall appearance of the piazza.

In contrast to the piazza's air of ordered rationalism, many of the events staged here were barbaric. In the 18th and 19th centuries, public executions were held. Condemned men were sometimes hammered to death by repeated blows to the temples. The last time a criminal was executed in this way was in 1826, even though the guillotine had by then been adopted as a more scientific means of execution.

The riderless horse races from the piazza down Via del Corso were scarcely more humane: the performance of the runners was enhanced by feeding the horses stimulants, wrapping them in nail-studded ropes, and letting off fireworks at their heels.

To the north of the piazza, Via Flaminia, built in 220 BC to connect Rome with Italy's Adriatic coast, enters the city at Porta del Popolo, a grand 16th-century gate built on the orders of Pope Pius IV de' Medici. The architect, Nanni di Baccio Bigio, modelled it on a Roman triumphal arch. The outer face has statues of St Peter and St Paul on either side and a Medici coat of arms.

A century later, Pope Alexander VII commissioned Bernini to decorate the inner face to celebrate the arrival in Rome of Queen Christina of Sweden. Lesser visitors were often delayed while customs officers rifled their luggage. The only way to speed things up was with a bribe.

⑫

Santa Maria dei Miracoli and Santa Maria in Montesanto

📍 G2 🏛 Piazza del Popolo
🚌 117, 119, 490, 495, 628, 926 🚋 2 Ⓜ Flaminio
Santa Maria dei Miracoli:
📞 06-361 0250 🕐 7am–12:30pm, 4–7:30pm daily
Santa Maria in Montesanto:
📞 06-361 0594 🕐 5:30–8pm Mon-Fri, 11am-1:30pm Sun

The two churches at the south end of Piazza del Popolo were designed by the architect Carlo Rainaldi (1611–91), the plans were revised by Bernini and it was Carlo Fontana who eventually completed the project. To provide a focal point for the piazza, the churches had to appear symmetrical. Although the two churches appear identical at first glance, there are differences if you look carefully. The site on the left was narrower. Hence, Rainaldi gave Santa Maria dei Miracoli (on the right) a circular dome and Santa Maria in Montesanto an oval one to squeeze it into the narrower site, while keeping the sides of the supporting drums that face the piazza identical.

> Over 3,000 years old, the obelisk in Piazza del Popolo was originally brought to Rome by Augustus to adorn the Circus Maximus after the conquest of Egypt.

The large Piazza del Popolo at sunset

The 19th-century water clock in the Pincio Gardens

 13

Pincio Gardens

G2 **Il Pincio** **117, 119, 490, 495, 628, 926** **2** **Flaminio**

The Pincio Gardens lie above Piazza del Popolo on a hillside that has been so skilfully terraced and richly planted with trees that, from below, the zig-zagging road climbing to the gardens is virtually invisible. In ancient Roman times, there were magnificent gardens on the Pincio Hill. The present gardens were designed in the early 19th century by Giuseppe Valadier (who also redesigned the Piazza del Popolo). The broad avenues, lined with umbrella pines, palm trees and evergreen oaks soon became a fashionable place to stroll, and even in the 20th century such diverse characters as Gandhi and Mussolini, Richard Strauss and King Farouk of Egypt patronized the Casina Valadier, an exclusive café and restaurant in the grounds.

From the Pincio's main square, Piazzale Napoleone I, the panoramic views of Rome stretch from the Monte Mario to the Janiculum.

One of the most striking features of the park itself is an Egyptian-style obelisk which Emperor Hadrian erected on the tomb of his favourite, the male slave Antinous. After the slave's premature death (according to some accounts he died saving the emperor's life), Hadrian deified him.

Marble busts of many historical Italian and other European figures line the paths of the gardens.

The 19th-century water clock on Via dell'Orologio was designed by a Dominican monk. It was displayed at the Paris Exhibition of 1889.

 14

Santi Ambrogio e Carlo al Corso

G3 **Via del Corso 437** **06-682 8101** **81, 117, 492, 628, 926** **7am-7pm daily**

This church belonged to the Lombard community in Rome, and is dedicated to two canonized bishops of Milan,

 GREAT VIEW
Pincio Gardens

Approach the Pincio Gardens from the grounds of Villa Borghese (p142) above the Pincio, or along Viale della Trinità dei Monti. The panoramic views of Rome are particularly beautiful at sunset.

Lombardy's capital. In 1471 Pope Sixtus IV gave the Lombards a church, and they dedicated it to Sant' Ambrogio, who died in 397. Then in 1610, when Carlo Borromeo was canonized, the church was rebuilt in his honour. Most of the work on the new church was carried out by father and son Onorio and Martino Longhi, but the fine dome is by Pietro da Cortona. The altarpiece by Carlo Maratta (1625–1713) is the Gloria dei Santi Ambrogio e Carlo. An ambulatory leads behind the altar to a chapel housing the heart of San Carlo, which is held in a richly decorated reliquary.

Mausoleum of Augustus

G3 **Piazza Augusto Imperatore** **06-0608** **81, 117, 492, 628, 926**

Only the brick core, which is overgrown with plants, is left today of what was once the most prestigious burial place in Rome. It Is currently being restored after many years of neglect. Augustus had the mausoleum built in 28 BC, the year he became sole ruler, as a tomb for himself and his descendants. The circular building was 87 m (285 ft) in diameter.

Inside were four concentric passageways linked by corridors where the urns containing the ashes of the Imperial family were placed. The first to be buried here was Augustus's favourite nephew, Marcellus, who had married Julia, the emperor's daughter. He died in 23 BC, possibly poisoned by Augustus's second wife Livia, who felt that her son, Tiberius, would make a more reliable emperor. When Augustus died in AD 14, his ashes were placed in the mausoleum, Tiberius duly became emperor, and dynastic poisonings continued to fill the family vault with urns.

This sinister monument was later used as a medieval fortress, a vineyard, a private garden, and even, in the 18th century, as an auditorium and theatre. It can now only be admired from the outside, but after restoration is complete (estimated by spring 2019) it will open to the public.

San Rocco

G3 **Largo San Rocco 1** **06-689 6416** **81, 117, 492, 628, 926** **7–9am & 4:30–8pm Mon-Sat, 8:30am–1pm & 4:30–8pm Sun** **17-31 Aug**

This church, with a restrained Neo-Classical façade by Giuseppe Valadier, the designer of Piazza del Popolo, began life as the chapel of a 16th-century hospital with beds for 50 men – San Rocco was a healer of the plague-stricken. A maternity wing was added for the wives of Tiber bargees to save them from having to give birth in the insanitary conditions of a boat. The hospital came to be used by unmarried mothers, and one section was set aside for women who wished to be unknown. They were even permitted to wear a veil for the duration of their stay.

Unwanted children were sent to an orphanage, and if any mothers or children died they were buried in anonymous graves. The hospital was abandoned in the early 20th century, and demolished in the 1930s during the excavation of the Mausoleum of Augustus.

The church sacristy contains an interesting Baroque altarpiece (c.1660) by Il Baciccia, the artist who decorated the ceiling of the Gesù (p106).

Casa di Goethe

G3 **Via del Corso 18** **117, 119, 490, 495, 628, 926** **2** **Flaminio** **10am–6pm Tue–Sun** **casadigoethe.it**

The German poet, dramatist and novelist Johann Wolfgang von Goethe (1749–1832) lived in this house from 1786 until 1788 and worked on a journal that eventually formed part of his travel book *The Italian Journey*. Rome's noisy street life irritated him, especially during Carnival time. He was a little perturbed by the number of murders in his neighbourhood, but Rome energized him and his book became one of the most influential ever written about Italy.

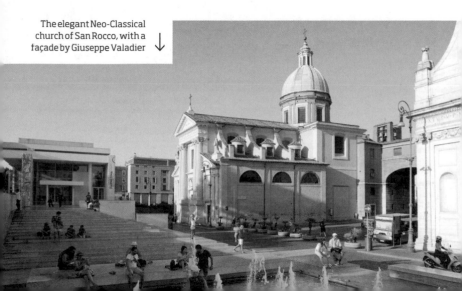

The elegant Neo-Classical church of San Rocco, with a façade by Giuseppe Valadier ↓

A SHORT WALK
PIAZZA DI SPAGNA

Distance 1.5 km (1 mile) **Nearest metro**
Spagna **Time** 30 minutes

Wandering around the network of narrow streets
between Piazza di Spagna and Via del Corso gives
you a feel for one of the liveliest areas in Rome, which
draws throngs of tourists and Romans to its discreet
and elegant shops. Since the 18th century the area,
has been popular with visitors, including famous
writers and composers.

↑ Via Condotti, one
of Rome's busiest
shopping streets

For almost three centuries the
Piazza di Spagna with its curious
Barcaccia fountain in the
centre has been the chief
meeting place for visitors
to Rome (p138).

Antico Caffè Greco has
busts and portraits
recalling the café's former
artistic patrons (p149).

Via delle Carrozze took its
name from the carriages of
wealthy tourists that used to
queue up here for repairs.

The shady, narrow Via Condotti has the
smartest shops in one of the chicest
shopping areas in the world (p148).

START

FINISH

← Fontana della Barcaccia
in Piazza di Spagna,
with Trinità dei Monti
in the distance

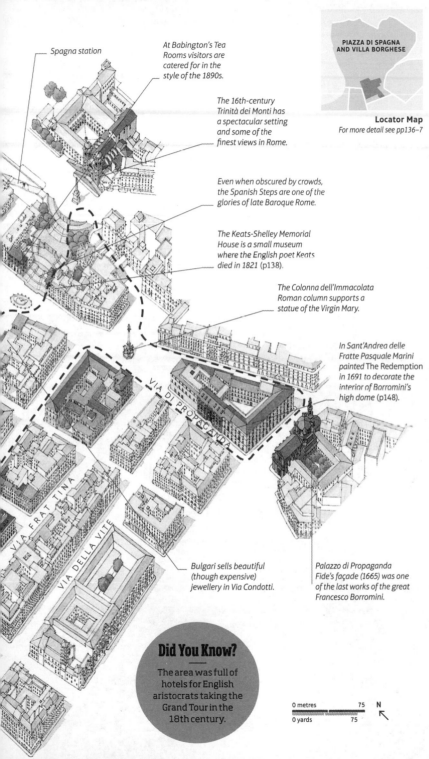

Spagna station

At Babington's Tea Rooms visitors are catered for in the style of the 1890s.

The 16th-century Trinità dei Monti has a spectacular setting and some of the finest views in Rome.

Even when obscured by crowds, the Spanish Steps are one of the glories of late Baroque Rome.

The Keats-Shelley Memorial House is a small museum where the English poet Keats died in 1821 (p138).

The Colonna dell'Immacolata Roman column supports a statue of the Virgin Mary.

In Sant'Andrea delle Fratte Pasquale Marini painted The Redemption in 1691 to decorate the interior of Borromini's high dome (p148).

Locator Map
For more detail see pp136–7

PIAZZA DI SPAGNA AND VILLA BORGHESE

VIA DI PROPAGANDA

VIA FRATTINA

VIA DELLA VITE

Bulgari sells beautiful (though expensive) jewellery in Via Condotti.

Palazzo di Propaganda Fide's façade (1665) was one of the last works of the great Francesco Borromini.

Did You Know?

The area was full of hotels for English aristocrats taking the Grand Tour in the 18th century.

| 0 metres | | 75 |
| 0 yards | | 75 |

N

CAMPO DE' FIORI

Between Corso Vittorio Emanuele II and the Tiber, the city displays many distinct personalities. The open-air market in Campo de' Fiori preserves the lively, bohemian atmosphere of the medieval inns that once flourished here, while the area also contains grand Renaissance palazzi, such as Palazzo Farnese and Palazzo Spada, where powerful Roman families built their fortress-like houses near the route of papal processions. Close by, overlooking the picturesque Tiber Island, lies the Jewish Ghetto, the oldest Jewish settlement in Europe, where many traces of daily life from past centuries can still be seen. The Portico of Octavia and the Theatre of Marcellus are spectacular examples of the city's many-layered history, built over the half-ruined remains of ancient Rome.

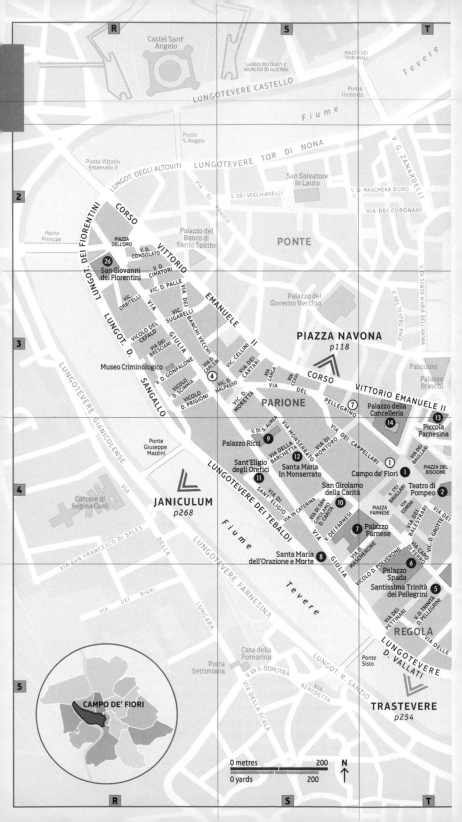

CAMPO DE'FIORI

Must See
1. Campo de' Fiori

Experience More
2. Teatro di Pompeo
3. Palazzo del Monte di Pietà
4. Sotterranei di San Paolo alla Regola
5. Santissima Trinità dei Pellegrini
6. Palazzo Spada
7. Palazzo Farnese
8. Santa Maria dell'Orazione e Morte
9. Palazzo Ricci
10. San Girolamo della Carità
11. Sant'Eligio degli Orefici
12. Santa Maria in Monserrato
13. Piccola Farnesina
14. Palazzo della Cancelleria
15. Teatro Argentina
16. Area Sacra di Largo Argentina
17. San Carlo ai Catinari
18. Fontana delle Tartarughe
19. Crypta Balbi
20. Santa Maria in Campitelli
21. San Nicola in Carcere
22. Theatre of Marcellus
23. Portico of Octavia
24. Tiber Island
25. Ghetto and Synagogue
26. San Giovanni dei Fiorentini
27. Casa di Lorenzo Manilio
28. Palazzo Cenci

Eat
1. Il Forno di Campo de' Fiori
2. Roscioli
3. Piperno

Stay
4. DOM Hotel
5. Hotel Teatro di Pompeo

Shop
6. Beppe e i suoi Formaggi
7. Atelier Patrizia Pieroni
8. Ibiz

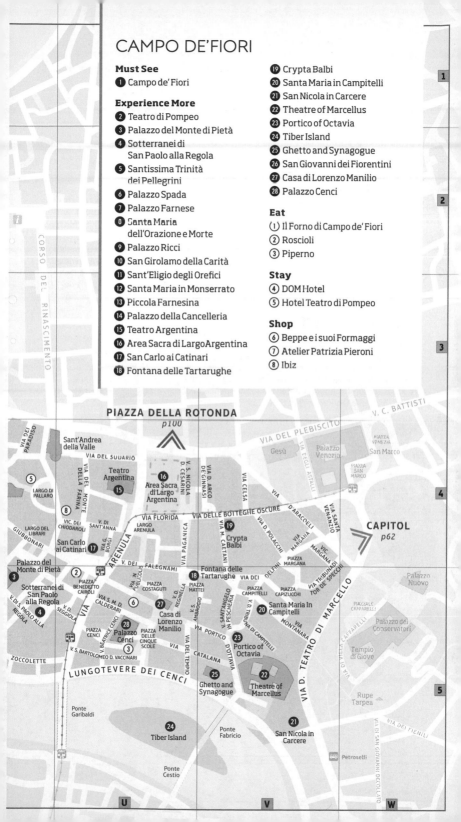

CAMPO DE' FIORI

📍 **T4** 🚌 **Bus 116 and routes to Largo di Torre Argentina or Corso Vittorio Emanuele II**

A lively square since medieval times, Campo de' Fiori bursts with colour during the morning market, and again after dark when its restaurants and bars make it a centre of Roman nightlife.

Occupying the site of a meadow in ancient times behind the vast structure of the Teatro di Pompeo (p164), Campo de' Fiori became the bustling, raffish – and at times rough – heart of Renaissance Rome, populated by artists, craftsmen and courtesans, and packed with cheap inns. Murders were not uncommon – Caravaggio killed his opponent on the piazza after losing a game of tennis, and the goldsmith Benvenuto Cellini murdered a business rival on nearby Via della Moretta. Today the square is home to Rome's best market for fresh produce between 7am and 1:30pm Monday to Saturday (p50).

Giordano Bruno Monument

In the centre of Campo de' Fiori is a statue of the philosopher Giordano Bruno. A former Catholic priest who dabbled in Calvinism and Lutheranism before being excommunicated by both, Bruno eventually concluded that philosophy and magic were superior to religion. He was tried for heresy and burned at the stake in 1600. His hooded statue is a grim reminder of the executions by the Inquisition that took place in the piazza.

INSIDER TIP
Shopping

The streets around the piazza, named for the medieval artisans who traded there, are lined with boutiques. One of the best is Via de' Giubbonari ("jerkin-makers"), which has many chic clothes shops.

VANOZZA CATANEI'S SHIELD

In the 15th century the area was full of inns, many of them owned by the successful courtesan Vanozza Catanei, mistress of Pope Alexander VI Borgia. On the corner of Campo de' Fiori and Via del Pellegrino you can see Catanei's shield, which she had decorated with her own coat of arms, along with those of both her husband and Borgia.

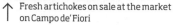

↑ Fresh artichokes on sale at the market on Campo de' Fiori

The market in Campo de' Fiori; statue of Giordano Bruno (inset) ↓

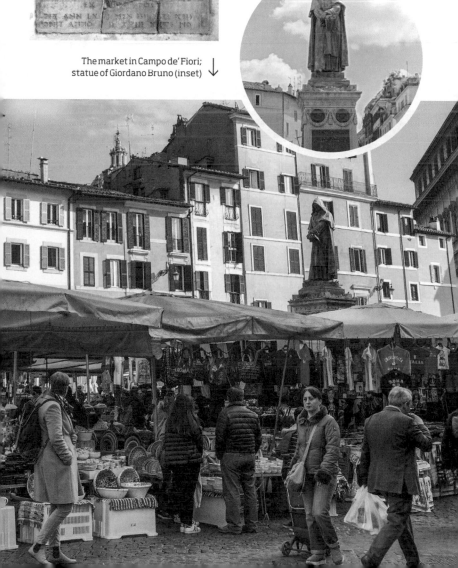

EXPERIENCE MORE

② Teatro di Pompeo

📍T4 🏛 Da Pancrazio, Piazza del Biscione 92 🚌116 and routes to Largo Torre Argentina or Corso Vittorio Emanuele II

A hint of Pompey's 55 BC theatre is evident in the curve of medieval Largo del Pollaro. The theatre could seat 17,000 people. Traces of it are visible in the ancient travertine corridors of the Pancrazio restaurant where you can see early examples of *opus reticulatum* – small square blocks of tufa (porous rock) set diagonally as a facing for a concrete wall.

③ Palazzo del Monte di Pietà

📍T5 🏛 Piazza del Monte di Pietà 33 ☎06-622 7252 🚌116 and routes to Largo di Torre Argentina or Corso Vittorio Emanuele II 🚊8

The Monte, as it is known, is a public institution, founded in 1539 by Pope Paul III Farnese as a pawnshop to staunch the usury then rampant in the city. The building still has offices and auction rooms for the sale of unredeemed goods.

The stars with diagonal bands on the huge central plaque decorating the façade are the coat of arms of Pope Clement VIII Aldobrandini, added when Carlo Maderno enlarged the palace in the 17th century. The clock under the bell tower on the left was added towards the end of the 18th century.

Within, the chapel (which is open for accredited groups; phone ahead) is a jewel of Baroque architecture, adorned with gilded stucco, marble panelling and reliefs. It is a perfect setting for the sculptures by Domenico Guidi – a bust of San Carlo Borromeo and a relief of the *Pietà*. There are also splendid reliefs by Giovanni Battista Théudon and Pierre Legros of biblical scenes illustrating the charitable nature of the institution.

④ Sotterranei di San Paolo alla Regola

📍11 C5 🏛 Via di San Paolo alla Regola ☎06-0608 🚌23, 116, 280 and routes to Largo di Torre Argentina 🚊8 ⏰by appt

The 16th-century Palazzo Specchi and the 18th-century church of San Paolo alla Regola hide the perfectly preserved underground remains of an ancient Roman house, dating from the 2nd to 3rd centuries. At present the site can only be visited by groups as part of a guided tour by prior arrangement (phone ahead).

A ramp leads down well below today's street level, to reveal the locations of residential buildings, warehouses and shops of the time with remains of amphoraes. One level above is the Stanza della Colonna, at one time an open courtyard, with traces of frescoes and mosaics on its walls. The structures were reused in medieval times.

↑ The 17th-century altarpiece depicting the *Holy Trinity* by Guido Reni in Santissima Trinità dei Pellegrini

↑ Borromini's forced-perspective colonnaded gallery at Palazzo Spada

Santissima Trinità dei Pellegrini

📍T5 🏛 Via dei Pettinari 36A
📞06-686 8451 🚌23, 116,
280 and routes to Largo di
Torre Argentina 🚋8
🕐4-8pm Mon-Sat, 8am-
1pm & 4-8pm Sun

The church was donated in the 16th century to a charitable organization founded by San Filippo Neri to care for the poor and sick. The 18th-century façade has niches with statues of the Evangelists by Bernardino Ludovisi. The interior, with Corinthian columns, ends in a horseshoe vault and apse, dominated by Guido Reni's striking altarpiece of the Holy Trinity (1625). The

frescoes in the lantern are also by Reni. Other interesting paintings include *St Gregory the Great Freeing Souls from Purgatory* by Baldassarre Croce (third chapel to the left); Cavalier d'Arpino's *Virgin and Saints* (second chapel to the left); and a painting by Borgognone (1677) of the Virgin and recently canonized saints. In the sacristy are depictions of the nobility washing the feet of pilgrims, a custom started by San Filippo.

Palazzo Spada

📍T5 🏛 Piazza Capo di Ferro
13 📞06-683 2409 🚌23,
116, 280 and routes to Largo
di Torre Argentina 🚋8
🕐 8:30am-7:30pm daily
(last adm: 7pm)

This majestic palazzo, built around 1550 for Cardinal Capo

di Ferro, has an elegant stuccoed courtyard and façade decorated with reliefs evoking Rome's glorious past.

Cardinal Bernardino Spada, who lived here in the 17th century with his brother Virginio (also a cardinal), hired architects Bernini and Borromini to work on the building. The brothers' whimsical delight in false perspectives resulted in a colonnaded gallery by Borromini that appears four times longer than it really is.

The cardinals also amassed a superb private collection of paintings, which is now on display in the Galleria Spada. The collection, housed in four rooms, features 16th- and 17th-century pieces by a wide range of artists, including Rubens, Dürer, Guercino, Guido Reni and Artemesia Gentileschi. The most significant of the artworks on display include *The Visitation* by Andrea del Sarto (1486–1530), *Cain and Abel* by Giovanni Lanfranco (1582–1647) and *The Death of Dido* by Guercino (1591–1666).

The palace is also the seat of the Italian state council.

> The brothers' whimsical delight in false perspectives resulted in a colonnaded gallery by Borromini that appears four times longer than it really is.

7

Palazzo Farnese

📍 T4 🏛 Piazza Farnese
🚌 23, 116, 280 and routes to Corso Vittorio Emanuele II
🎫 for guided tours only (Mon, Wed & Fri in English, times vary); book online at least one week ahead
🌐 inventerrome.com

The prototype for numerous princely palaces, Palazzo Farnese was originally built for Cardinal Alessandro Farnese (who became Pope Paul III in 1534). He commissioned the greatest artists to work on it, starting with Antonio da Sangallo the Younger as architect in 1517. Michelangelo, who took over after him, contributed the great cornice and central window of the main façade, and the third level of the courtyard. The interior is decorated with frescoes by leading artists including Annibale Carracci and Daniele da Volterra.

Michelangelo had a plan for the Farnese gardens to be connected by a bridge to the Farnese home in Trastevere, Villa Farnesina (p272), but the scheme was unrealized. The palazzo was completed in 1589, on a less ambitious scale, by Giacomo della Porta. It is has been the home of the French Embassy since 1635.

8

Santa Maria dell'Orazione e Morte

📍 S4 🏛 Via Giulia 262
☎ 06-6880 6862 🚌 23, 116, 280 🎫 for restoration

A pious confraternity was formed here in the 16th century to collect the bodies of the unknown dead and give them a Christian burial. The theme of death is stressed in this church, dedicated to St Mary of Prayer and Death. The doors and windows of Ferdinando Fuga's dramatic

Baroque façade are decorated with winged skulls. Above the central entrance there is a *clepsydra* (an ancient hourglass) – symbolic of death.

9

Palazzo Ricci

📍 S4 🏛 Piazza de' Ricci
🚌 23, 40, 46, 62, 64, 116, 280, 870 🎫 to the public

Palazzo Ricci was famous for its frescoed façade – now rather faded – originally painted in the 16th century by Polidoro da Caravaggio, a follower of Raphael.

In Renaissance Rome it was common to commission artists to decorate the outsides of houses with

The corner of Via del Pellegrino and Via di Monserrato, as seen from Via dei Banchi Vecchi

 11

Sant'Eligio degli Orefici

📍 S4 🏛 Via di Sant'Eligio 8A 📞 06-686 8260 🚌 23, 40, 46, 62, 64, 116, 280 🕐 9:30am-1pm Mon-Fri (ring bell first at Via di Sant'Eligio 7) 🚫 Aug

The name of the church marks the fact that it was commissioned by a rich corporation of goldsmiths (orefici) in the early 16th century. The original design was by Raphael, who, like his master Bramante, had acquired a sense of the grandiose from the remains of Roman antiquity. The influence of some of Bramante's works, such as the choir of Santa Maria del Popolo (p140), is evident in the simple way the arches and pilasters define the structure of the walls. The cupola of Sant' Eligio is attributed to Baldassarre Peruzzi, while the façade was added in the early 17th century by Flaminio Ponzio.

 12

Santa Maria in Monserrato

📍 S4 🏛 Via di Monserrato 115 📞 06-686 5865 🚌 23, 40, 46, 62, 64, 116, 280 🕐 5-7pm Sat; 10am-1pm & 5-7pm Sun. To arrange a visit Mon-Fri, call 06-688 9651

The origins of the Spanish national church in Rome go back to 1506, when a hospice for Spanish pilgrims was begun by a brotherhood of the Virgin of Montserrat in Catalonia. Inside is Annibale Carracci's painting San Diego de Alcalà and a copy of a Sansovino statue of St James. Some beautiful 15th-century tombs by Andrea Bregno and Luigi Capponi are in the courtyard and side chapels. Do not miss Bernini's bust of church benefactor Pedro Foix de Montoya in the annexe.

heroes of Classical antiquity. A fresco by a leading artist such as Polidoro, reputedly the inventor of this style of painting, was a conspicuous status symbol, in the nobility's attempts to outshine each other with their palazzi.

 10

San Girolamo della Carità

📍 S4 🏛 Via di Monserrato 62A 📞 06-687 9786 🚌 23, 40, 46, 62, 64, 116, 280 🕐 Oct-Jun: 10:30am-12:30pm Sun & public hols

The church was built on a site incorporating the home of San Filippo Neri, the 16th-century saint from Tuscany who renewed Rome's spiritual and cultural life by his friendly, open approach to religion. He would have loved the frolicking putti shown around his statue in the Antamoro chapel dedicated to him –

they would have reminded him of the Roman urchins he had cared for during his lifetime.

The breathtaking Spada Chapel, designed by Borromini, is unique both as a work of art and as an illustration of the spirit of the Baroque age. All architectural elements are concealed so that the space of the chapel's interior is defined solely by decorative marble-work and statues. Veined jasper and precious multi-coloured marbles are sculpted to imitate flowery damask and velvet hangings. Even the altar rail is a long swag of jasper drapery held up by a pair of kneeling angels with wooden wings.

Although there are memorials to former members of the Spada family, oddly there is no indication as to which of the Spadas was responsible for endowing the chapel. It was probably art-lover Virgilio Spada, a follower of San Filippo Neri.

↑ The courtyard of the Renaissance Palazzo della Cancelleria

 13

Piccola Farnesina

📍 T4 🏛 Corso Vittorio Emanuele II 168 🚌 40, 46, 62, 64, 70, 81, 87, 116, 492 🕐 Oct-May: 10am-4pm Tue-Sun; Jun-Sep: 1-7pm Tue-Sun 🌐 museobarracco.it

This miniature palazzo acquired its name from the lilies decorating its cornices that were mistakenly identified as part of the Farnese family crest. In fact they were part of the coat of arms of a French clergyman, Thomas Le Roy, for whom the palazzo was built in 1523.

The entrance is in a façade built to overlook Corso Vittorio Emanuele II when the road was built at the start of the 1900s. The original façade on the left of today's entrance is attributed to Antonio da Sangallo the Younger.

The Piccola Farnesina now houses the Museo Barracco, a sculpture collection assembled during the 19th century by the politician Baron Giovanni Barracco. A bust of the baron is in the courtyard. The collection includes an ancient Egyptian relief of the scribe Nofer, some Assyrian artifacts and, among the Etruscan exhibits, a delicate ceramic female head. On the first floor is the Greek collection with a head of Apollo.

 14

Palazzo della Cancelleria

📍 T4 🏛 Piazza della Cancelleria 📞 06-6988 7566 🚌 40, 46, 62, 64, 70, 81, 87, 116, 492 Courtyard: 🕐 7:30am-8pm Mon-Sat, 9:30am-7pm Sun **Sala Riaria and Salone dei Cento Giorni:** 🕐 Tue pm & Sat am (call 06-6989 3405 at least a month in advance)

The palazzo, a prime example of Early Renaissance architecture, was begun in 1485. It was financed partly with the gambling winnings of Cardinal Raffaele Riario, who was in charge of the Papal Chancellery. Roses, the emblem of the Riario family, adorn the vaults and capitals of the beautiful Doric courtyard. The palazzo's interior was decorated after the Sack of Rome in 1527. Giorgio Vasari boasted that he had completed work on one enormous room in just 100 days (thus it was named Salone dei Cento Giorni); Michelangelo allegedly retorted: "It looks like it." Mannerist artists Perin del Vaga and Francesco Salviati frescoed the cardinal's rooms. The splendid Sala Riaria has a clock face painted by Baciccia.

On the right of the palazzo's main entrance is the church of San Lorenzo in Damaso, founded by Pope Damasus (reigned 366–84). It was reconstructed in 1495.

 15

Teatro Argentina

📍 U4 🏛 Largo di Torre Argentina 52 🚌 40, 46, 62, 64, 70, 81, 87, 186, 492, 810 🚋 8 🕐 Museum by appt only (call 06-0608) 🌐 teatrodiroma.net

One of Rome's most influential theatres was founded by the Sforza Cesarini family in 1732, though the façade dates from

Beppe e i suoi Formaggi

This enoteca and gourmet cheese shop is a wonderful place for special wine and foodie souvenirs, particularly cheeses, all made from the milk of Alpine cows, sheep and goats.

📍 U5 🏛 Via Santa Maria del Pianto 9A 🌐 beppeeisuoi formaggi.it

---

Atelier Patrizia Pieroni

Roman designer Patrizia Pieroni creates chic womenswear. Her boutique holds rails full of colourful offerings and stunning accessories to lift any outfit. The second floor is an art gallery hosting exhibitions and events.

📍 S3 🏛 Via del Pellegrino 172 🌐 patriziapieroni.it

Ibiz

If you're in the market for a unique bag to take home, look no further: this little shop is brimming with colourful bags and purses handcrafted in leather on the premises.

📍 U4 🏛 Via dei Chiavari 39 🌐 ibizroma.it

a century later. Many famous operas, including those of Verdi, were first performed here. In 1816 the theatre saw the ill-fated debut of Rossini's *Barber of Seville*, during which the composer insulted the unappreciative audience, who then pursued him hissing and jeering through the streets.

Area Sacra di Largo Argentina

⬛ U4 ⬛ Largo di Torre Argentina 🚌 40, 46, 62, 64, 70, 81, 87, 186, 492, 810 🚋 8 ⬛ to the public, but ruins clearly visible from street

The remains of four temples were discovered here in the 1920s, the oldest (temple C) dating from the early 3rd century BC. It was placed on a high platform preceded by an altar. In medieval times the church of San Nicola de' Cesarini was built over temple A's podium. The north column stumps belonged to a great portico, the Hecatostylum (portico of 100 columns). In Imperial times two marble lavatories were built here – the remains of one is visible behind temple A. Behind temples B and C are remains of a great platform of tufa blocks identified as part of the Curia of Pompey – a rectangular building with a statue of Pompey. It was here that the Senate met and Julius Caesar was murdered on 15 March 44 BC. At the southwest corner of the site is a cat sanctuary for Rome's abandoned felines.

San Carlo ai Catinari

⬛ U4 ⬛ Piazza B. Cairoli 📞 06-6830 7070 🚌 40, 46, 62, 64, 70, 81, 87, 186, 492, 810 🚋 8 🕐 7:30am–noon & 4–7pm daily

In 1620 Rome's Milanese congregation decided to honour Cardinal Carlo Borromeo with this great church. It was called "ai Catinari" on account of the many bowl-makers' *(catinari)* shops in the area surrounding the church. The solemn travertine façade was completed in 1638 by the Roman architect Soria. The 16th-century basilican plan is flanked by chapels. The St Cecilia Chapel was designed and decorated by Antonio Gherardi. The church's paintings and frescoes by Pietro da Cortona and Guido Reni depict the life and acts of San Carlo.

The ornate crucifix on the sacristy altar is inlaid with marble and mother-of-pearl and is by the 16th-century sculptor Algardi.

> ### ASSASSINATION OF JULIUS CAESAR
>
> According to legend, the night before Caesar was killed, his wife Calpurnia dreamed she was holding his dead body, and she tried to persuade him to stay at home. Refusing to listen, he went to a meeting at the Curia of Pompey, as scheduled. He was attacked by a group of senators, including his former ally Brutus, who were opposed to his growing megalomania. His dying words were allegedly, "Tu quoque, Brute?" ("You too, Brutus?")

The Baroque interior of the basilica of San Carlo ai Catinari ↓

18 Fontana delle Tartarughe

📍V5 🏛 Piazza Mattei
🚌 46, 62, 63, 64, 70, 87, 186, 492, 810 🚋 8

The delightful Fontana delle Tartarughe (*tartarughe* means "tortoises") was commissioned by the Mattei family between 1581 and 1588 to decorate "their" piazza. The design was by Giacomo della Porta, but the fountain owes much of its charm to the four bronze youths each resting one foot on the head of a dolphin, sculpted by Taddeo Landini. Nearly a century after the fountain was built an unknown sculptor added the tortoises to complete the composition.

19 Crypta Balbi

📍V4 🏛 Via delle Botteghe Oscure ⏰ Open 9am–7:45pm Tue–Sun 🌐 museo nazionaleromano.beni culturali.it

Part of the Museo Nazionale Romano, Crypta Balbi is an inventive museum devoted to urban archaeology, and illustrates how a piece of land in central Rome has been used over the centuries. It stands on

↑ An ancient jug – one of the finds on display at the Crypta Balbi museum

the remains of a theatre built in 13 BC, the ruins of which can still be seen. Further excavations revealed that in the 1st century AD the *esedra* (the curved auditorium) had been converted into what appears to have been a smart public lavatory, with marble seats. Then, it seems, the area went downhill, as in the 3rd century blocks of flats (*insulae*) for the poor were constructed, one of them with a Mithraeum in the basement. By the 7th century the area had become a glassworks, evidenced by a huge dump of discarded glass.

20 Santa Maria in Campitelli

📍V5 🏛 Piazza di Campitelli 9 📞 06-6880 3978 🚌 40, 46, 62, 63, 64, 70, 87, 186, 780, 810 ⏰ 7am–7pm daily

In 17th-century Rome the plague could still strike fiercely and there were no reliable, effective remedies. Many Romans simply prayed for a cure to a sacred medieval icon of the Virgin, the Madonna del Portico. When a particularly lethal outbreak of plague abated in 1656, popular gratitude was so strong that a new church was built to house the icon.

The church, designed by Bernini's pupil Carlo Rainaldi, was completed in 1667. The main elements of the lively Baroque façade are the graceful columns, symbolizing the supporters of the true faith.

Inside the church stands a fabulously ornate, gilded altar tabernacle with spiral columns, designed by Giovanni Antonio de Rossi to contain the image of the Virgin. The side chapels are decorated by some of Rome's finest Baroque artists: Sebastiano Conca, Giovanni Battista Gaulli (known as Il Baciccia) and Luca Giordano.

↑ Domed ceiling of the church of Santa Maria in Campitelli

STAY

DOM Hotel

From the intimate, dimly lit bar area, hung with Warhol prints and stags' heads, to the luxuriously appointed guest rooms decorated with splashy modern art, DOM has an appealingly rock-star feel. There's also a bijou roof terrace for sipping cocktails under the stars.

📍U5 🏛 Via Giulia 131
🌐 domhotelroma.com

Hotel Teatro di Pompeo

Built on the site of the ancient Teatro di Pompeo, this friendly three-star hotel offers great value for money. Guest rooms feature beamed ceilings and big windows, while the breakfast room has ancient Roman remains.

📍R3 🏛 Largo del Pallaro 8
🌐 hotelteatrodi pompeo.it

Aerial view towards the Capitoline Hill, with the Theatre of Marcellus in the foreground ↑

San Nicola in Carcere

📍 V5 🏛 Via del Teatro di Marcello 46 📞 06-6830 7198 🚌 44, 63, 81, 160, 170, 628, 780, 781 🕐 10am-5pm daily Excavations: call 347-381 1874 to book

The medieval church of San Nicola in Carcere stands on the site of three Roman temples of the Republican era which were converted into a prison (carcere) in the Middle Ages. The temples of Juno, Spes and Janus faced a city gate leading from the Forum Holitorium, the city's vegetable and oil market, to the road down to the port on the Tiber. The underground excavations are well worth a visit.The columns embedded in the walls of the church belonged to two flanking temples whose platforms are now marked by lawns. The church was rebuilt in 1599, with a new façade by Giacomo della Porta, and restored during the 19th century, but the bell tower and Roman columns, incorporated into the church's façade, are part of the original design.

Theatre of Marcellus

📍 V5 🏛 Via del Teatro di Marcello 📞 06-0608 🚌 44, 63, 81, 160, 170, 628, 780, 781 🕐 9am-6pm daily (summer: to 7pm)

The curved outer wall of this vast amphitheatre has supported generations of Roman buildings. It was built by Emperor Augustus (27 BC–AD 14), who dedicated it to Marcellus, his nephew and son-in-law, who had died aged 19 in 23 BC.

The Middle Ages were a turbulent time of invasions and local conflicts and by the 13th century the theatre had been converted into the fortress of the Savelli family. In the 16th century Baldassarre Peruzzi built a great palace on the theatre ruins for the Orsini family. This included a garden that faced the Tiber.

Close to the theatre stand three Corinthian columns and a section of frieze. These are from the Temple of Apollo, which once housed many great works of art that the Romans had plundered from Greece in the 2nd century BC.

Portico of Octavia

📍 V5 🏛 Via del Portico d'Ottavia 🚌 46, 62, 63, 64, 70, 87, 186, 780, 810

Built in honour of Octavia (the sister of Augustus and the abandoned wife of Mark Antony), this is the only surviving portico of what used to be the monumental piazza of Circus Flaminius. The rectangular portico enclosed temples dedicated to Jupiter and Juno, decorated with bronze statues. The part you see today is the great central atrium originally covered by marble facings.

In the Middle Ages a great fish market and a church, Sant'Angelo in Pescheria, were built in the ruins of the portico. As the church was associated with the fishing activities of the nearby river port, aquatic flora and fauna feature in many of its inlays. Links with the Tiber are also apparent in the stucco façade on the adjacent Fishmonger's Oratory, built in 1689. The church has a fresco of the Madonna and angels by the school of Benozzo Gozzoli.

24 Tiber Island

📍 U5 🏛 Isola Tiberina
🚌 23, 63, 280, 780 🚊 8

In ancient times the island, which lay opposite the city's port, had large structures of white travertine at either end, built to resemble the stern and prow of a ship. Since 293 BC, when a temple was dedicated to Aesculapius, the god of healing and protector against the plague, the island has been associated with the sick. San Bartolomeo all'Isola, the church in the island's central piazza, was built on the ruins of the Temple of Aesculapius in the 10th century. Its bell tower is visible from across the river.

From the Ghetto area you can reach the island by a foot-bridge, the Ponte Fabricio. The oldest original bridge over the Tiber still in use, it was built in 62 BC. In medieval times the Pierleoni and then the Caetani, two powerful families, controlled this strategic point by use of a tower, still *in situ*. The other bridge to the island, the Ponte Cestio, is inscribed with the names of the Byzantine emperors associated with its restoration in AD 370.

25 Ghetto and Synagogue

📍 V5 🚌 23, 63, 280, 780 and routes to Largo di Torre Argentina 🚊 8

The first Jews came to Rome as traders in the 2nd century BC and there has been a Jewish community in Rome ever since. Jews were much appreciated for their financial and medical skills during the time of the Roman Empire.

Systematic persecution began in the 16th century. From 25 July 1556 all Rome's Jews were forced to live inside a high-walled enclosure erected on the orders of Pope Paul IV. The Ghetto was in a damp, unhealthy part of Rome. Inhabitants were only allowed out during the day, and on Sundays they were driven into the Church of Sant'Angelo in Pescheria to listen to Christian sermons – a practice that was abolished only in 1848.

Persecution started again in 1943 with the German occupation. Although many Jews were helped to escape or were hidden by Roman citizens, thousands were deported to German concentration camps.

The **Synagogue** on Lungotevere was completed in 1904 and houses a **Jewish Museum** that describes the history of the community, Torahs and other artifacts.

Synagogue and Jewish Museum

🏛 Synagogue: Lungotevere dei Cenci 📞 06-6840 0661 Jewish Museum: 🕐 Apr–mid-Sep: 10am–6pm Sun–Thu, 10am–4pm Fri; mid-Sep–Mar: 10am–5pm Sun–Thu, 10am–2pm Fri 🚫 Jewish public hols 🌐 museoebraico.roma.it

26 San Giovanni dei Fiorentini

📍 R2 🏛 Via Acciaioli 2 📞 06-6889 2059 🚌 23, 40, 46, 62, 64, 116, 280, 870 🕐 7:25am–noon & 5–7pm daily

The church of St John of the Florentines was built for the large Florentine community in

this area. Pope Leo X wanted it to be an expression of the cultural superiority of Florence over Rome. Started in the early 16th century, the church took over a century to build. The principal architect was Antonio da Sangallo the Younger, but many others contributed before Carlo Maderno's elongated cupola was finally completed in 1620. The present façade was added in the 18th century.

The church was decorated mainly by Tuscan artists. One interesting exception is the 15th-century statue of San Giovannino by the Sicilian Mino del Reame in a niche above the sacristy. The spectacular high altar houses a marble group by Antonio

Raggi, *The Baptism of Christ*. The altar itself is by Borromini, who is buried in the church.

The church also has a small museum of sacred art (open 9:30am–noon Mon–Sat).

27
Casa di Lorenzo Manilio

📍 U5 🏛 Via del Portico d'Ottavia 1D 🚌 46, 62, 63, 64, 70, 87, 186, 780, 810 🚫 to the public

Before the Renaissance, most Romans had only vague ideas of their city's past, but the 15th-century revival of interest in the philosophy and arts of antiquity inspired some to build houses recalling the splendour of ancient Rome. In 1468 a certain Lorenzo Manilio built a great house for his family, decorating it with an elegant Classical plaque. The Latin inscription dates the building according to the ancient Roman method – 2,221 years after the foundation of the city – and gives the owner's name. Original reliefs are embedded in the façades. The Piazza Costaguti façade's windows are inscribed *Ave Roma* (Hail Rome).

28
Palazzo Cenci

📍 U5 🏛 Vicolo dei Cenci 🚌 23, 63, 280, 780 and routes to Largo di Torre Argentina 🚫 to the public

Palazzo Cenci belonged to the family of Beatrice Cenci, who was accused, together with her brothers and stepmother, of witchcraft and the murder of her tyrannical father. She was beheaded in 1599.

The Ponte Fabricio footbridge that links the Ghetto to Tiber Island

EAT

Il Forno di Campo de' Fiori

This is the best place locally for a takeaway lunch: delicious *pizza bianca* stuffed with anything from mortadella to Nutella. Also try the delicious biscuits and pastries.

📍 T4 🏛 Vicolo del Gallo 14 🌐 fornocampo defiori.com

Roscioli

This family-owned restaurant/food shop/deli is renowned for its wines, meats and cheeses. You're best off ordering antipasti and pasta rather than a main course.

📍 T4 🏛 Via dei Giubbonari 21 🌐 salumeriaroscioli.com

€€€

Piperno

Tucked away in the Ghetto, this traditional eatery is a good place to sample Roman cuisine.

📍 U5 🏛 Via Monte dè Cenci 9 🌐 ristorantepiperno.it

€€€

Most of the original medieval palazzo has been demolished, and the building you see today dates back to the 1570s. Heraldic half-moons decorate the main façade on Via del Progresso, while balconies open on the opposite side where a medieval arch joins the palace to Palazzetto Cenci, designed by Martino Longhi the Elder. Many of the rooms retain the decoration that the unfortunate Beatrice would have known as a child.

Tiber Island with Ponte Garibaldi in the foreground

A SHORT WALK
CAMPO DE' FIORI

Distance 1.5 km (1 mile) **Nearest bus** 116
Time 30 minutes

A stroll through this fascinating part of Renaissance Rome will take you through some lovely shopping streets, including Via dei Giubbonari with its fashionable clothes shops, past numerous restaurants and bars and to Piazza di Campo de' Fiori, which has a famous morning market. Popular restaurants keep the area alive late into the night. On your walk there will be plenty of great buildings to admire, though few are open to the public. Two exceptions are the Piccola Farnesina, with its collection of Classical statues, and Palazzo Spada, home to many significant paintings.

Palazzo Ricci has painted Classical scenes on its façade, a favourite form of decoration of Renaissance houses (p166).

Sant'Eligio degli Orefici, a small Renaissance church designed by Raphael, is concealed behind a later façade (p167).

Did You know?

The market on Campo de' Fiori is one of the oldest in Rome, dating to the 1860s.

Santa Maria in Monserrato has strong connections with Spain, and houses a Bernini bust of Cardinal Pedro Foix de Montoya (p167).

The chief attraction of San Girolamo della Carità is Borromini's fabulous Spada Chapel (p167).

A pair of dramatic winged skulls flank the doorway to Santa Maria dell'Orazione e Morte, dedicated to the burial of the dead (p166).

VIA DI MONSERRATO
VIA GIULIA
LUNGOTEVERE DEI TEBALDI
TEVERE
START
FINISH

← Stalls of fresh produce at the market on Campo de' Fiori

0 metres 75
0 yards 75
N ↑

```
```

The vast Palazzo della Cancelleria housed the papal administration that ran the affairs of the Church (p168).

The plaque on Piccola Farnesina honours Giovanni Barracco. His sculpture collection is housed in the palazzo (p168).

Locator Map
For more detail see pp160–61

CAMPO DE' FIORI

The bustling market makes Piazza Campo de' Fiori one of Rome's most entertaining squares (p162).

Heraldic eagles stare down from the pediments of the Palazzo Pio Righetti's windows.

Michelangelo and other great artists helped create the monumental Renaissance Palazzo Farnese (p166).

Palazzo Spada's picture gallery houses a collection started by two wonderfully eccentric 17th-century cardinals (p165).

Palazzo del Monte di Pietà was a papal institution, where the poor pawned their possessions in order to borrow small sums of money (p164).

Santissima Trinità dei Pellegrini's principal role was to look after poor pilgrims arriving in Rome (p165).

Sotterranei di San Paolo alla Regola are the remains of a Roman house in the basement of an old palace (p164).

PIAZZA DELLA CANCELLERIA

VIA DEI BAULLARI

PIAZZA CAMPO DE' FIORI

VIA DEI GIUBBONARI

PIAZZA FARNESE

VIA CAPO DI FERRO

PIAZZA DEL MONTE DI PIETÀ

VIA DEGLI SPECCHI

VIA DEI PETTINARI

PONTE SISTO

EL PELLE GRINO

QUIRINAL AND MONTI

One of the original seven hills of Rome, the Quirinal was a largely residential area in Imperial times, home to the vast complex of the Baths of Diocletian, which still rise in front of the city's main railway station, Termini. Abandoned in the Middle Ages, the area returned to favour in the 16th century, when the prime site atop the hill was taken by the papacy to create the huge Palazzo del Quirinale, now home to Italy's president, while great aristocratic families such as the Colonna and Aldobrandini built palaces lower down the hill. Following Unification the surrounding area was completely transformed and many old palazzi were replaced by monumental buildings, especially along busy Via Nazionale, now one of the city's main arteries. The small Monti district, hidden behind Trajan's markets, was a crowded slum teeming with prostitutes in ancient Roman times, separated from the Forum by a long wall. It is now a fashionable bohemian oasis, with trendy shops, bars and cafés clustering around traffic-free Piazza Madonna dei Monti and the hilly streets of Via dei Serpenti and Via del Boschetto.

QUIRINAL AND MONTI

Must Sees
1. Trevi Fountain
2. Palazzo Massimo alle Terme (Museo Nazionale Romano)

Experience More
3. Castor and Pollux
4. Palazzo del Quirinale
5. Palazzo Colonna
6. Santi Apostoli
7. San Marcello al Corso
8. Santi Vincenzo e Anastasio
9. Scuderie del Quirinale
10. Santa Maria in Trivio
11. Accademia Nazionale di San Luca
12. Sant'Andrea al Quirinale
13. San Carlo alle Quattro Fontane
14. Le Quattro Fontane
15. Moses Fountain
16. Santa Maria degli Angeli e dei Martiri
17. Piazza della Repubblica
18. Sant'Agata dei Goti
19. Palazzo delle Esposizioni
20. Santi Domenico e Sisto
21. Villa Aldobrandini
22. Santa Maria dei Monti

Eat
1. Alle Carrette
2. L'Asino d'Oro
3. La Carbonara

Drink
4. Trimani Il Winebar

Stay
5. Villa Spalletti Trivelli

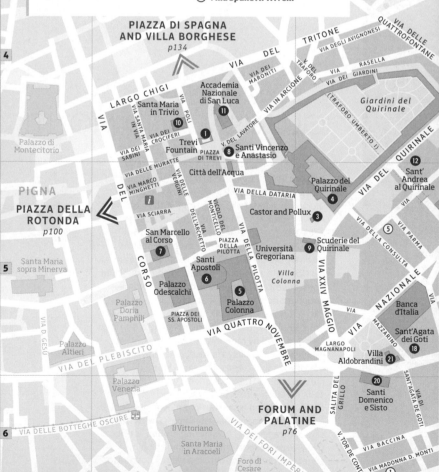

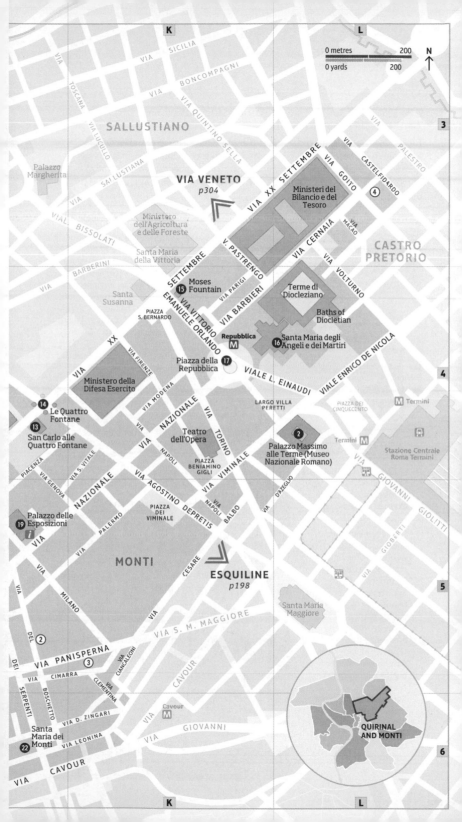

❶

TREVI FOUNTAIN

⊙H4 🚌 52, 53, 61, 62, 63, 71, 80, 116, 119 and other routes along Via del Corso and Via del Tritone

Tucked away on a tiny piazza, this is the most famous – and the largest – fountain in Rome. Built in 1762 by Italian architect Nicola Salvi, in the flamboyant Rococo style, the Trevi Fountain is a travertine extravaganza of rearing seahorses, conch-blowing Tritons, craggy rocks and palm trees built into the side of the Palazzo Poli.

↑ Relief of Trivia pointing to the spring from which the water flows

The fountain's waters come from the Acqua Vergine, a Roman aqueduct built in 19 BC and fed by springs 22 km (14 miles) from the city. Legend has it that the Acqua Vergine is named after a young virgin called Trivia who showed Roman engineers the location of a freshwater spring. The word Trevi is a corruption of her name.

The fountain contains about 3 million litres (666,000 gallons) of water. Once reputed to be the sweetest water in Rome, it is now treated with chemicals. Legend has it that throwing a coin into the fountain guarantees a return to Rome.

€3,000

of coins are thrown into the fountain every day. The money is collected and given to charity.

LA CITTÀ DELL'ACQUA

⊕ ⊙H5 🏠 Vicolo del Puttarello 25
🕐 Tue-Sun
🌐 vicuscaprarius.com

In 2001 a stretch of the Acqua Vergine aqueduct (built in Augustan times and still feeding the Trevi Fountain) was discovered during restoration work on an old cinema nearby. Part of the underground archaeological area of "The City of Water" can now be visited, including the aqueduct and the ruins of an ancient Roman apartment block (insula) that was later converted into a single family home. Artifacts uncovered in the area are also on display.

LA DOLCE VITA

Federico Fellini's 1960 film is about a paparazzo (played by Marcello Mastroianni) drifting through the decadent nightlife of Rome, and meeting a beautiful Swedish actress played by Anita Ekberg. The most famous scene - Ekberg taking a shower in the Trevi Fountain - may be largely responsible for making the Trevi the best known and most photographed fountain in the city.

Oceanus and Chariot pulled by Tritons and Horses

The central statue standing in a triumphal arch is of Oceanus, the personification of an enormous river encircling the world from which all streams of water are derived in ancient mythology. The statue was carved by Pietro Bracci, who took over work on the fountain after the death of Nicola Salvi, his long-time friend, in 1751.

Oceanus's conch-shell chariot is powered by two horses steered by Tritons. One Triton struggles to master an unruly beast, while the other leads a far more docile animal. The horses were intended to symbolize the different moods of the sea.

The Trevi Fountain; and a detail (inset) of its sculpture showing a Triton steering a horse ↑

The Trevi fountain illuminated at night

② ⟨⟩ Ⓜ 🖐

PALAZZO MASSIMO ALLE TERME

📍 L4 🏠 Largo di Villa Peretti 1 📞 06-3996 7700 🚌 36, 38, 40, 64, 170, H and other routes to Piazza del Cinequecento Ⓜ Repubblica, Termini 🕐 9am-7:45pm Tue-Sun

The main site of the Museo Nazionale Romano, the airy 19th-century Palazzo Massimo alle Terme holds an exceptional collection of antiquities dating from the 2nd century BC to the end of the 4th century AD.

Founded in 1889, the museum contains one of the world's leading collections of Classical art, comprising frescoes, mosaics, statues and other artifacts found in Rome since 1870. The exhibits are beautifully displayed on several floors. The courtyard, with its portico of statues dappled with light and shade, is a wonderful introduction to this spectacular collection. The museum has many highlights, but the exquisite frescoes from Livia's Villa are a particular must see.

The Museo Nazionale Romano has four sites. The other branches are in the Baths of Diocletian, just around the corner from Palazzo Massimo alle Terme *(see box)*, the Crypta Balbi *(p170)* and Palazzo Altemps *(p131)*. The same entry ticket is valid for all four sites for three consecutive days.

←

Courtyard of the 19th-century Palazzo Massimo alle Terme, lined with statues

BATHS OF DIOCLETIAN

📍L4 🏛 Terme di Diocleziano,
Viale E de Nicola 79 📞06-3996 7700
🕐9am-7:30pm Tue-Sun

Built under Emperor Diocletian
between AD 298 and 306, this bath
complex was the largest in ancient
Rome. Parts were later converted into
the church of Santa Maria degli Angeli e
dei Martiri *(p193)*. The Baths now house
the Museo Nazionale Romano's
collection of funerary monuments
and inscriptions. Highlights include
a display about the history of writing
and a section on amulets and magic.

Collection Highlights

Frescoes and Mosaics

Some of the most joyous displays are on the
second floor, where wall paintings and mosaics
have been brought from ancient villas excavated
in and around Rome. The most incredible are
the four exquisite floor-to-ceiling illusionistic
frescoes from the underground dining room of a
villa that belonged to Emperor Augustus's wife
Livia. They portray a garden with flowers, fruit
trees and birds, and were created to give diners
the impression they were eating al fresco.

Objects

In the basement, objects evoke
the reality of everyday life in
ancient Rome. There are ivory
dice, sewing needles, sets of
compasses and a miniature
abacus, along with tiny spoons
used for mixing cosmetics.
Don't miss the haunting
Grottarossa Mummy, the
mummified remains of an
eight-year-old girl, buried
with her jewellery and doll.

↑ Fresco depicting a garden
with birds and fruit trees
from the dining room of
Livia's Villa at Prima Porta,
north of Rome

Sculpture

Exhibits on the first floor evoke the luxury
enjoyed by the elite of ancient Rome, typified
by the elaborate bronze fittings - including lion
heads and a Medusa - from the opulent boats
which Emperor Caligula used for parties on the
Lake of Nemi. Other highlights include an ivory
Mask of Apollo and a striking bronze sculpture of
a Boxer whose lips and wounds have a red hue.

EXPERIENCE MORE

③ Castor and Pollux

📍J5 🏛Piazza del Quirinale
🚌H, 40, 64, 70, 170 and
many routes along Via
del Tritone

Castor and Pollux and their
prancing horses stand in the
Piazza del Quirinale. Over
5.5 m (18 ft) high, these statues
are huge Roman copies of 5th-
century BC Greek originals.
They once stood at the
entrance to the nearby Baths
of Constantine. Pope Sixtus V
had them restored and placed
here in 1588. They gave the
square its familiar name of
Monte Cavallo (horse hill).

The obelisk between them
was brought here in 1786 from
the Mausoleum of Augustus.
In 1818 the composition was
completed by the addition of
a massive granite basin, once
a cattle trough in the Forum.

④ Palazzo del Quirinale

📍J5 🏛Piazza del Quirinale
🚌H, 40, 64, 70, 170 and
many routes along Via del
Tritone ⏰mid-Sep-late
Jun: 9:30am-4pm Tue, Wed,
Fri-Sun 🚫pub hols
🌐quirinale.it

By the 1500s, the Vatican had
a reputation as an unhealthy
location because of the high
incidence of malaria, so Pope
Gregory XIII chose this site as
a papal summer residence.
Work began in 1573. Piazza
del Quirinale has buildings on
three sides, while the fourth
is open, with a splendid view
of the city. Many great architects worked on the palace.

After Rome became the
capital city of the new united
Italy in 1870, the palace
became the official residence
of the king, then, in 1947, of
the president of the republic.

The immaculately mani-
cured gardens are open to
the public only once a year,
on Republic Day (2 June).

⑤ Palazzo Colonna

📍H5 🏛Via della Pilotta 17
🚌H, 40, 64, 70, 170 and
many routes to Piazza
Venezia ⏰9am-1:15pm Sat
only (guided tour in English
at noon) or by appt (call
06-679 4350 to book)
🌐galleriacolonna.it

Pope Martin V Colonna
(reigned 1417–31)
began building the
palazzo, but most
of the structure
dates from the
18th century. It

↑ Annibale Carracci's *The
Bean Eater*, on display
in Galleria Colonna

has belonged to over twenty
generations of the Colonna
family. The Galleria Colonna,
built by Antonio del Grande
between 1654 and 1665, is the
only part of the palazzo open
to the public. The pictures are
numbered but unlabelled, so
remember to pick up a guide
at the start of your visit. Go
up the stairs and through
the antechamber leading to
a series of three gleaming
marble rooms with prominent
yellow columns, the Colonna
family emblem (*colonna*
means "column").

The ceiling frescoes
celebrate Marcantonio
Colonna's victory over the
Turks at the Battle of Lepanto
(1571). On the walls are 16th-
to 18th-century paintings,
including Annibale Carracci's
The Bean Eater. The room of
landscape paintings, many by
Poussin's brother-in-law
Gaspare Dughet, reflects the
18th-century taste of Cardinal
Girolamo Colonna. Beyond is
a room with a ceiling fresco
of *The Apotheosis of Martin V.*
The throne room has a chair
reserved for visiting popes
and a copy of Pisanello's
portrait of Martin V. The
gallery offers a fine view of the
private palace garden, site of
the ruined Temple of Serapis.

← Statue of Castor and his horse
in the Piazza del Quirinale

 The Baroque nave and interior of the church of the Santi Apostoli

Santi Apostoli

 H5 Piazza dei Santi Apostoli 06-699571 H, 40, 64, 70, 170 and many other routes to Piazza Venezia 7am-noon & 4-7pm daily

The 6th-century church that was originally on this site was rebuilt in the 15th century by popes Martin V Colonna and Sixtus IV della Rovere, whose oak-tree crest

PALAZZO COLONNA

It was not merely the deliciously frescoed ceilings, lashings of gilt, Venetian glass chandeliers and painted mirrors that made the the home of the noble Colonna family such a hit with aristocratic party-goers in the 1930s. The polished marble floors were superb for roller-skating parties.

decorates the capitals of the late 15th-century portico. Inside the portico on the left is Canova's 1807 memorial to the engraver Giovanni Volpato. The church itself contains a much larger monument by Canova, his Tomb of Clement XIV (1789).

The Baroque interior by Francesco and Carlo Fontana was completed in 1714. Note the 3D effect of Giovanni Odazzi's painted *Rebel Angels*, who really look as though they are falling from the sky. A huge 18th-century altar-piece by Domenico Muratori illustrates the martyrdom of the Apostles James and Philip, whose tombs are in the crypt.

San Marcello al Corso

H5 Piazza di San Marcello 5 06-679 3910 62, 63, 81, 85, 117, 119, 160, 492, 628 7am-midnight Mon-Fri, 9am-midnight Sat & Sun

This church was originally one of the first places of Christian worship in Rome,

which were known as *tituli*. A later Romanesque building on the site burned down in 1519, but it was rebuilt by Jacopo Sansovino with a single nave and many richly decorated private chapels on either side. The imposing travertine façade was designed by Carlo Fontana in late Baroque style.

The third chapel on the right features fine frescoes of the Virgin Mary by Francesco Salviati. The decoration of the next chapel was interrupted by the Sack of Rome in 1527. Raphael's follower Perin del Vaga fled, leaving the ceiling frescoes to be completed by Daniele da Volterra and Pellegrino Tibaldi when peace returned to the city. In the nave stands a splendid marble Venetian-style double tomb made by Sansovino around 1520; this is a memorial to Cardinal Giovanni Michiel (who was the victim of a Borgia poisoning in 1503) and his nephew, Bishop Antonio Orso.

8

Santi Vincenzo e Anastasio

QH4 **A**Vicolo dei Modelli 73 **B**52, 53, 61, 62, 63, 71, 80, 116, 119 **C**9am–8pm daily

Overlooking the Trevi Fountain is one of the most over-the-top Baroque façades in Rome. Its thickets of columns are crowned by the huge coat of arms of Cardinal Raimondo Mazzarino, better known as Cardinal Mazarin, chief minister of France, who commissioned Martino Longhi the Younger to build the church in 1650. The female bust above the door is of one of the cardinal's famous nieces, either Louis XIV's first love, Maria Mancini (1639–1715), or her younger sister, Ortensia. In the apse, memorial plaques record the popes whose *praecordia* (a part of the heart) are enshrined behind the wall. This gruesome tradition was started at the end of the 16th century by Pope Sixtus V and continued until Pius X stopped it in the early 20th century.

9

Scuderie del Quirinale

QJ5 **A**Via 24 Maggio 16 **B**H, 40, 60, 64, 70, 170 **C**for exhibitions only – check website **W**scuderie quirinale.it

The Scuderie started life as stables for the nearby Palazzo del Quirinale. Built in the early 1700s by Ferdinando Fuga over the remains (still partially visible) of the ancient Temple of Serapis, the stables were remodelled by Gae Aulenti in the 1990s. The Scuderie del Quirinale now host some of the best temporary art exhibitions in the country. The top floor has great views of Rome.

> **The Scuderie del Quirinale now host some of the best temporary art exhibitions in the country.**

10

Santa Maria in Trivio

QH4 **A**Piazza dei Crociferi 49 **C**06-678 9645 **B**52, 53, 61, 62, 63, 71, 80, 116, 119 **C**8am–noon & 4–8pm daily

It has been said that Italian architecture is one of façades, and nowhere is this clearer than in the 1570s façade of Santa Maria in Trivio, delightfully stuck on to the building behind it. Note the false windows. There is illusion inside too, particularly in the ceiling frescoes, which show scenes from the New Testament by Antonio Gherardi (1644–1702).

The name of this beautiful little church probably means "St Mary-at- the-meeting-of-three-roads".

EXPERIENCE Quirinal and Monti

← The Baroque Santi Vincenzo e Anastasio, with the Trevi Fountain in the foreground

Self-portrait by Lavinia Fontana in the Accademia Nazionale di San Luca

the many IHS emblems *(Iesus Hominum Salvator* – Jesus Saviour of Mankind).

The site for the church was wide but shallow, so Bernini pointed the long axis of his oval plan not towards the altar, but towards the sides; he then leads the eye round to the altar and. Here Bernini ordered works of art in various media which function not in isolation, but together. The crucified St Andrew (Sant'Andrea) of the altarpiece looks up at a stucco version of himself, who in turn ascends towards the lantern and the Holy Spirit.

The rooms of St Stanislas Kostka in the adjacent convent should not be missed. The quarters of the Jesuit novice, who died in 1568 at the age of 19, reflect not his own spartan taste, but the richer style of the 17th-century Jesuits. The Polish saint has been brilliantly immortalized in marble by Pierre Legros (1666–1719).

 Accademia Nazionale di San Luca

Ọ H4 **☐** Piazza dell' Accademia di San Luca 77 **🚌** 52, 53, 61, 62, 63, 71, 80, 116, 119 and many routes along Via del Corso and Via del Tritone **⌚** 10am–12:30pm Mon-Sat **🌐** accademiasanluca.eu

St Luke is supposed to have been a painter, hence the name of Rome's academy of fine arts. Appropriately, the gallery contains a painting of *St Luke Painting a Portrait of the Virgin* by Raphael and his followers. The academy's heyday was in the 17th and 18th centuries, when many members gave their work to the collection. Canova donated a model for his famous marble group, *The Three Graces*.

Of particular interest are three fascinating self-portraits painted by women: the 17th-century Italian Lavinia Fontana; the 18th-century Swiss Angelica Kauffmann, whose painting is copied from a portrait of her by Joshua Reynolds; and Elisabeth Vigée-Lebrun, the French painter of the years before the 1789 Revolution.

---

12 **Sant'Andrea al Quirinale**

Ọ J5 **☐** Via del Quirinale 29 **☎** 06-487 4565 **🚌** 116, 117 and routes to Via del Tritone **⌚** 9am-noon & 3-6pm Tue-Sun

Known as the "Pearl of the Baroque" because of its beautiful roseate marble interior, Sant'Andrea was designed by Bernini and executed by his assistants between 1658 and 1670. It was built for the Jesuits, hence

STAY

Villa Spalletti Trivelli
With the feel of an elegant country-house retreat, this luxury villa has atmosphere and style in abundance. Fine antiques grace every room, a sweeping staircase leads to sumptuous guest rooms upstairs, and there's even a garden - a rarity in central Rome.

Ọ J5 **☐** Via Piacenza 4 **🌐** villaspalletti.it

 The light interior of the small church of San Carlo alle Quattro Fontane

→
The once-controversial Fontana delle Naiadi in the Piazza della Repubblica

⑬

San Carlo alle Quattro Fontane

📍J4 🏛Via del Quirinale 23 📞06-488 3261 🚌116, 117 and routes to Piazza Barberini Ⓜ️Barberini 🕙10am-1pm & 3-6pm Mon-Fri (mornings only Jul & Aug), 10am-1pm Sat & Sun

In 1634, the Trinitarians, a Spanish order whose role was to pay the ransom of Christian hostages to the Arabs, commissioned Borromini to design a church and convent at the Quattro Fontane crossroads. The church, so small it would fit inside one of the piers of St Peter's, is also known as "San Carlino".

Although dedicated to Carlo Borromeo, the 16th-century Milanese cardinal canonized in 1620, San Carlo is as much a monument to Borromini. Both the façade and interior employ bold curves that give light and life to a small, cramped site. The oval dome and tiny lantern are particularly ingenious. Finished in 1667, the façade is one of Borromini's last works.

There are further delights in the playful inverted shapes in the cloister and the stucco work in the refectory.

In a small room off the sacristy hangs a portrait of Borromini himself wearing the Trinitarian cross. Borromini committed suicide in 1667, and in the crypt a small curved chapel reserved for him remains empty.

---

⑭

Le Quattro Fontane

📍J4 🏛Intersection of Via delle Quattro Fontane and Via del Quirinale 🚌Routes to Piazza Barberini or Via Nazionale Ⓜ️Barberini

These four small fountains are attached to the corners of the buildings at the intersection of two narrow, busy streets. They date from the great redevelopment of Rome in the reign of Sixtus V (1585–90). Each fountain has a statue of a reclining deity. The river god accompanied by the she-wolf is clearly the Tiber; the other male figure may be the Arno. The female figures represent Strength and Fidelity or the goddesses Juno and Diana.

The crossroads is at the highest point of the Quirinal hill and commands splendid views of three distant landmark obelisks: those placed by Sixtus V in front of Santa Maria Maggiore and Trinità dei Monti, and the one that stands in Piazza del Quirinale.

---

⑮

Moses Fountain

📍K4 🏛Fontana dell'Acqua Felice, Piazza San Bernardo 🚌36, 60, 61, 62, 492 Ⓜ️Repubblica

Officially known as the Fontana dell'Acqua Felice, this fountain owes its popular name to the grotesque statue of Moses in the central niche. The massive structure with its three elegant arches was designed by Domenico Fontana to mark the terminal of the Acqua Felice aqueduct, so called because it was one of the many great improvements commissioned by Felice Peretti, Pope Sixtus V.

Completed in 1587, the acqueduct brought clean piped water to this quarter of Rome for the first time.

The notorious statue of Moses striking water from the rock is larger than life and the proportions of the body are obviously wrong. Sculpted either by Prospero Bresciano or Leonardo Sormani, it is a clumsy attempt at re-creating the awesome appearance of Michelangelo's *Moses* in the church of San Pietro in Vincoli *(p205)*. As soon as it was unveiled to the public, it met with ridicule; it was said to be frowning at having been brought into the world by such an inept sculptor. The side reliefs by minor sculptors also illustrate water stories from the Old Testament: Aaron leading the Israelites to water and Joshua pointing the army towards the Red Sea. The fountain's four lions are copies of Egyptian originals (now in the Vatican Museums), which Sixtus V had put there for the public's "convenience" and "delight".

16
Santa Maria degli Angeli e dei Martiri

📍 L4 🚇 Piazza della Repubblica 📞 06-488 0812 🚌 36, 60, 61, 62, 64, 90, 116, 170, 492, 910 Ⓜ Repubblica, Termini 🕐 7am-6:30pm Mon-Sat, 7am-7:30pm Sun

Parts of the ruined Baths of Diocletian *(p187)* provided building material and setting for this church, constructed by Michelangelo in 1563. The church was so altered in the 18th century that it has lost most of its original character.

17
Piazza della Repubblica

📍 5K4 🚌 36, 60, 61, 62, 64, 90, 170, 492, 646, 910 Ⓜ Repubblica

Romans often refer to the piazza by its old name, Piazza Esedra, so called because it follows the shape of an *exedra*

(a semicircular recess) that was part of the Baths of Diocletian. The piazza was included in the great redevelopment undertaken when Rome became capital of a unified Italy. Under its sweeping 19th-century colonnades there were once elegant shops, but they have been ousted by banks, travel agencies and cafés.

In the middle of the piazza stands the Fontana delle Naiadi. Mario Rutelli's four naked bronze nymphs caused a scandal when unveiled in 1901. Each reclines on an aquatic creature symbolizing water in its various forms: a seahorse for the oceans, a water snake for rivers, a swan for lakes, and a curious frilled lizard for subterranean streams. The figure in the middle, added in 1911, is of the sea god Glaucus.

→
Santi Domenico e Sisto, with a painting of the Madonna above the altar

EAT

Alle Carrette

This cheerful pizzeria serves up delicious thin-crust Roman-style pizzas. The tables outside on the cobbled street are in high demand in summer.

📍 J6 🏠 Via della Madonna dei Monti 95
📞 06-679 2270

€ € €

L'Asino d'Oro

Italian dishes with a twist – such as wild boar with chocolate, or rabbit with pistachio – are what set apart this Monti favourite. Its cool, contemporary interior, lively atmosphere and inexpensive fixed lunchtime menu are further draws.

📍 J5 🏠 Via del Boschetto 73
📞 06-4891 3832

€ € €

La Carbonara

The scribblings of diners that cover every inch of the walls say it all: this buzzy, relaxed restaurant has plenty of satisfied customers.
The speciality is, of course, carbonara, but there are plenty of other pastas, as well as good meaty mains.

📍 K5 🏠 Via Panisperna 214
🌐 lacarbonara.it

€ € €

 18

Sant'Agata dei Goti

📍 J5 🏠 Via Mazzarino 16 and Via Panisperna 29
📞 06-4893 0456 🚌 40, 60, 64, 70, 71, 117, 170 🕐 7am–1pm & 4–7pm daily

The Goths (*Goti*) who gave their name to this church occupied Rome in the 6th century AD. They were Aryan heretics who denied the divinity of Christ. The church was founded between AD 462 and 470, shortly before the main Gothic invasions, and the beautiful granite columns date from this period. The most delightful part of the church is the 18th-century courtyard built around a well.

19

Palazzo delle Esposizioni

📍 J5 🏠 Via Nazionale 194
🚌 40, 60, 64, 70, 116T, 170
🕐 10am–8pm Tue–Sun (Fri & Sat: to 10:30pm)
🌐 palazzoesposizioni.it

This grandiose building, with wide steps, Corinthian columns and statues, was designed as an exhibition centre by the architect Pio Piacentini and built by the city of Rome in 1882 during the reign of Umberto I. The main entrance looks like a triumphal arch.

The restored palazzo still hosts high-profile exhibitions of modern and contemporary art that change every three to six months and include sculptures, paintings and photography. Live performances, films and lectures also take place here.

20

Santi Domenico e Sisto

📍 J6 🏠 Largo Angelicum 1
📞 06-670 2201 🚌 40, 60, 64, 70, 71, 117, 170
🕐 3–6pm Sat

The church has a tall, slender Baroque façade rising above a steep flight of steps. This divides into two curving flights that sweep up to the terrace in front of the entrance. The pediment of the façade is crowned by eight flaming candlesticks.

The interior has a vaulted ceiling with a large fresco of *The Apotheosis of St Dominic* by Domenico Canuti (1620–84). The first chapel on the right was decorated by Bernini, who may also have designed the sculpture of Mary Magdalene meeting the risen Christ in the Garden of Gethsemane. This

→
The tranquil gardens of Villa Aldobrandini, with fountains and statues

fine marble group was executed by Antonio Raggi (1649). Above the altar is a 15th-century terracotta plaque of the Virgin and Child. On the left, over a side altar, is a large painting of the Madonna from the same period, attributed to Benozzo Gozzoli (1420–97), a pupil of Fra Angelico.

Villa Aldobrandini

J5 ⌂ Via Panisperna
🚌 40, 60, 64, 70, 71, 117, 170 ⌛ to the public
Gardens: Via Mazzarino 1
🕐 dawn-dusk daily

Built in the 16th century for the Dukes of Urbino and acquired for his family by Pope Clement VIII Aldobrandini (reigned 1592–1605), the villa is now government property and houses an international law library.

The villa, decorated with the family's six-starred coat of arms, is closed to the public, but the gardens and terraces, hidden behind a high wall that runs along Via Nazionale, can be reached through an iron gate in Via Mazzarino. Steps lead up past 2nd-century AD ruins into the gardens, highly recommended as an oasis of tranquillity in the city centre. Raised some 10 m (30 ft) above street level, the Villa Aldobrandini garden offers excellent views of the Forum and Piazza Venezia. Gravel paths lead between formal lawns and clearly marked specimen trees.

> Raised some 10 m (30 ft) above street level, the Villa Aldobrandini garden offers excellent views of the Forum and Piazza Venezia.

Santa Maria dei Monti

J6 ⌂ Via Madonna dei Monti 41 ☎ 06-485 531
🚌 75, 117 Ⓜ Cavour 🕐 7am-noon & 4:30-7:30pm daily

Designed by Giacomo della Porta, this church, dating from 1580, has a particularly splendid dome. Over the high altar is a stunning medieval painting of the Madonna dei Monti, patroness of this quarter of Rome. The altar in the left transept houses the tomb and effigy of the unworldly French saint Benoît-Joseph Labre, who died here in 1783, having spent his life as a solitary pilgrim. He slept rough in the ruins of the Colosseum, gave away any charitable gifts he received, and came regularly to worship. His faith could not sustain his body: in his mid-thirties, he collapsed and died outside the church. The foul rags he wore are preserved.

A SHORT WALK
THE QUIRINAL HILL

Distance 0.7 km (0.4 mile) **Nearest bus** H, 40, 64, 70, 170
Time 15 minutes

Even though Palazzo del Quirinale is usually closed to the public, it is well worth walking up the hill to the palace to see the giant Roman statues of Castor and Pollux in the piazza and enjoy fine views of the city. Come down the hill by way of the narrow streets and stairways that lead to one of Rome's unforgettable sights, the Trevi Fountain. Many small churches lie hidden away in the back streets. Towards Piazza Venezia there are grand palazzi, including that of the Colonna, one of Rome's most ancient and powerful families.

The Accademia Nazionale di San Luca art academy has works by famous former members (p191).

Santa Maria in Via is famous for its medieval well and miraculous 13th-century icon of the Madonna.

The attractive façade of the tiny Santa Maria in Trivio conceals a rich Baroque interior (p190).

The Trevi, Rome's grandest and best-known fountain, almost fills the tiny Piazza di Trevi (p182).

San Marcello al Corso contains a stark Crucifixion by Van Dyck in the sacristy (p189).

Palazzo Odescalchi has a Bernini façade from 1664, with a balustrade and richly decorated cornice. The building faces Santi Apostoli.

VIA POLI
VIA DELLE MURATTE
VIA DELLE VERGINI
VIA DELL'UMILTÀ
VIA DEL CORSO

```
0 metres    75    N
0 yards     75    ↑
```

↑ Obelisk and statues of Castor and Pollux on Piazza del Quirinale

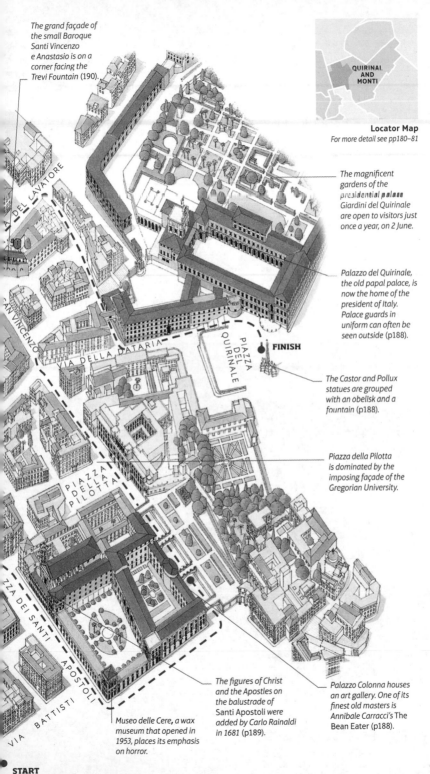

The grand façade of the small Baroque Santi Vincenzo e Anastasio is on a corner facing the Trevi Fountain (190).

Locator Map
For more detail see pp180–81

QUIRINAL AND MONTI

The magnificent gardens of the presidential palace Giardini del Quirinale are open to visitors just once a year, on 2 June.

Palazzo del Quirinale, the old papal palace, is now the home of the president of Italy. Palace guards in uniform can often be seen outside (p188).

FINISH

The Castor and Pollux statues are grouped with an obelisk and a fountain (p188).

Piazza della Pilotta is dominated by the imposing façade of the Gregorian University.

VIA DELLA DATARIA

PIAZZA DEL QUIRINALE

PIAZZA DELLA PILOTTA

Palazzo Colonna houses an art gallery. One of its finest old masters is Annibale Carracci's The Bean Eater (p188).

The figures of Christ and the Apostles on the balustrade of Santi Apostoli were added by Carlo Rainaldi in 1681 (p189).

Museo delle Cere, a wax museum that opened in 1953, places its emphasis on horror.

VIA BATTISTI

START

197

MARIA VIRGO ASSVPTA E AD ETheREV ThALAMV IN QVO REX REGV STELLATO SEDET SOLIO

EXALTATA EST SANCTA DEI GENITRIX SVPER ChOROS ANGELORVO AD CELESTIA REGNA

ESQULINE

The Esquiline is the largest and highest of Rome's
seven hills. In Imperial Rome the western slopes
overlooking the Forum housed the crowded slums
of the Suburra. On the eastern side there were
a few villas belonging to wealthy citizens such
as Maecenas, patron of the arts and adviser to
Augustus. The essential character of the place
has persisted through two millennia; it is still
one of the poorer quarters of the city. The area
is now heavily built up, except for a rather seedy
park on the Colle Oppio, a smaller hill to the south
of the Esquiline, where you can see the remains
of the Baths of Titus, the Baths of Trajan and
Nero's Domus Aurea. The district's main interest,
however, lies in its churches. Many of these were
founded on the sites of private houses where
Christians met to worship secretly in the days
when their religion was banned.

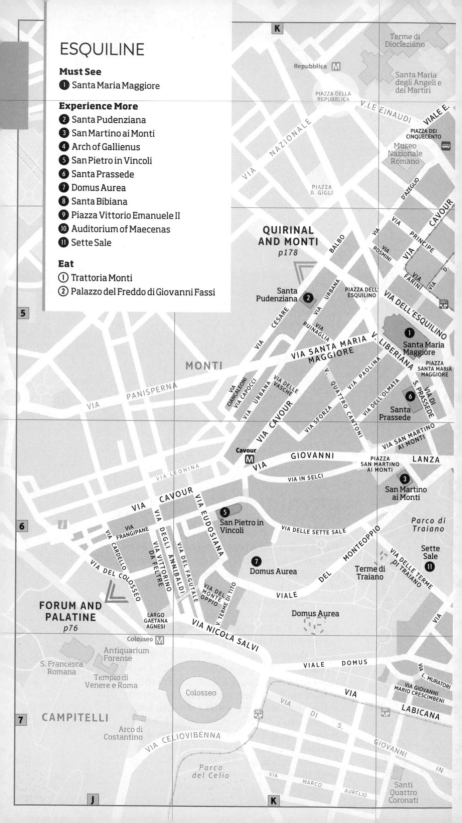

ESQUILINE

Must See
1. Santa Maria Maggiore

Experience More
2. Santa Pudenziana
3. San Martino ai Monti
4. Arch of Gallienus
5. San Pietro in Vincoli
6. Santa Prassede
7. Domus Aurea
8. Santa Bibiana
9. Piazza Vittorio Emanuele II
10. Auditorium of Maecenas
11. Sette Sale

Eat
1. Trattoria Monti
2. Palazzo del Freddo di Giovanni Fassi

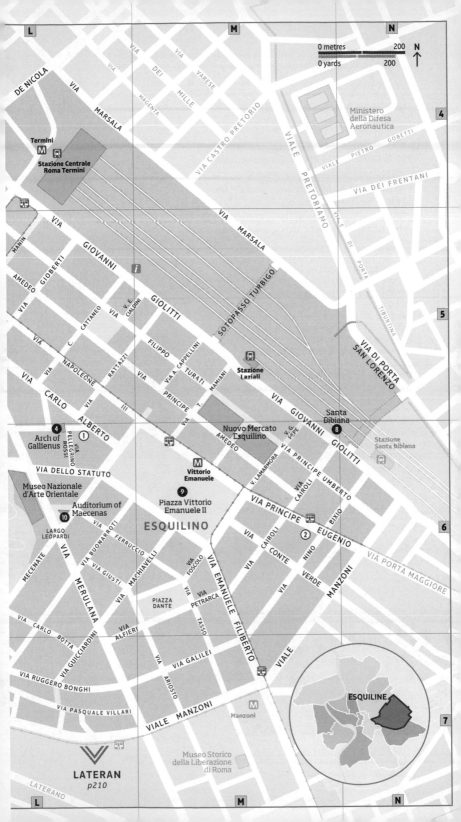

SANTA MARIA MAGGIORE

EXPERIENCE Esquiline

📍L5 🏛Piazza di Santa Maria Maggiore ☎06-6988 6800 🚌16, 70, 71, 714 🚊14 Ⓜ Termini, Cavour 🕐7am–6:45pm daily

Of all the great Roman basilicas, Santa Maria Maggiore has the most successful blend of different architectural styles. One of the four papal basilicas, it has a beautiful interior with sparkling mosaics.

This is the biggest of the 26 churches in Rome dedicated to the Virgin Mary. Originally built by Pope Liberius in the 4th century, Santa Maria Maggiore was renovated and improved upon by many popes over the centuries, although it still retains its early medieval structure. The colonnaded nave is part of the original 5th-century building. The Cosmatesque marble floor and delightful Romanesque bell tower, with its blue ceramic roundels, are medieval. The Renaissance saw a new coffered ceiling, and the Baroque gave the church twin domes and its imposing front and rear façades. The mosaics are Santa Maria's most famous feature and are some of the oldest in Rome. From the 5th century come the biblical scenes in the aisle and the spectacular mosaics on the triumphal arch. Medieval highlights include a 13th-century enthroned Christ in the loggia.

Flaminio Ponzio designed this richly decorated chapel (1611) for Pope Paul V Borghese.

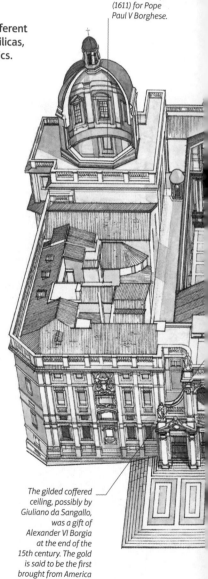

The gilded coffered ceiling, possibly by Giuliano da Sangallo, was a gift of Alexander VI Borgia at the end of the 15th century. The gold is said to be the first brought from America by Columbus.

↑ The 18th-century exterior of Santa Maria Maggiore on the piazza of the same name

1288–92
▽ Nicholas IV adds
apse and transepts

1743
Ferdinando Fuga adds main
façade on orders of Benedict XIV

Timeline

420
Probable
founding date

432–40
▲ Sixtus III
completes church

1347
Cola di Rienzo
crowned Tribune
of Rome in Santa
Maria Maggiore

1673
Carlo Rainaldi
rebuilds apse

*A series of wonderful
apse mosaics of the
Virgin by Jacopo
Torriti (1295) is here.*

*The Baldacchino
was the work of
Ferdinando Fuga.*

*The Gothic Tomb of
Cardinal Rodriguez
(1299) contains
Cosmatesque
marblework.*

*This Sistine Chapel
was built for Pope
Sixtus V (1584–7)
by Domenico
Fontana and
houses his tomb.*

↑ Detail of the mosaic
in the apse showing
angels, by Jacopo Torriti

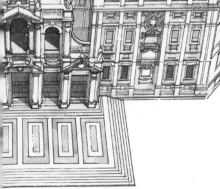

↑ Illustration showing the
layout of the vast Santa
Maria Maggiore basilica

**LEGEND OF
THE SNOW**

In 356 Pope
Liberius had a
dream in which
the Virgin told him to build a church
on the spot where he found snow.
When it fell on the Esquiline, on the
morning of 5 August in the middle
of a baking Roman summer, he
naturally obeyed. The miracle of
the snow is commemorated each
year by a service during which
thousands of white petals float
down from the ceiling of Santa
Maria. Originally roses were used,
but nowadays the petals are more
usually taken from dahlias.

Interior of Santa Pudenziana showing the splendid 4th-century apse mosaic

meet in the house of a man named Equitius. In the 4th century, after Constantine had legalized Christianity, Pope Sylvester I built a church, one of the very few things he did during his pontificate. In fact he was so insignificant that in the 5th century a more exciting life was fabricated for him – which included tales of him converting Constantine and curing him of leprosy.

Pope Sylvester's church was replaced in about AD 500 by St Symmachus, rebuilt in the 9th century and then transformed completely in the 1630s. The only immediate signs of its age are the ancient Corinthian columns dividing the nave and aisles. The most interesting interior features are a series of frescoed landscapes of the countryside around Rome (campagna romana) by the 17th-century French artist Gaspare Dughet, Poussin's brother-in-law, in the right aisle.

EXPERIENCE MORE

Santa Pudenziana

📍K5 🚪Via Urbana 160 📞06-481 4622 🚌16, 75, 105, 714 Ⓜ Cavour ⏱8:30am-noon & 3-6pm daily

Churches tend to be dedicated to existing saints, but this church, through a linguistic accident, created a brand new saint. In the 1st century AD a Roman senator called Pudens lived here, and is said to have allowed St Peter to lodge with him. In the 2nd century a bath house was built on this site and in the 4th century a church was established inside the baths, known as the Ecclesia Pudentiana (the church of Pudens). In time it was assumed that "Pudentiana" was a woman's name and a life was created for her – she

became the sister of Prassede and was credited with caring for Christian victims of persecution. In 1969 both saints were declared invalid.

The 19th-century façade of the church retains an 11th-century frieze depicting both Prassede and Pudenziana. The apse has a remarkable 4th-century mosaic influenced by Classical pagan art.

San Martino ai Monti

📍L6 🚪Viale del Monte Oppio 28 📞06-478 4701 🚌16, 714 Ⓜ Cavour, Vittorio Emanuele ⏱7.30am-noon & 4-7pm daily

Christians have worshipped on the site of this church since the 3rd century, when they used to

Arch of Gallienus

📍L6 🚪Via Carlo Alberto 🚌16, 71, 714 Ⓜ Vittorio Emanuele

Squashed between two buildings just off Via Carlo Alberto is the central arch of an originally three-arched gate erected in memory of Emperor Gallienus, who was

Did You Know?

The horns on Michelangelo's Moses' head should be beams of light, but the Old Testament text was mistranslated.

assassinated by his Illyrian officers in AD 262. It was built on the site of the old Esquiline Gate in the Servian Wall, parts of which are visible nearby.

San Pietro in Vincoli

📍K6 🏠 Piazza di San Pietro in Vincoli 4A 📞 06-9784 4950 🚌 75, 117 Ⓜ Cavour, Colosseo 🕐 8am-12.30pm & 3-7pm (Oct-Mar: until 6pm) daily

According to tradition, the two chains *(vincoli)* used to shackle St Peter while he was being held in the depths of the Mamertine Prison *(p99)*

were subsequently taken to Constantinople. In the 5th century, Empress Eudoxia deposited one in a church there and sent the other to her daughter Eudoxia in Rome. She in turn gave hers to Pope Leo I, who had this church built to house it. Some years later the second chain was brought to Rome, where it linked miraculously with its partner.

The chains are still here, displayed below the high altar, but the church is now best known for Michelangelo's *Tomb of Pope Julius II*. When it was commissioned in 1505, Michelangelo spent eight months searching for perfect blocks of marble at Carrara in Tuscany, but Pope Julius became more interested in the building of a new St Peter's and the project was laid aside. After the pope's death in 1513, Michelangelo resumed work on the tomb, but had only finished the statues of *Moses* and *The Dying Slaves* when Pope Paul III persuaded him to start work on the Sistine Chapel's *Last Judgment*. Michelangelo had planned a vast monument with over 40 statues, but the tomb that was built – mainly by his pupils – is simply a façade with six niches for statues. *The Dying Slaves* are in Paris and Florence, but the tremendous bearded *Moses* is here, nearly 2.5 m (8 feet) in height, with his huge muscular arms and intense expression.

Santa Prassede

📍L5 🏠 Via Santa Prassede 9A 📞 06-488 2456 🚌 16, 70, 71, 75, 714 Ⓜ Vittorio Emanuele 🕐 7am-noon, 4-6:30pm daily (from 7:30am Sun; Aug: pm only)

The church was founded by Pope Paschal II in the 9th

century, on the site of a 2nd-century oratory. Although the interior has been altered and rebuilt, the structure of the 9th-century church is visible. Its three aisles are separated by rows of granite columns. In the central nave, there is a round stone slab covering the well where, according to legend, Santa Prassede is said to have buried the remains of 2,000 martyrs.

Artists from Byzantium decorated the church with glittering, jewel-coloured mosaics. Those in the apse and choir depict stylized white-robed elders, the haloed elect looking down from the gold and blue walls of heaven, spindly legged lambs, feather-mop palm trees and bright-red poppies.

In the apse, Santa Prassede and Santa Pudenziana stand on either side of Christ, with the fatherly arms of St Paul and St Peter on their shoulders. Beautiful mosaics of saints, the Virgin and Christ, and the Apostles also cover the walls and vault of the Chapel of St Zeno, built as a mausoleum for Pope Paschal's mother, Theodora. Part of a column brought back from Jerusalem, allegedly the one to which Christ was bound and flogged, also stands here.

→

Michelangelo's *Moses* in San Pietro in Vincoli

7

Domus Aurea

K6 **Viale della Domus Aurea** 85, 87, 117, 186, 810, 850 3 **Colosseo** **for guided tours on weekends only – phone in advance (06-3996 7700); virtual tours are available online coopculture.it**

After allegedly setting fire to Rome in AD 64, Nero decided to build himself an outrageous new palace. The Domus Aurea (sometimes called Nero's Golden House) occupied part of the Palatine and most of the Celian and Esquiline hills – an area approximately 25 times the size of the Colosseum. The vestibule on the Palatine side of the complex contained a colossal gilded statue of Nero. There was an artificial lake, with gardens and woods where imported wild beasts were allowed to roam free. According to Suetonius in his *Life of Nero*, the Domus Aurea's walls were adorned with gold and mother-of-pearl, rooms had ceilings that showered guests with flowers or perfumes, the dining hall rotated and the baths were fed with both sulphurous water and sea water.

Tacitus described Nero's debauched garden parties, with banquets served on barges and lakeside brothels serviced by aristocratic women. Since Nero killed himself in AD 68, however, he did not have long to enjoy his new home.

Nero's successors, anxious to distance themselves from the monster-emperor, did their utmost to erase all traces of the palace. Vespasian drained the lake and built the Colosseum (*p88*) in its place, Titus and Trajan each erected a complex of baths over the palace, and Hadrian placed the Temple of Venus and Rome (*p87*) over the vestibule.

Rooms from one wing of the palace have survived, buried beneath the ruins of the Baths of Trajan on the Oppian Hill. Excavations have revealed large frescoes and mosaics that are thought to be a panorama of Rome from a bird's-eye perspective.

Visitors are advised to bring a jacket as the temperature inside the building is around 10° C (50° F).

> **The Domus Aurea's walls were adorned with gold and mother-of-pearl, rooms had ceilings that showered guests with flowers or perfumes.**

8

Santa Bibiana

M6 **Via Giovanni Giolitti 154** 06-446 5235 71 5, 14 **Vittorio Emanuele** 7:30–10am & 4:30-7:30pm Mon-Sat; 7:30am-12:30pm & 4:30-7:30pm Sun

The deceptively simple façade of Santa Bibiana was Bernini's first foray into architecture. It is a clean, economic design with superimposed pilasters and deeply shadowed archways. The church itself was built on the site of the palace belonging to Bibiana's family. This is where the saint was buried after being flogged to death with leaded cords during the brief persecution of the Christians in the reign of Julian the Apostate (361–3). Just inside the church is a small column against which Bibiana is said to have been whipped. Her remains, along with those of her mother Dafrosa and her sister Demetria, who also suffered martyrdom, are preserved in an alabaster urn below the altar.

In a niche above the altar stands a statue of Santa Bibiana by Bernini – the first fully clothed figure he ever sculpted. He depicts her standing beside a column, holding the cords with which she was whipped, apparently on the verge of a deadly swoon.

← A bust of Emperor Nero at the park entrance to the Domus Aurea

↑ The Porta Magica in Piazza Vittorio Emanuele II

 9

Piazza Vittorio Emanuele II

🅟 M6 🚌 4, 9, 71 🚋 5, 14
Ⓜ Vittorio Emanuele

Rome's largest square, Piazza Vittorio, as it is called for short, was once one of the city's main open-air food markets. The market has moved around the corner to covered premises and is now called Nuovo Mercato Esquilino (p51). The arcaded square was built as part of the urban development that was undertaken following the unification of Italy in 1861. It was named after Italy's first king, but there is nothing regal about its appearance today. The garden area in the centre of the square contains a number of mysterious ruins, including a large mound, part of a Roman fountain from the 3rd century AD and the Porta Magica, a curious 17th-century doorway inscribed with alchemical signs and formulae, which belonged to a marquis whose home was often visited by alchemists and magicians.

 10

Auditorium of Maecenas

🅟 L6 🏠 Largo Leopardi 2
📞 06-0608 🚌 16, 714
Ⓜ Vittorio Emanuele 🕐 by appt; phone in advance

Maecenas, a fop, gourmet and patron of the arts, was also an astute adviser and colleague of the Emperor Augustus. Fabulously rich, he created a fantastic villa and gardens on the Esquiline Hill, most of which have long disappeared beneath the modern city. The partially reconstructed auditorium, isolated on a traffic island, is all that remains.

Inside, a semicircle of tiered seats suggests that it may have been a place for readings and performances. If it was, then Maecenas would have been entertained here by his protégés, the lyric poet Horace and Virgil, author of the *Aeneid*, reading their latest works. However, water ducts have also been discovered and it may well have been a *nympheum* – a kind of summerhouse – with

fountains. Traces of frescoes remain on the walls: you can make out garden scenes and a procession of miniature figures.

 11

Sette Sale

🅟 L6 🏠 Via delle Terme di Traiano 📞 06-0608 🚌 85, 87, 117, 186, 810, 850 🚋 3
Ⓜ Colosseo 🕐 by appt; phone in advance

Not far from Nero's Domus Aurea is the cistern of the Sette Sale, built here to supply the enormous quantities of water needed for the Baths of Trajan. These were built for Emperor Trajan in AD 104 on parts of the Domus Aurea that had been damaged by a fire.

A set of stairs leads down into the cistern, well below street level. There is not much to see here now, but you can walk through the huge, echoing cistern where light rays illuminate the watery surfaces. The nine sections, 30 m (98 ft) long and 5 m (16 ft) wide, had a capacity of eight million litres.

A SHORT WALK
THE ESQUILINE HILL

Distance 1 km (0.6 mile) **Nearest metro** Vittorio Emmanule **Time** 20 minutes

The sight that draws most people to this rather scruffy part of Rome is the great basilica of Santa Maria Maggiore. But it is also well worth searching out some of the smaller churches on the Esquiline: Santa Pudenziana and Santa Prassede with their celebrated mosaics, and San Pietro in Vincoli, home to one of Michelangelo's most famous sculptures. To the south, in the Colle Oppio park, are the scattered remains of the Baths of Trajan.

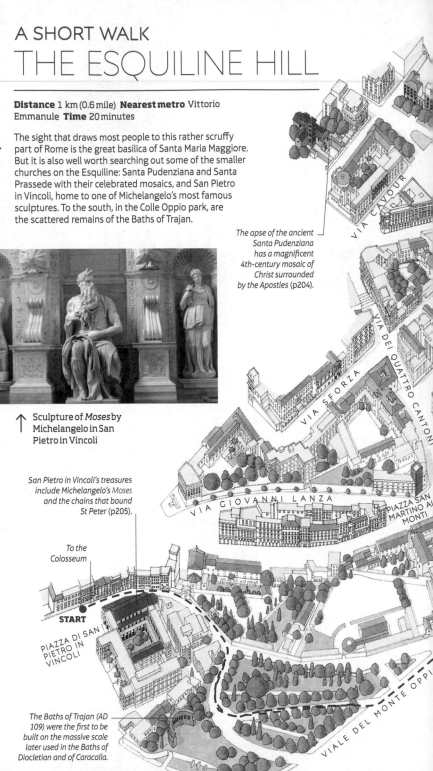

The apse of the ancient Santa Pudenziana has a magnificent 4th-century mosaic of Christ surrounded by the Apostles (p204).

↑ Sculpture of *Moses* by Michelangelo in San Pietro in Vincoli

San Pietro in Vincoli's treasures include Michelangelo's Moses and the chains that bound St Peter (p205).

To the Colosseum

START

PIAZZA DI SAN PIETRO IN VINCOLI

VIA CAVOUR

VIA DEI QUATTRO CANTONI

VIA SFORZA

VIA GIOVANNI LANZA

PIAZZA SAN MARTINO AI MONTI

VIALE DEL MONTE OPPIO

The Baths of Trajan (AD 109) were the first to be built on the massive scale later used in the Baths of Diocletian and of Caracalla.

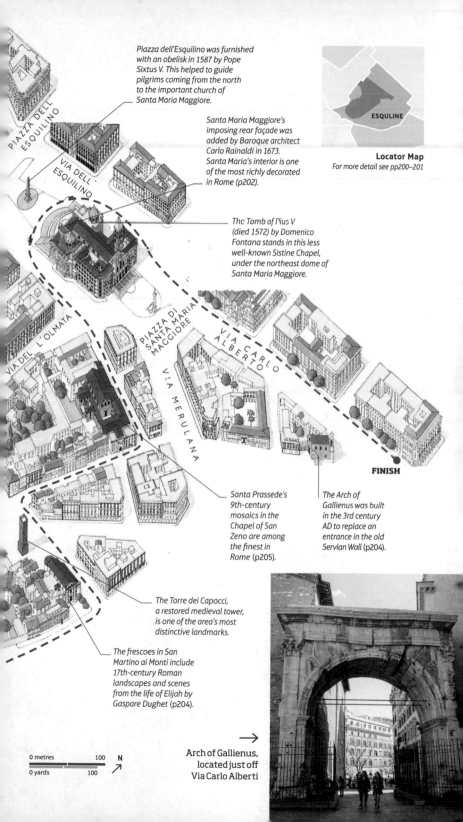

Piazza dell'Esquilino was furnished with an obelisk in 1587 by Pope Sixtus V. This helped to guide pilgrims coming from the north to the important church of Santa Maria Maggiore.

Santa Maria Maggiore's imposing rear façade was added by Baroque architect Carlo Rainaldi in 1673. Santa Maria's interior is one of the most richly decorated in Rome (p202).

Locator Map
For more detail see pp200–201

ESQUILINE

PIAZZA DELL' ESQUILINO

VIA DELL' ESQUILINO

The Tomb of Pius V (died 1572) by Domenico Fontana stands in this less well-known Sistine Chapel, under the northeast dome of Santa Maria Maggiore.

VIA DEL L'OLMATA

PIAZZA DI SANTA MARIA MAGGIORE

VIA CARLO ALBERTO

VIA MERULANA

FINISH

Santa Prassede's 9th-century mosaics in the Chapel of San Zeno are among the finest in Rome (p205).

The Arch of Gallienus was built in the 3rd century AD to replace an entrance in the old Servian Wall (p204).

The Torre dei Capocci, a restored medieval tower, is one of the area's most distinctive landmarks.

The frescoes in San Martino ai Monti include 17th-century Roman landscapes and scenes from the life of Elijah by Gaspare Dughet (p204).

0 metres   100
0 yards   100

N

→ Arch of Gallienus, located just off Via Carlo Alberti

LATERAN

In the Middle Ages the Lateran Palace was the
residence of the popes, and the Basilica of San
Giovanni beside it rivalled St Peter's in splendour.
After the return of the popes from Avignon at
the end of the 14th century, the area declined
in importance. Pilgrims still continued to visit
San Giovanni and Santa Croce in Gerusalemme,
but the area remained sparsely inhabited. Ancient
convents were situated amid gardens and
vineyards until Rome became capital of Italy in
1870 and a network of residential streets was
laid out here to house the influx of newcomers.
Archaeological interest lies chiefly in the Aurelian
Wall and the ruins of the Aqueduct of Nero.

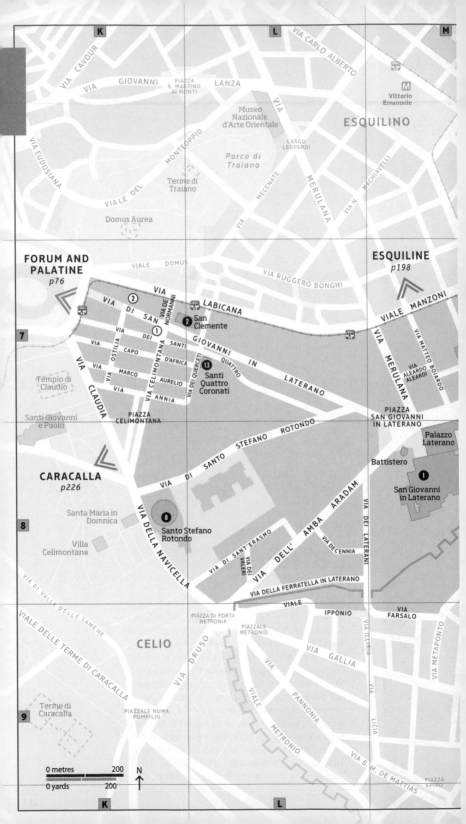

K **L** **M**

VIA CAVOUR

VIA GIOVANNI LANZA

PIAZZA S. MARTINO AI MONTI

VIA CARLO ALBERTO

Vittorio Emanuele **M**

ESQUILINO

VIA EUDOSIANA

VIA MONTEOPPIO

Museo Nazionale d'Arte Orientale

LARGO LEOPARDI

VIA MERULANA

VIA MECENATE

Parco di Traiano

Terme di Traiano

Domus Aurea

VIALE DEL

VIA N. MACHIAVELLI

FORUM AND PALATINE
p76

VIALE DOMUS

VIA RUGGERO BONGHI

ESQUILINE
p198

VIA DEI NORMANNI

VIA DI SAN

②

VIA LABICANA

② San Clemente

VIALE MANZONI

VIA MERULANA

VIA MATTEO BOIARDO

7

VIA DEI

①

VIA OSTILIA

VIA CAPO D'AFRICA

VIA CELIMONTANA

VIA SANTI QUATTRO

VIA GIOVANNI IN LATERANO

VIA ALEARDO ALEARDI

VIA CLAUDIA

Tempio di Claudio

VIA MARCO AURELIO

VIA ANNIA

VIA DEI QUERCETI

⑬ Santi Quattro Coronati

PIAZZA SAN GIOVANNI IN LATERANO

Santi Giovanni e Paolo

PIAZZA CELIMONTANA

VIA DI SANTO STEFANO ROTONDO

Palazzo Laterano

CARACALLA
p226

Santa Maria in Domnica

VIA DELLA NAVICELLA

⑧

Santo Stefano Rotondo

VIA DI SANT'ERASMO

VIA DEI VALERI

VIA DELL' AMBA ARADAM

VIA DECENNIA

VIA DEI LATERANI

Battistero

① San Giovanni in Laterano

8

Villa Celimontana

VIA DELLA FERRATELLA IN LATERANO

VIA DI VALLE DELLE CAMENE

VIALE DELLE TERME DI CARACALLA

CELIO

VIA DRUSO

PIAZZA DI PORTA METRONIA

PIAZZALE METRONIA

VIALE IPPONIO

VIA GALLIA

VIA ITALTRA

VIA FARSALO

VIA METAPONTO

VIA LICIA

9

Terme di Caracalla

PIAZZALE NUMA POMPILIO

VIALE METRONIO

VIA PANNONIA

VIA B. M. DE MATTIAS

PIAZZA EPIRO

0 metres 200
0 yards 200

N ↑

K **L**

LATERAN

Must Sees

1. San Giovanni in Laterano
2. San Clemente

Experience More

3. Museum of Musical Instruments
4. Santa Croce in Gerusalemme
5. Amphiteatrum Castrense
6. Porta Asinaria
7. Scala Santa and Sancta Sanctorum
8. Santo Stefano Rotondo
9. Porta Maggiore
10. Aqueduct of Nero and the Freedmen's Tombs
11. Museo Storico della Liberazione di Roma
12. Baker's Tomb
13. Santi Quattro Coronati

Eat

① Trattoria Luzzi

Stay

② Palazzo Manfredi

SAN GIOVANNI IN LATERANO

📍M8 🏠Piazza di San Giovanni in Laterano 4 📞06-6988 6433 🚌16, 81, 85, 87, 186, 650, 850 🚋3 Ⓜ️San Giovanni ⏰Cathedral: 7am-6:30pm; Cloister: 9am-6pm; Museum: 10am-5:30pm; Baptistry: 9am-12:30pm & 4-6:30pm

In the 4th century, the Laterani family were disgraced and their land taken by Emperor Constantine to build Rome's first Christian basilica, San Giovanni in Laterano. This is the cathedral of Rome's bishopric.

↑ Fresco detail showing the pope proclaiming the Holy Year of 1300, attributed to Giotto

Today's church retains the original shape, but has been destroyed by fire twice and rebuilt several times. Borromini undertook the last major rebuild of the interior in 1646, and the main façade is an 18th-century addition. Before the pope's move to Avignon in 1309, the adjoining Lateran Palace was the official papal residence, and until 1870 all popes were crowned in the church. This is the city's main cathedral, and the seat of the Bishop of Rome, the pope, who celebrates Maundy Thursday Mass here. This is also where the pope attends the annual blessing of the people. The church has the world's first baptistry – its ocatgonal shape formed the model for all those to come.

> **This is the city's main cathedral, and the seat of the Bishop of Rome, the pope, who celebrates Maundy Thursday Mass here.**

TRIAL OF A CORPSE

Fear of rival factions led the early popes to extraordinary lengths. At the Lateran Palace in 897 Pope Stephen VI tried the corpse of his predecessor, Formosus, for disloyalty to the Church. The corpse was found guilty, its right hand was mutilated and it was thrown into the Tiber.

↑ The elegant north façade, added by Domenico Fontana in 1586

Did You Know?

Only the pope can celebrate Mass at the altar in San Giovanni in Laterano.

↑ Papal altar with the Gothic baldacchino, decorated with frescoes dating from the 14th century

2

SAN CLEMENTE

📍 K7 🏛 Via di San Giovanni in Laterano 🚌 85, 87, 117, 186, 810, 850 🚊 3 🚇 Colosseo 🕐 9am-12:30pm & 3-6pm Mon-Sat, noon-6pm Sun 🌐 basilicasanclemente.com

San Clemente gives visitors a chance to travel back through three layers of history, providing an insight into how buildings were modified over the years.

↑ Courtyard of the San Clemente basilica

At street level, the present-day basilica dates to the 12th century. It features medieval mosaics and Renaissance frescoes, notably those depicting St Catherine of Alexandria by the 15th-century Florentine artist Masolino da Panicale. Underneath lies a 4th-century church built to honour San Clemente, the fourth pope, who was exiled to the Crimea and martyred by being tied to an anchor and drowned. His life is illustrated in some of the frescoes. This 4th-century church was built over a temple dedicated to the cult of Mithras, which in turn was built inside a 1st-century AD aristocratic house.

The site was taken over in the 17th century by Irish Dominicans, who still continue the excavations begun by Father Mullooly in 1857.

← A fresco by Masolino da Panicale showing a scene from the life of St Catherine of Alexandria

Timeline

Late 2nd century
▲ Temple of Mithras built

4th century
First church built over courtyard of earlier Roman building

1084
Church destroyed during Norman invasion led by Robert Guiscard

1108
New church built over 4th-century church

1857
Original 4th-century church rediscovered by Father Mullooly

1861
▲ Church is excavated. Roman ruins discovered

THE CULT OF MITHRAS

In 3rd-century Rome the all-male cult of Mithras rivalled Christianity. Followers believed that Mithras had brought life to the world by spilling the blood of a bull and that faith in Mithras guaranteed salvation. Would-be cult members underwent initiation ceremonies, including trials by ice, fire, hunger and thirst. Ritual banquets were held in the triclinium, a room with stone benches on either side of an altar.

↑ The 12th-century apse mosaic of the *Triumph of the Cross* representing the crucified Christ as a Tree of Life

EXPERIENCE MORE

↑ The cross and angels adorning Santa Croce in Gerusalemme

3

Museum of Musical Instruments

? P7 **↑** Piazza di Santa Croce in Gerusalemme 9A **🚌** 16, 81, 649, 810 **🚊** 3 **🕐** 9am-7pm Tue-Sun **w** museostrumenti musicali.beniculturali.it

One of Rome's lesser-known museums, the Museum of Musical Instruments stands on the site of the Sessorianum, the great Imperial villa belonging to Empress St Helena, later included in the Aurelian Wall. It houses a collection of more than 3,000 outstanding musical instruments from all over the world, including instruments typical of the various regions of Italy, and wind, string and percussion instruments of all ages (including ancient Egyptian, Greek and Roman).

There are also sections dedicated to church and military music. The greater part of the collection comprises Baroque instruments: be sure to see the gorgeous Barberini harp (dating to 1605–20), which is remarkably well-preserved, on the first floor in Room 13. There are also fine examples of spinets, harpsichords and clavichords, and one of the first pianos ever made, dating from 1722.

4

Santa Croce in Gerusalemme

? P7 **↑** Piazza di Santa Croce in Gerusalemme 12 **🚌** 16, 81, 649, 810 **🚊** 3 **🕐** 7am-12:45pm & 3:30-7:30pm daily **w** santacroce roma.it

Emperor Constantine's mother St Helena founded this church in AD 320 in the grounds of her private palace. Although the church stood at the edge of the city, the relics of the Crucifixion that St Helena had brought back from Jerusalem made it a centre of pilgrimage. Most important were the pieces of Christ's Cross (*croce* means "cross") and part of Pontius Pilate's inscription in Latin, Hebrew and Greek: "Jesus of Nazareth King of the Jews".

In the crypt is a Roman statue of Juno, found at Ostia (*p314*), transformed into a statue of St Helena by replacing the head and arms.

The 15th-century apse fresco shows the medieval legends that arose around the Cross. Helena is shown holding it over a dead youth and restoring him to life. Another episode shows its recovery from the Persians by the Byzantine Emperor Heraclitus after a bloody battle. In the centre of the apse is a tomb by Jacopo Sansovino made for Cardinal Quiñones, Emperor Charles V's confessor (died 1540).

5

Amphiteatrum Castrense

? P7 **↑** Between Piazza di Santa Croce in Gerusalemme and Viale Castrense **🚌** 649 **🚊** 3 **🕐** first and third Sat of month by appt (call 06-3996 7700)

This small 3rd-century amphitheatre was used for games and baiting animals. It owes its preservation to being part of the Aurelian Wall (*p236*), but its graceful arches framed by brick semi-columns were blocked up. The amphitheatre is best seen from outside the walls, from where there is also a good view of the bell tower of Santa Croce in Gerusalemme.

6

Porta Asinaria

? M8 **↑** Between Piazza di Porta San Giovanni and Piazzale Appio **🚌** 16, 81, 85, 87 **🚊** 3 **Ⓜ** San Giovanni

The Porta Asinaria (Gate of the Donkeys) is one of the minor gateways built between

18th-century piano at the Museum of Musical Instruments

↑ The 28 steps of the Scala Santa, with devotees kneeling and praying

270 and 273 in the Aurelian Wall (p236) . Twin circular towers were added and a small enclosure built around the entrance; the remains are still visible. From outside the walls you can see the gate's white travertine façade and two rows of small windows, giving light to two corridors built into the wall above the gateway. In AD 546 treacherous barbarian soldiers serving in the Roman army opened this gate to the hordes of the Goth Totila, who mercilessly looted the city. In 1084 the Holy Roman Emperor Henry IV entered Rome via Porta Asinaria with the antipope Guibert to oust Pope Gregory VII. The gate was badly damaged in the conflicts that followed.

The area close to the gate, in the Via Sannio is the home of a large flea market 8am–1pm Mon–Fri and till 6pm Sat.

7

Scala Santa and Sancta Sanctorum

M7 🏛Piazza di San Giovanni in Laterano 14 📞06-772 6641 🚌16, 81, 85, 87, 186 and other routes to Piazza di San Giovanni in Laterano 🚋3 Ⓜ San Giovanni ⏰6:30am-6:30pm Mon-Sat, 7am-7pm Sun & hols

On the east side of Piazza di San Giovanni in Laterano, a building by Domenico Fontana (1589) houses two surviving parts of the old Lateran Palace. One is the Sancta Sanctorum, the other the holy staircase, the Scala Santa. The 28 steps, said to be those that Christ ascended in Pontius Pilate's house during his trial, are said to have been brought from Jerusalem by St Helena, the mother of Constantine.

This belief, however, cannot be traced back any earlier than the 7th century.

The steps were moved to their present site by Pope Sixtus V (reigned 1585–90) when the old Lateran Palace was destroyed. No foot may touch the holy steps, so they are covered by wooden boards. They may only be climbed by the faithful on their knees, especially on Good Friday. In the vestibule there are various 19th-century sculptures including an *Ecce Homo* by Giosuè Meli (1874).

The Scala Santa and two side stairways lead to the Chapel of St Lawrence or Sancta Sanctorum (Holy of Holies), built by Pope Nicholas III in 1278. Decorated with fine Cosmatesque marble-work, the chapel contains many important relics, the most precious being an image of Jesus – the *Acheiropoeton* or "picture painted without hands", said to be the work of St Luke, with the help of an angel. It was taken on procession in medieval times to ward off plagues.

On the walls and in the vault, restoration work has revealed 13th-century frescoes which for 500 years had been covered by later paintings.

Porta Asinaria, part of the Aurelian Wall

 8

Santo Stefano Rotondo

📍 K8 🏛 Via di Santo Stefano Rotondo 7 📞 06-421 199 🚌 81, 117, 673 🕐 10am–1pm & 3:30–6:30pm (2:30–5:30pm winter) daily ⏰ three weeks in Aug

One of Rome's earliest Christian churches, Santo Stefano Rotondo was built between 468 and 483. It has an unusual circular plan with four chapels in the shape of a cross. It is lit by 22 high windows, a few of them restored or blocked by restorations carried out under Pope Nicholas V (reigned 1447–55), who consulted the Florentine architect Leon Battista Alberti. The archway in the centre may have been added during this period.

In the 16th century the church walls were frescoed by Niccolò Pomarancio with particularly gruesome illustrations of the martyrdom of innumerable saints. Some of the medieval decor remains: in the first chapel to the left of the entrance is a 7th-century mosaic of Christ with San Primo and San Feliciano.

 9

Porta Maggiore

📍 N7 🏛 Piazza di Porta Maggiore 🚌 105 🚊 3, 5, 14, 19

Originally the two arches of Porta Maggiore were not part of the city wall, but part of an aqueduct built by the Emperor Claudius in AD 52. They carried the water of the Aqua Claudia over the Via Labicana and Via Prenestina, two of ancient Rome's main south-bound roads. You can still see the original roadway beneath the gate. In the large slabs of basalt – a hard volcanic rock used in all old Roman roads – note the great ruts created by centuries of cartwheel traffic. On top of the arches separate conduits carried the water of two aqueducts: the Aqua Claudia, and its offshoot, the Aqueduct of Nero. They bear inscriptions from the time of the Emperor Claudius and also from the reigns of Vespasian and Titus. In all, six aqueducts from different water sources entered the city at Porta Maggiore.

The Aqua Claudia was 68 km (43 miles) long, with over 15 km (9 miles) above ground. Its majestic arches are a notable feature of the Roman countryside, and a popular mineral water bears its name. One stretch of the Aqua Claudia had its arches bricked up when it was incorporated into the 3rd-century Aurelian Wall (p236).

↑ The unusual circular plan of the church of Santo Stefano Rotondo

---

STAY

Palazzo Manfredi
This chic bolthole boasts dead-ahead views of the Colosseum from its airy and impeccably tasteful rooms and suites. Guests can also enjoy the view from Aroma, the glass-walled Michelin-starred restaurant on the roof.

📍 K7 🏛 Via Labicana 125 🌐 palazzo manfredi.com

€€€

Aqueduct of Nero and the Freedmen's Tombs

♀ N6 ⚑ Intersection of Via Statilia and Via di Santa Croce in Gerusalemme 🚌 105, 649 🚊 3, 5, 14, 19 🕐 by appt (call 06-0608)

The aqueduct was built by Nero in the 1st century AD as an extension of the Aqua Claudia to supply Nero's Golden House (p206). Partly incorporated into later buildings, the arches make their way via the Lateran to the Celian Hill. Along the first section of the aqueduct, in Via Statilia, is a small tomb in the shape of a house, dating from the 1st century BC, bearing the names and likenesses of a group of slaves freed by the Statilii, the family of Claudius's notorious wife Messalina.

Museo Storico della Liberazione di Roma

♀ M7 ⚑ Via Tasso 145 ☎ 06-700 3866 Ⓜ Manzoni, San Giovanni 🚊 3 🕐 9:30am–12:30pm Tue–Sun, 3:30–7:30pm Tue, Thu & Fri 🚫 Aug

This museum, dedicated to the resistance to the Nazi occupation of Rome, is housed in the ex-prison of the Gestapo. The makeshift cells with bloodstained walls make a strong impact (see also Fosse Ardeatine p320).

Baker's Tomb

♀ P7 ⚑ Piazzale Labicano 🚌 105 🚊 3, 5, 14, 19

In the middle of the tram junction near Porta Maggiore stands the well preserved tomb of the rich baker Eurysaces and his wife Atistia, which was built in 30 BC. Roman custom forbade burials within city walls, and the roads leading out of cities became lined with tombs and monuments for the middle and upper classes. This tomb is shaped like a baking oven, and a low-relief frieze at the top shows Eurysaces presiding over his slaves through the various phases of the breadmaking process. The inscription on the tomb proudly asserts his origins and also reveals him as a freed slave, probably of Greek origin. Many men like Eurysaces saved money from their meagre slave salaries to earn their freedom and set up their own businesses, becoming the backbone of Rome's economy.

> The implied idea of the pope as heir to the Roman Empire would affect the whole course of medieval European history.

Santi Quattro Coronati

♀ L7 ⚑ Via Santi Quattro Coronati 20 ☎ 06-7047 5427 🚌 85, 117 🚊 3 Cloister and church: 🕐 10–11:45am & 4–5:45pm Mon–Sat, 4–5:45pm Sun

The name of this convent (Four Crowned Saints) refers to the Christian soldiers martyred for refusing to worship a pagan god. Erected in the 4th century AD, it was rebuilt after the invading Normans set fire to the neighbourhood in 1084. Hidden within is the garden of the delightful inner cloister (admission on request), one of the earliest of its kind, built c.1220.

The convent's main feature is the Chapel of St Sylvester – its remarkable frescoes (1246) recount the legend of the conversion to Christianity of the Emperor Constantine by Pope Sylvester I (reigned 314–35). Stricken by the plague, Constantine is prescribed a bath in children's blood. Unable to bring himself to obey, Constantine is visited in a dream by St Peter and St Paul. They advise him to find Sylvester, who cures him and baptizes him. The final scene shows the emperor kneeling before the pope. The implied idea of the pope as heir to the Roman Empire would affect the whole course of medieval European history.

← A tram running through an arch of the 1st-century AD Aqueduct of Nero

A SHORT WALK
PIAZZA DI SAN GIOVANNI

The Chapel of Santa Rufina, originally the portico of the baptistry, has a 5th-century mosaic of spiralling foliage in the apse.

Distance 0.5 km (0.6 mile) **Nearest metro** San Giovanni
Time 15 minutes

Stroll along San Giovanni's modern avenues to the Basilica of San Giovanni and the Lateran Palace, which look out over a huge open area, the Piazza di San Giovanni, laid out at the end of the 16th century with an Egyptian obelisk, the oldest in Rome, in the centre. Sadly the traffic streaming in and out of the city through Porta San Giovanni tends to detract from its grandeur. Across the square is the building housing the Scala Santa (the Holy Staircase), one of the most revered relics in Rome and the goal for many pilgrims. The area is also a venue for political rallies.

VIA DI SANTO STEFANO ROTONDO

VIA DELL´AMBA ARADAM

VIA DEI LATERANI

The Chapel of San Venanzio is decorated with a series of 7th- century mosaics on a gold background. This detail from the apse shows one of the angels flanking the central figure of Christ. San Venanzio was an accomplished 6th-century Latin poet.

The Cloister of San Giovanni fortunately survived the two fires that destroyed the early basilica. A 13th-century masterpiece of mosaic work, the cloister now houses fragments from the medieval basilica.

Grand 18th-century façade of San Giovanni in Laterano

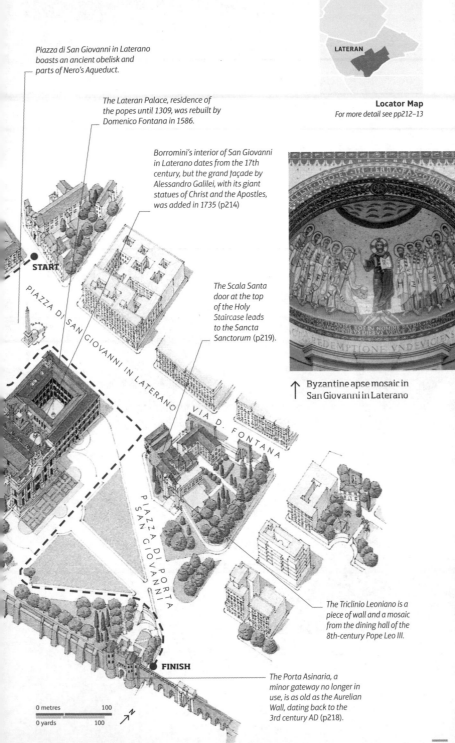

Piazza di San Giovanni in Laterano boasts an ancient obelisk and parts of Nero's Aqueduct.

The Lateran Palace, residence of the popes until 1309, was rebuilt by Domenico Fontana in 1586.

Borromini's interior of San Giovanni in Laterano dates from the 17th century, but the grand façade by Alessandro Galilei, with its giant statues of Christ and the Apostles, was added in 1735 (p214)

The Scala Santa door at the top of the Holy Staircase leads to the Sancta Sanctorum (p219).

LATERAN

Locator Map
For more detail see pp212–13

↑ Byzantine apse mosaic in San Giovanni in Laterano

START

PIAZZA DI SAN GIOVANNI IN LATERANO

VIA D. FONTANA

PIAZZA DI PORTA SAN GIOVANNI

The Triclinio Leoniano is a piece of wall and a mosaic from the dining hall of the 8th-century Pope Leo III.

FINISH

The Porta Asinaria, a minor gateway no longer in use, is as old as the Aurelian Wall, dating back to the 3rd century AD (p218).

| 0 metres | 100 |
| 0 yards | 100 |

CARACALLA

The Celian Hill overlooks the Colosseum, and takes its name from Caelius Vibenna, the legendary hero of Rome's struggle against the Tarquins. In Imperial Rome this was a fashionable place to live, and some of its vanished splendour is still apparent in the vast ruins of the Baths of Caracalla. Today, thanks to the Archaeological Zone established at the beginning of the 20th century, it is a peaceful area, a green wedge from the Aurelian Wall to the heart of the city. Through it runs the cobbled Via di Porta San Sebastiano, part of the old Via Appia. This road leads to Porta San Sebastiano, one of the best-preserved gates in the ancient city wall.

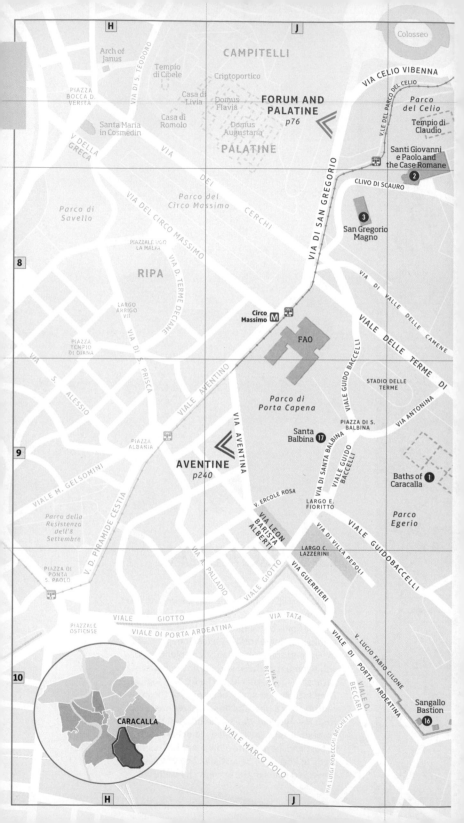

Colosseo

CAMPITELLI

VIA CELIO VIBENNA

VIA DEL PARCO DEL CELIO

Arch of Janus

Tempio di Cibele

Criptoportico

Parco del Celio

VIA DI S. TEODORO

PIAZZA BOCCA D. VERITA

Casa di Livia

Domus Flavia

FORUM AND PALATINE *p76*

Tempio di Claudio

VI-LE DEL PARCO DEL CELIO

Santa Maria in Cosmedin

Casa di Romolo

Domus Augustana

Santi Giovanni e Paolo and the Case Romane **2**

V DELLA GRECA

VIA

PALATINE

CLIVO DI SCAURO

VIA DEI CERCHI

Parco di Savello

Parco del Circo Massimo

VIA DEL CIRCO MASSIMO

San Gregorio Magno **3**

VIA DI SAN GREGORIO

VIA DI VALLE DELLE CAMENE

8

PIAZZALE UGO LA MALFA

RIPA

VIA D. TERME DECIANE

LARGO ARRIGO VII

Circo Massimo **M**

VIALE DELLE TERME DI

VIALE GUIDO BACCELLI

PIAZZA TEMPIO DI DIANA

FAO

STADIO DELLE TERME

VIA DI S. PRISCA

VIA S. ALESSIO

Parco di Porta Capena

PIAZZA DI S. BALBINA

VIA ANTONINA

VIALE AVENTINO

Santa Balbina **17**

9

PIAZZA ALBANIA

VIA DI SANTA BALBINA

VIA GUIDO BACCELLI

VIALE M. GELSOMINI

AVENTINE *p240*

VIA AVENTINA

V. ERCOLE ROSA

Baths of Caracalla **1**

Parco della Resistenza dell'8 Settembre

V. D. PIRAMIDE CESTIA

VIA LEON BATISTA ALBERTI

LARGO E. FIORITTO

Parco Egerio

PIAZZA DI PONTA S. PAOLO

VIA A. PALLADIO

LARGO C. LAZZERINI

VIA DI VILLA PEPOLI

VIALE GUIDOBACCELLI

10

PIAZZALE OSTIENSE

VIALE GIOTTO

VIALE DI PORTA ARDEATINA

VIA GUERRIERI

VIA TATA

CARACALLA

VIALE GIOTTO

VIALE C. BELTRAMI

V. LUCIO FABIO CILONE

Sangallo Bastion **16**

VIALE DI PORTA ARDEATINA

VIALE MARCO POLO

VIA LUIGI ROBECCHI BRICHETTI

VIALE O. BECCARI

VIA DI PORTA ARDEATINA

H

J

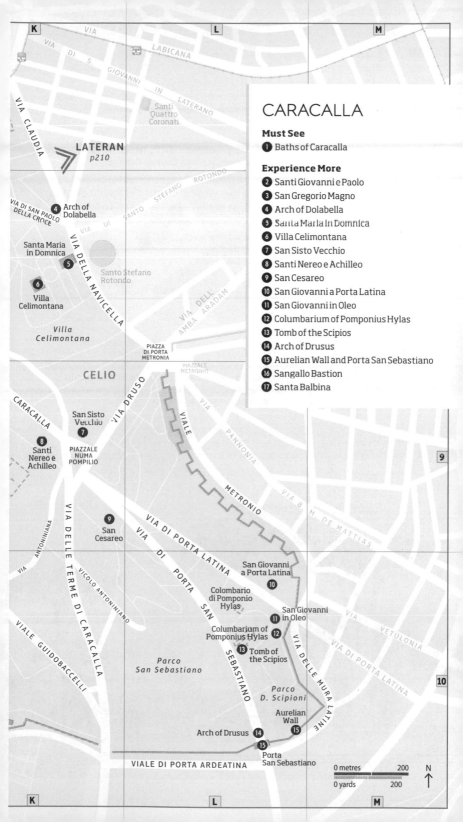

CARACALLA

Must See
❶ Baths of Caracalla

Experience More
❷ Santi Giovanni e Paolo
❸ San Gregorio Magno
❹ Arch of Dolabella
❺ Santa Maria in Domnica
❻ Villa Celimontana
❼ San Sisto Vecchio
❽ Santi Nereo e Achilleo
❾ San Cesareo
❿ San Giovanni a Porta Latina
⓫ San Giovanni in Oleo
⓬ Columbarium of Pomponius Hylas
⓭ Tomb of the Scipios
⓮ Arch of Drusus
⓯ Aurelian Wall and Porta San Sebastiano
⓰ Sangallo Bastion
⓱ Santa Balbina

LATERAN
p210

0 metres   200
0 yards   200

N

❶ ⬦ ⬧ ⬨

BATHS OF CARACALLA

📍K9 🏛 Viale delle Terme di Caracalla 52 🚌160-628 🚋3 Ⓜ Circo Massimo 🕘9am–2pm Mon, 9am–approximately 1 hour before sunset Tue–Sun 🌐isromantique.it

Completed by Emperor Caracalla in AD 217, the baths functioned for around 300 years until the acqueducts feeding them were sabotaged by invading Goths. This is one of the most enjoyable and best preserved ancient sites in the city.

Over 1,600 bathers at a time could enjoy the facilities, which included not only baths and gymnasia but gardens, shops selling food and drink, a library, art galleries, lecture rooms and, inevitably doing a roaring trade, a host of pimps, gigolos and prostitutes. In summer the Baths of Caracalla now hosts a hugely popular festival of opera and ballet in the *caldarium (p52)*.

Inside the Baths

The *apodyterium* (changing room) was where people removed their clothes before bathing. They would then head to a hot steam room *(laconia)*, designed like Turkish baths, to induce sweat. This was followed by a hot bath in a bronze tub *(caldarium)*. The skin was then scraped to remove dead skin and dirt. Bathers then headed into the luke-warm waters of the *tepidarium*, followed by a plunge into the freezing-cold indoor pool, the *frigidarium*. The final stage was a swim in the outdoor pool *(natatio)*.

> INSIDER TIP
> **Virtual Reality Tours**
>
> The Baths of Caracalla is the first archaeological site in Italy to be brought to life with virtual reality goggles. Reconstructions of the entire site are viewable in 3D through the headsets with audio commentary.

↑ The two *apodyteria* (changing rooms), with remains of mosaic floor tiles

PALAESTRA

Propped up against the walls of the gymnasia *(palaestra)* are fractured mosaics of athletes. Opening off the main space are smaller rooms where wrestlers were massaged with oil and wax to make the skin more supple, then sprinkled with dust to stop them being slippery, before engaging in matches. During the 1960 Olympics the *palaestra* were used for gymnastics events.

← The *caldarium*, where skin was scraped clean with a *strigil* after a hot bath

↑ Ruins of the Baths of Caracalla, surrounded by towering umbrella pines

EXPERIENCE MORE

Santi Giovanni e Paolo

📍 K8 🏛 Piazza Santi Giovanni e Paolo 13 📞 06-772711 🚌 75, 81, 117, 673 🚋 3 Ⓜ Colosseo or Circo Massimo 🕐 8:30am-noon & 3:30-6pm daily

Santi Giovanni e Paolo is dedicated to two martyred Roman officers whose house originally stood on this site. Giovanni (John) and Paolo (Paul) had served the first Christian emperor, Constantine. When they were later called to arms by the pagan emperor Julian the Apostate, they refused and were beheaded and buried in secret in their own house in AD 362.

Built towards the end of the 4th century, the church retains many elements of its original structure. The Ionic portico dates from the 12th century, and the apse and bell tower were added by Nicholas Breakspeare, the only English pope, who reigned as Adrian IV (1154–9). The base of the impressive 13th-century Romanesque bell tower was part of the Temple of Claudius that stood on this site. The interior, which was remodelled in 1718, has granite piers and columns. A tomb slab in the nave marks the burial place of the martyrs, whose relics are preserved in an urn under the high altar. In a tiny room near the altar, a magnificent 13th-century fresco depicts the figure of Christ flanked by his Apostles (to see it, ask the sacristan who will be able to unlock the door).

Excavations carried out beneath the church have revealed two 2nd- and 3rd-century Roman houses, the **Case Romane del Celio**, that were used as a Christian burial place. Well worth a visit, the Roman houses, which include 20 rooms and a labyrinth of corridors, have beautifully restored pagan and Christian frescoes. The walls are painted to resemble precious marble. The arches that are found to the left of the church were originally part of a 3rd-century street of shops.

Case Romane del Celio

🏛 Clivo di Scauro 🕐 10am-1pm & 3-6pm Thu-Mon 🌐 caseromane.it

> **Well worth a visit, the Roman houses, which include 20 rooms and a labyrinth of corridors, have beautifully restored pagan and Christian frescoes.**

The basilica of Santi Giovanni e Paolo on the Celian Hill

❸ San Gregorio Magno

📍 J8 🏛 Piazza di San Gregorio 1 ☎ 06-700 8227 🚌 75, 81, 117, 673 🚋 3 Ⓜ Circo Massimo 🕐 9am–1pm, 3:30–7pm daily

Historically, this church has links with England, for it was from here that St Augustine was sent on his mission to convert England to Christianity. The church was founded in AD 575 by San Gregorio Magno (St Gregory the Great), who turned his family home on this site into a monastery. It was rebuilt in medieval times and restored in 1629–33 by Giovanni Battista Soria. The church is reached via steps from the street.

The forecourt contains some interesting tombs. To the left is that of Sir Edward Carne, who came to Rome several times between 1529 and 1533 as King Henry VIII's envoy to gain the pope's consent to the annulment of Henry's marriage to Catherine of Aragon.

The interior, remodelled by Francesco Ferrari in the mid-18th century, is Baroque, apart from the fine mosaic floor and some ancient columns. At the end of the right aisle is the chapel of St Gregory. Leading off it, another small chapel, believed to have been the saint's own cell, houses his episcopal throne – a Roman chair of sculpted marble. The Salviati Chapel, on the left, contains a picture of the Virgin said to have spoken to St Gregory.

Outside, amid the cypresses to the left of the church, stand three small chapels, dedicated to St Andrew, St Barbara and St Sylvia (Gregory the Great's mother). The chapels contain frescoes by Domenichino and Guido Reni.

Did You Know?

In summer Villa Celimontana hosts an excellent jazz festival.

❹ Arch of Dolabella

📍 K8 🏛 Via di San Paolo della Croce 🚌 81, 117, 673 🚋 3 Ⓜ Colosseo

The arch was built in AD 10 by consuls Caius Junius Silanus and Cornelius Dolabella, possibly on the site of one of the old Servian Wall's gateways. It was made of travertine blocks and later used to support Nero's extension of the Claudian aqueduct, built to supply the Imperial Palace on the Palatine Hill.

❺ Santa Maria in Domnica

📍 K8 🏛 Piazza della Navicella 12 ☎ 06-7720 2685 🚌 81, 117, 673 🚋 3 Ⓜ Colosseo 🕐 for Mass only while construction work is undertaken on Metro C; call for latest information

The church overlooks the Piazza della Navicella (little boat) and takes its name from the 16th-century fountain. Dating from the 7th century, the church was probably built on the site of an ancient Roman firemen's barracks, which later became a meeting place for Christians. In the 16th century Pope Leo X added the portico and the coffered ceiling.

In the apse behind the modern altar is a superb 9th-century mosaic commissioned by Pope Paschal I. Wearing the square halo of the living, the pope appears at the feet of the Virgin and Child. The Virgin, surrounded by a throng of angels, holds a handkerchief like a fashionable lady at a Byzantine court.

❻ Villa Celimontana

📍 K8 🏛 Piazza della Navicella 🚌 81, 117, 673 Park: 🕐 7am–dusk daily

The Dukes of Mattei bought this land in 1553 and transformed the vineyards that covered the hillside into a formal garden. As well as palms and other exotic trees, the garden has its own Egyptian obelisk. Villa Mattei, built in the 1580s and now known as Villa Celimontana, houses the Italian Geographical Society.

The Mattei family used to open the park to the public on the day of the Visit of the Seven Churches, an annual event instituted by San Filippo Neri in 1552. Starting from the Chiesa Nuova (p128), Romans went on foot to the city's seven major churches and, on reaching Villa Mattei, were given bread, wine, salami, cheese, an egg and two apples. The pine-shaded park, now owned by the city of Rome, makes an ideal place for a picnic and has a playground with swings.

↑ The Egyptian obelisk in the grounds of Villa Celimontana

Detail of a 9th-century mosaic in the church of Santi Nereo e Achilleo

7

San Sisto Vecchio

📍K9 🏛Piazzale Numa Pompilio 8 ☎06-7720 5174 🚌160, 628, 671, 714 🕐9-11am & 3-5:30pm daily

This small church is of great historical interest, as it was granted to St Dominic in 1219 by Pope Honorius III. The founder of the Dominican order soon moved his own headquarters to Santa Sabina (p247), San Sisto becoming the first home of the order of Dominican nuns, who still occupy the monastery. The church, with its 13th-century bell tower and frescoes, is also a popular place for weddings.

8

Santi Nereo e Achilleo

📍K9 🏛Via delle Terme di Caracalla 28 ☎06-687 3124 🚌160, 628, 671, 714 🕐noon-12:30pm Sun (for half an hour only)

According to legend, St Peter, after escaping from prison, was fleeing the city when he lost a bandage from his wounds. The original church was founded here in the 4th century on the spot where the bandage fell, but it was later re-dedicated to the 1st-century AD martyrs St Nereus and St Achilleus.

Restored at the end of the 16th century, the church has retained many medieval features, including several fine 9th-century mosaics on the triumphal arch. A magnificent pulpit rests on an enormous porphyry pedestal which was found nearby in the Baths of Caracalla. The walls of the side aisles are decorated with grisly 16th-century frescoes by Niccolò Pomarancio, showing in clinical detail how each of the Apostles was martyred.

9

San Cesareo

📍K9 🏛Via di Porta San Sebastiano ☎338-491 6838 🚌218, 628 🕐10am-4pm Sat, 10am-noon Sun 🚫Aug

This splendid old church was built over Roman ruins of the 2nd century AD. The lovely Renaissance façade was designed by Giacomo della Porta. The fine Cosmatesque mosaic work and carving inside rival that of any church in Rome. The episcopal throne, altar and pulpit are decorated with delightful animals. The church was restored in the 16th century by Pope Clement VIII, whose coat of arms decorates the ceiling.

> The church of St John at the Latin Gate, founded in the 5th century, rebuilt in 720 and restored in 1191, is one of the most picturesque of the old Roman churches.

San Giovanni a Porta Latina

L10 **Via di San Giovanni a Porta Latina** **06-7047 5938** **218, 360, 628** **7:30am–12:30pm & 3-7pm daily**

The church of St John at the Latin Gate, founded in the 5th century, rebuilt in 720 and restored in 1191, is one of the most picturesque of the old Roman churches. Classical columns support the medieval portico, and the 12th-century bell tower is superb. A tall cedar tree shades an ancient well standing in the forecourt. The interior has been restored, but it preserves the rare simplicity of its early origins, with ancient columns of varying styles lining the aisles. Traces of early medieval frescoes can still be seen within the church. The beautiful 12th-century

frescoes created by several different artists under the direction of one master, show 46 different biblical scenes, from both the Old and New Testaments and are among the finest of their kind in Rome.

San Giovanni in Oleo

L10 **Via di Porta Latina** **06-7740 0032** **628** **Ask at San Giovanni a Porta Latina**

The name of this charming octagonal Renaissance chapel or oratory means "St John in Oil". The tiny building marks

the spot where, according to legend, St John was boiled in oil – and came out unscathed, or even refreshed. An earlier chapel is said to have existed on the site; the present one was built in the early 16th century. The design has been attributed to Baldassare Peruzzi or Antonio da Sangallo the Younger. In the mid-17th century it was restored by Borromini, who altered the roof, crowning it with a cross supported by a sphere decorated with roses. Borromini also added a terracotta frieze of roses and palm leaves. The wall paintings inside the chapel include one of St John in a cauldron of boiling oil.

$\rightarrow$

Detail of a medieval fresco in San Giovanni a Porta Latina (right) and Classical columns inside the church (below)

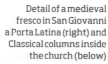

Columbarium of Pomponius Hylas

L10 **Via di Porta Latina 10** **06-0608.** **218, 360, 628** **for guided tours only; phone ahead**

Known as a columbarium because it resembles a dove-cote (*columba* is the Latin word for "dove"), this kind of vaulted tomb was usually built by rich Romans to house the cremated remains of their freedmen. Many similar tombs have been uncovered in this part of Rome, which up until the 3rd century AD lay outside the city wall. This one dates from the 1st century AD. An inscription states that it is the tomb of Pomponius Hylas and his wife, Pomponia Vitalinis. Above her name is a "V" which indicates that she was still living when the inscription was made.

Tomb of the Scipios

L10 **Via di Porta San Sebastiano 9** **06-0608** **218, 360, 628** **for guided tours only; phone ahead**

The Scipios were a family of conquering generals. Southern Italy, Corsica,

Algeria, Spain and Asia Minor all fell to their Roman armies. The most famous of these generals was Publius Cornelius Scipio Africanus, who defeated the great Carthaginian general Hannibal at the Battle of Zama in 202 BC. Scipio Africanus was not buried here in the family tomb, but at Liternum near Naples, where he owned a favourite villa.

The Tomb of the Scipios was discovered in 1780, complete with various sarcophagi, statues and terracotta burial urns. Many of the originals have now been moved to the Vatican Museums and copies stand in their place.

The earliest sarcophagus was that of Cornelius Scipio Barbatus, consul in 298 BC, for whom the tomb was built. Members of his illustrious family continued to be buried here up to the middle of the 2nd century BC.

Arch of Drusus

L10 **Via di Porta San Sebastiano** **218, 360**

Once mistakenly identified as a triumphal arch, the so-called Arch of Drusus merely supported the branch aqueduct that supplied the Baths of Caracalla. It was built in the 3rd century AD, so had

no connection with Drusus, a stepson of the Emperor Augustus. Its monumental appearance was due to the fact that it carried the aqueduct across the important route, Via Appia. The arch still spans the old cobbled road, just 50 m (160 ft) short of the gateway Porta San Sebastiano.

Aurelian Wall and Porta San Sebastiano

L10 **Museo delle Mura, Via di Porta San Sebastiano 18** **218, 360** **9am-2pm Tue-Sun (last adm: 30 mins before closing)** **1 Jan, 1 May, 25 Dec** **museodellemuraroma.it**

Most of the Aurelian Wall, begun by the Emperor Aurelian (AD 270–75) and completed by his successor Probus (AD 276–82), has survived. Aurelian ordered its construction as a defence against Germanic tribes, whose raids were penetrating deeper and deeper into Italy. Some 18 km (11 miles) round, with 18 gates and 381 towers, the wall took in all the seven hills of Rome. It was raised to almost twice its original height by Maxentius (AD 306–12).

The wall was Rome's main defence until 1870, when it was breached by Italian artillery just by Porta Pia, close to today's British Embassy. Many of the gates are still in use, and although the city has spread, most of its noteworthy historical and cultural sights still lie within the wall.

Porta San Sebastiano, the gate leading to the Via Appia Antica (p321), is the largest and best-preserved gateway in the Aurelian Wall. It was rebuilt by Emperor Honorius

← Visitors at the Columbarium of Pomponius Hylas

↑ The fortified Porta San Sebastiano, the best preserved gateway in the Aurelian Wall

in the 5th century AD. Originally the Porta Appia, in Christian times it gradually became known as the Porta San Sebastiano, because the Via Appia led to the basilica and catacombs of San Sebastiano, which were popular places of pilgrimage.

It was at this gate that the last triumphal procession to enter the city by the Appian Way was received in state – that of Marcantonio Colonna after the victory of Lepanto over the Turkish fleet in 1571. Today the gate's towers house a museum with prints and models showing the wall's history. From here you can take a short walk along the restored wall.

 16
Sangallo Bastion

♀ K10 ♠ Viale di Porta Ardeatina 🚌 160

Haunted by the memory of the Sack of Rome in 1527 and fearing attack by the Turks, Pope Paul III asked Antonio da Sangallo the Younger to reinforce the Aurelian Wall. Work on the huge projecting bastion began in 1537. Its massive bulk can only be admired from outside.

 17
Santa Balbina

♀ J9 ♠ Piazza di Santa Balbina 8 📞 06-575 09 69 🚌 160 🚊 3 Ⓜ Circo Massimo 🕐 by appt only; phone ahead

Overlooking the Baths of Caracalla, this isolated church is dedicated to Santa Balbina, a 2nd-century virgin martyr. It is one of the oldest in Rome, dating back to the 5th century, and was built on the remains of a Roman villa. Consecrated by Pope Gregory the Great, in the Middle Ages Santa Balbina was a fortified monastery and over time has changed in appearance several times, regaining its Romanesque aspect in the 1920s. It contains many works of art.

From the piazza in front of the church, a staircase leads up to a three-arched portico. Inside, light streams in from a series of high windows along the length of the nave. The remains of St Balbina and her father, St Quirinus, are in an urn at the high altar, though the church's real treasure is situated in the far right-hand corner: the magnificent sculpted and inlaid tomb of Cardinal Stefanis de Surdis by Giovanni di Cosma (1303).

Other features worth noting are a 13th-century episcopal throne and various fragments of medieval frescoes. These include a lovely *Madonna and Child*, an example of the school of Pietro Cavallini, in the second chapel on the left. Fragments of 1st-century Roman mosaics were also discovered in the 1930s. Depicting birds and signs of the zodiac, these are now set into the church floor.

 PICTURE PERFECT
Aurelian Wall

A highlight of a visit to the Porta San Sebastiano ramparts of the restored Aurelian Wall is the matchless views of the Appian Way and the green hills beyond, which make for a superb photo opportunity.

A SHORT WALK
THE CELIAN HILL

Distance 1 km (0.6 mile) **Nearest metro** Circo Massimo
Time 20 minutes

In the course of a morning exploring the green slopes of the Celian Hill, you will see a fascinating assortment of archaeological remains and beautiful churches. A good starting point is the church of San Gregorio Magno, from where the Clivo di Scauro leads up to the top of the hill. The steep narrow street passes the ancient porticoed church of Santi Giovanni e Paolo with its beautiful Romanesque bell tower soaring above the surrounding medieval monastery buildings. Of the parks on the hill, the best kept and most peaceful is the Villa Celimontana with its formal walks and avenues. There are few bars or restaurants in the area but the green spaces are great for a picnic.

Clivo di Scauro, the Roman Clivus Scauri, leads up to Santi Giovanni e Paolo, passing under the flying buttresses that support the church.

La Vignola is a delightful Renaissance pavilion, reconstructed here in 1911 after it had been demolished during the creation of the Archaeological Zone around the Baths of Caracalla.

To Circo Massimo Metro

San Gregorio Magno monastery and chapel were founded here by Pope Gregory the Great at the end of the 6th century (p233).

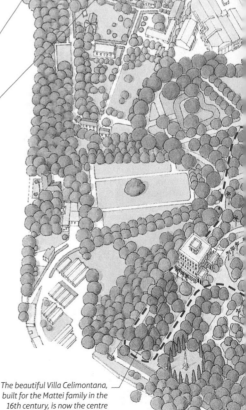

VIA DI SAN GREGORIO

CLIVO DI SCAURO

START

The beautiful Villa Celimontana, built for the Mattei family in the 16th century, is now the centre of a public park (p233).

↑ Villa Celimontana, located in a pine-shaded public park

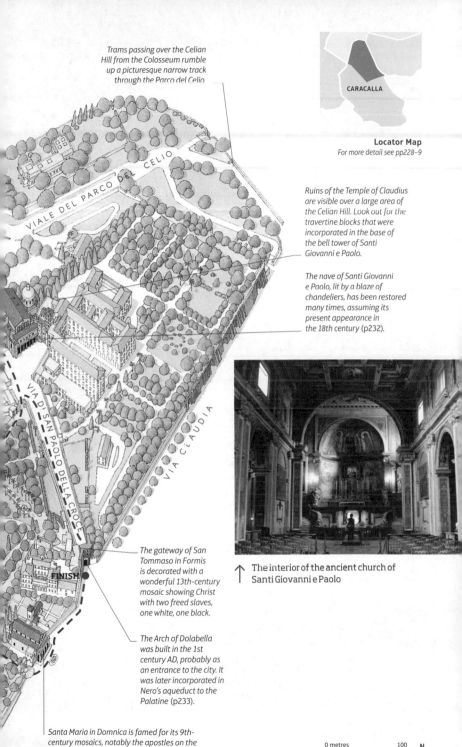

Trams passing over the Celian Hill from the Colosseum rumble up a picturesque narrow track through the Parco del Celio

Locator Map
For more detail see pp228–9

CARACALLA

Ruins of the Temple of Claudius are visible over a large area of the Celian Hill. Look out for the travertine blocks that were incorporated in the base of the bell tower of Santi Giovanni e Paolo.

The nave of Santi Giovanni e Paolo, lit by a blaze of chandeliers, has been restored many times, assuming its present appearance in the 18th century (p232).

VIALE DEL PARCO DEL CELIO

VIA DI SAN PAOLO DELLA CROCE

VIA CLAUDIA

FINISH

The gateway of San Tommaso in Formis is decorated with a wonderful 13th-century mosaic showing Christ with two freed slaves, one white, one black.

The Arch of Dolabella was built in the 1st century AD, probably as an entrance to the city. It was later incorporated in Nero's aqueduct to the Palatine (p233).

Santa Maria in Domnica is famed for its 9th-century mosaics, notably the apostles on the triumphal arch above the apse flanking a medallion containing the figure of Christ (p233).

↑ The interior of the ancient church of Santi Giovanni e Paolo

0 metres 100
0 yards 100

N

AVENTINE

This is one of the most peaceful, leafy areas within the walls of the city. Although it is largely residential, with romantic villas, there are some unique historic sights. From the top of the Aventine Hill, crowned by the magnificent basilica of Santa Sabina, there are fine views across the river to Trastevere and St Peter's. At the foot of the hill, ancient Rome is preserved in the two tiny Temples of the Forum Boarium and the Circus Maximus. The liveliest streets are in Testaccio, which has shops, restaurants and clubs, while to the south, beside Rome's solitary pyramid, the Protestant Cemetery is another oasis of calm.

AVENTINE

Experience
1. San Giorgio in Velabro
2. San Teodoro
3. Santa Maria in Cosmedin
4. Arch of Janus
5. Santa Maria della Consolazione
6. Area Archeologica di Sant'Omobono
7. Temples of the Forum Boarium
8. San Giovanni Decollato
9. Casa dei Crescenzi
10. Santa Sabina
11. Santi Bonifacio e Alessio
12. Piazza dei Cavalieri di Malta
13. Protestant Cemetery
14. Monte Testaccio
15. Il Mattatoio
16. Pyramid of Caius Cestius
17. San Saba
18. Circus Maximus

Eat and Drink
1. Flavio Al Velavevodetto
2. Romeo Chef & Baker
3. Oasi della Birra
4. Tram Depot

Stay
5. San Anselmo

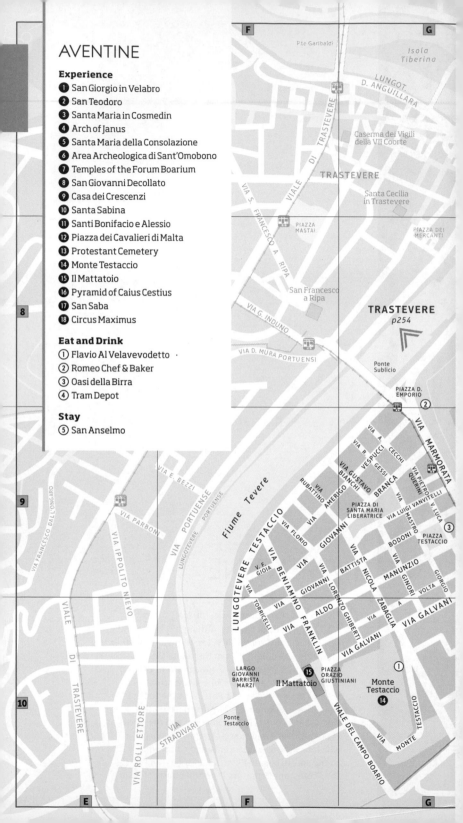

TRASTEVERE
p254

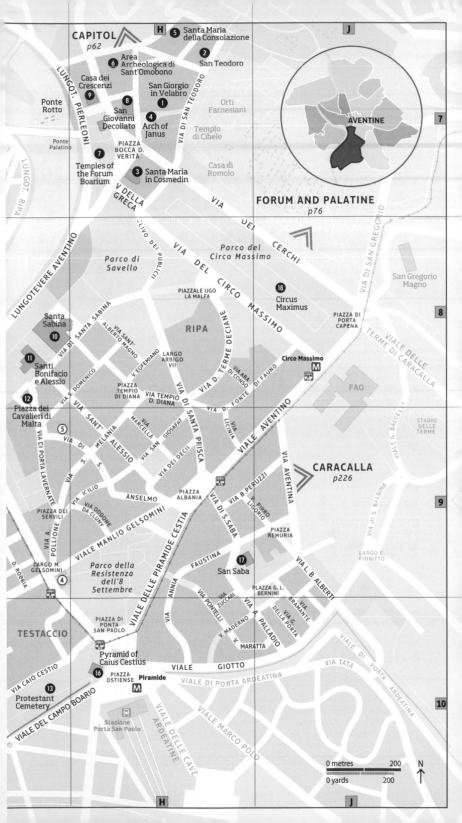

H

J

5 Santa Maria della Consolazione

2 San Teodoro

6 Area Archeologica di Sant'Omobono

Casa dei Crescenzi **9**

1 San Giorgio in Velabro

Orti Farnesiani

8 San Giovanni Decollato

4 Arch of Janus

Tempio di Cibele

AVENTINE

7

Ponte Rotto

LUNGOT. PIERLEONI

Ponte Palatino

PIAZZA BOCCA D. VERITÀ

Casa di Romolo

7 Temples of the Forum Boarium

3 Santa Maria in Cosmedin

V. DELLA GRECA

VIA DEI CERCHI

FORUM AND PALATINE
p76

LUNGOT. RIPA

Parco di Savello

Parco del Circo Massimo

VIA DI SAN GREGORIO

San Gregorio Magno

LUNGOTEVERE AVENTINO

CLIVO DEI PUBLICII

VIA DEL CIRCO MASSIMO

PIAZZALE UGO LA MALFA

18 Circus Maximus

PIAZZA DI PORTA CAPENA

8

VIALE DELLE TERME DI CARACALLA

Santa Sabina **10**

VIA DI SANTA SABINA

VIA SANT'ALBERTO MAGNO

RIPA

VIA D. TERME DECIANE

VIA ARA MASSIMA

VIA D. CONSO

Circo Massimo **M**

FAO

STADIO DELLE TERME

11 Santi Bonifacio e Alessio

V. EUFEMIANO

LARGO ARRIGO VII

VIA D. FONTE DI FAUNO

VIA LICINIA

VIALE G. BACCELLI

12 Piazza dei Cavalieri di Malta

VIA S. DOMENICO

PIAZZA TEMPIO DI DIANA

VIA TEMPIO D. DIANA

VIA DI SANTA PRISCA

VIALE AVENTINO

VIA AVENTINA

CARACALLA
p226

9

VIA DI S. BALBINA

5

VIA SANT'ALESSIO

VIA MELANIA

VIA S. S.

VIA MARELLA

VIA SAN GIOSAFAT

VIA DEI DECII

VIA B. PERUZZI

V. PIRRO LIGORIO

⑤ VIA DI

VIA DI PORTA LAVERNALE

VIA ICILIO

VIA ODDONE DA CLUNY

ANSELMO

PIAZZA ALBANIA

VIA DI S. SABA

PIAZZA REMURIA

LARGO E. FIORITTO

PIAZZA DEI SERVILI

VIA A. POLLIONE

LARGO M. GELSOMINI

④

VIALE MANLIO GELSOMINI

Parco della Resistenza dell'8 Settembre

VIALE DELLE PIRAMIDE CESTIA

FAUSTINA

VIA ANNIA

VIA PONTELLI

VIA A. PALLADIO

VIA L. B. ALBERTI

17 San Saba

PIAZZA G. L. BERNINI

VIA BRAMANTE

VIA G. DELLA PORTA

TESTACCIO

PIAZZA DI PONTA SAN PAOLO

VIA MADERNO

V. ZUCCARI

V. MARATTA

VIA GIOTTO

VIALE

VIALE DI PORTA ARDEATINA

VIA TATA

VIALE DI PORTA ARDEATINA

10

Pyramid of Caius Cestius

16 PIAZZA OSTIENSE

Piramide **M**

VIA CAIO CESTIO

13 Protestant Cemetery

VIALE DEL CAMPO BOARIO

Stazione Porta San Paolo

VIALE DELLE CAVE ARDEATINE

VIALE MARCO POLO

H

J

EXPERIENCE

❶

San Giorgio in Velabro

⑨H7 **⌂Via del Velabro 19**
☎06-6979 7536 **🚌23, 44,
81, 160, 170, 280, 628, 715,
716, 780** **🕐10am-12:30pm
& 4-6:15pm Tue, Fri & Sat**

In the hollow of the street
named after the Velabrum,
the swamp where Romulus
and Remus are said to have
been found by the she-wolf,
is a small church dedicated
to St George, whose bones
lie under the altar.

The 7th-century basilica
has suffered over time from
floods. Careful restoration
has, however, returned it to its
original appearance. A double
row of granite and marble
columns (taken from ancient
Roman temples) divides the
triple nave. The austerity of
the grey interior is relieved by
golden frescoes in the apse
(attributed to Pietro Cavallini,
1295). The façade and the bell
tower date from the 1100s.

❷

San Teodoro

⑨H7 **⌂Via di San Teodoro
7** **☎06-678 6624** **🚌23, 44,
81, 160, 170, 280, 628, 715,
716** **🕐9:30am-12:30pm
Sun-Fri**

This small, round 6th-century
church at the foot of the
Palatine has breathtaking 6th-
century mosaics in the apse,

and a Florentine cupola dating
from 1454. The fetching outer
courtyard was designed by
Carlo Fontana in 1705.

❸

Santa Maria
in Cosmedin

⑨H7 **⌂Piazza della Bocca
della Verità 18** **☎06-678
7759** **🚌23, 44, 81, 160,
170, 280, 628, 715, 716**
**🕐9:30am-6pm daily
(winter: to 5pm); gates shut
10 mins before closing**

This beautiful unadorned
church was built in the 6th
century on the site of the
ancient city's food market.
The elegant Romanesque bell
tower and portico were added
during the 12th century. In
the 19th century a Baroque
façade was removed and the
church restored to its original

↑ The ancient Bocca della
   Verità, a lie detector
   according to legend

simplicity. It contains many
fine examples of Cosmati
work, in particular the mosaic
pavement, the raised choir,
the bishop's throne and the
canopy over the main altar.

Set into the wall of the
portico is the Bocca della
Verità (Mouth of Truth). This
may have been a drain cover,
dating back to before the 4th
century BC. Medieval tradition
had it that the formidable
jaws would snap shut over the
hand of those who told lies –
a useful trick for testing the
faithfulness of spouses.

❹

Arch of Janus

⑨H7 **⌂Via del Velabro**
**🚌23, 44, 63, 81, 160, 170,
280, 628, 715, 716, 780**

Probably dating from the
reign of Constantine, this
imposing four-faced marble
arch stood at the crossroads

→

The Renaissance exterior
of the church of Santa Maria
della Consolazione

❘ COSMATI MOSAICS

Glass mosaics and fragments of coloured marble were
salvaged from ancient Roman buildings to adorn the
pavements, cloisters, fonts and tombs of medieval
churches in Rome with complex geometric patterns.
Discs of porphyry and serpentine were often sliced from
ancient columns to make the patchwork designs. The
most famous practitioners were the Cosmati family,
who worked in Rome in the 12th and 13th centuries.

on the edge of the Forum Boarium, near the ancient docks. Merchants did business in its shade. On the keystones above the four arches you can see small figures of the goddesses Roma, Juno, Ceres and Minerva. In medieval times the arch formed the base of a tower fortress. It was finally restored to its original shape in 1827.

 5

Santa Maria della Consolazione

⊙ H7 ⚑ Piazza della Consolazione 94 ☎ 06-678 4654 🚌 23, 44, 63, 81, 160, 170, 280, 628, 715, 716, 780 🕓 6:30am–6:30pm Mon-Sat, 10am–6:30pm Sun

The church stands near the foot of the Tarpeian Rock, the site of public execution of traitors in ancient Rome.

In 1385, Giordanello degli Alberini, a condemned nobleman, paid two gold florins for an image of the Virgin Mary to be placed here, to provide consolation to prisoners in their final moments before execution. Hence the name

of the church that was constructed here in 1470. It was reconstructed between 1583 and 1600 by Martino Longhi, who provided the early Baroque façade at the same time.

The church's 11 side-chapels are owned by noble families and local crafts guild members. Taddeo Zuccari was responsible for the 1556 frescoes depicting scenes from the Passion (first chapel on the right), while the Mannerist artist Niccolò Circignani painted the scenes from the life of Mary and Jesus housed in the fifth chapel. In the presbytery is the image of Mary, attributed to Antoniazzo Romano.

 6

Area Archeologica di Sant'Omobono

⊙ H7 ⚑ Vico Jugario 4 ☎ 06-0608 🚌 23, 44, 63, 81, 160, 170, 280, 628, 715, 716, 780 🕓 by appt only; call in advance

Unearthed in 1937, this important archaeological area contains the remains of a temple dedicated to Mater Matuta, goddess protectress of navigation, which date from the 6th century BC and are attributed to the time of King Tullius. The excavations have also revealed traces of a pre-Roman cult.

EAT & DRINK

Flavio Al Velavevodetto

This stellar trattoria, famed for its pasta dishes, backs onto Monte Testaccio; you can see the ancient amphorae through glass panels in the wall.

⊙ G10 ⚑ Via di Monte Testaccio 97 🌐 ristorante velavevodetto.it

€€€

Romeo Chef & Baker

Come to this vast restaurant at lunch for quality meats and cheeses, at aperitivo hour for the superior nibbles at the chic bar, or at dinner for Michelin-starred culinary bravado.

⊙ G8 ⚑ Piazza dell'Emporio 28 🌐 romeo.roma.it

€€€

Oasi della Birra

The shelves of this enoteca are stacked with beers and wines. Fill up on the generous free buffet at aperitivo time on the terrace.

⊙ G9 ⚑ Piazza Testaccio 38 ☎ 06-574 61 22

Tram Depot

A friendly spot for an afternoon beer, and buzzing at aperitivo time in summer, this little café-bar (once part of a 1903 vintage tram) has quirky seating on the pavement.

⊙ G9 ⚑ Via Marmorata 13 ☎ 06-575 44 06

7 Temples of the Forum Boarium

H7 Piazza della Bocca della Verità 23, 44, 81, 160, 170, 280, 628, 715, 716 coopculture.it

These very well-preserved Republican temples date from the 2nd century BC and were saved for posterity when they were reconsecrated as Christian churches in the Middle Ages. They offer rare examples of combined elements from Greek and Roman architecture.

The rectangular temple (formerly known as the Temple of Fortuna Virilis) was dedicated to Portunus, god of rivers and ports. Set on a podium, it has four Ionic travertine columns and 12 half-columns, embedded in the tufa wall of the *cella* – the room that housed the image of the god.

Nearby is the small circular **Temple of Hercules**, its slender Corinthian columns surrounding the central *cella*. Built around 120 BC, it is thought to be the earliest Roman marble edifice still surviving. It is often referred to as the Temple of Vesta owing to its similarity to the one in the Forum.

Temple of Hercules
for guided tours, first and third Sun of month by appt; call 06-3996 7700

8 San Giovanni Decollato

H7 Via di San Giovanni Decollato 22 06-679 1890 23, 44, 63, 81, 160, 170, 280, 628, 715, 716, 780 only for the feast of St John, 24 Jun: 9:30am–12:30pm

Giorgio Vasari's *The Beheading of St John* (1553), from which the church takes its name, dominates the main altar. In 1490 Pope Innocent VIII gave this site to build a church for a Florentine confraternity. Clad in black robes and hoods, the Florentine monks would encourage prisoners to repent of their sins and give them a decent burial after they had been hanged. In the cloisters there are seven manholes that were used to receive the bodies. The confraternity still exists, with church funds going towards assisting prisoners' families.

The oratory features a cycle of frescoes by Florentine Mannerists Francesco Salviati

↑ The tower of 11th-century Casa dei Crescenzi

and Jacopino del Conte depicting events in the life of St John the Baptist.

9 Casa dei Crescenzi

H7 Via Luigi Petroselli 23, 44, 63, 81, 160, 170, 280, 628, 715, 716, 780

Studded with archaeological fragments, this house is what remains of an 11th-century tower fortress. The Crescenzi family built it to keep an eye on the docks and bridge where they collected a toll. It is only viewable from outside.

↓ Temple of Hercules and fountain in the Forum Boarium

Santa Sabina

G8 **Piazza Pietro d'Illiria 1** **06-579 401** **23, 280, 716** **Circo Massimo** **8:15am–12:30pm & 3:30–6pm daily**

High on the Aventine stands an early Christian basilica, founded by Peter of Illyria in AD 425 and restored to its original simplicity in the early 20th century. Light filters through 9th-century windows upon a wide nave framed by white Corinthian columns supporting an arcade decorated with a marble frieze. Over the main door is a 5th-century blue and gold mosaic dedicatory inscription. The pulpit, carved choir and bishop's throne date from the 9th century.

The church was given to the Dominicans in the 13th century and in the nave is the magnificent mosaic tombstone of one of the first leaders of the order, Muñoz de Zamora (died 1300).

The side portico has 5th-century panelled doors carved from cypress wood, representing scenes from the Bible, including one of the earliest Crucifixions in existence.

 The 13th-century Romanesque bell tower of Santi Bonifacio e Alessio

Santi Bonifacio e Alessio

G8 **Piazza di Sant'Alessio 23** **06-574 3446** **23, 280, 716** **Circo Massimo** **for special events only**

The church is dedicated to two early Christian martyrs, whose remains lie under the main altar. Legend has it that Alessio, son of a rich senator living on the site, fled east to avoid an impending marriage and became a pilgrim. Returning home after many years, he died as a servant, unrecognized, under the stairs of the family entrance hall, clutching the manuscript of his story for posterity.

The original 5th-century church has undergone many changes over time. Note-worthy are the 18th-century façade with its five arches, the restored Cosmati doorway and pavement, and the magnificent Romanesque five-storey bell tower (1217).

An 18th-century Baroque chapel by Andrea Bergondi houses part of the staircase.

Piazza dei Cavalieri di Malta

G8 **23, 280, 716** **Circo Massimo**

Surrounded by cypress trees, this ornate walled piazza decorated with obelisks and military trophies was designed by Piranesi in 1765. It is named after the Order of the Knights of Malta (Cavalieri di Malta), whose priory (at No. 3) is famous for the bronze keyhole through which there is a miniature view of St Peter's, framed by a tree-lined avenue. The priory church, Santa Maria del Priorato, was restored in Neo-Classical style by Piranesi in the 18th century. To visit the church, ask permission in person at the Order's building at Via Condotti 48. At the southwest corner of the square is Sant'Anselmo, the international Benedictine church, where Gregorian chant may be heard on Sundays.

Protestant Cemetery

📍 G10 🏛 Cimitero Acattolico, Via Caio Cestio 6 📞 06-574 1900 🚌 23, 280, 716 🚊 3 Ⓜ Piramide 🕐 9am-5pm Mon-Sat, 9am-1pm Sun (last adm: 30 mins before closing); donation expected

The peace of this well-tended cemetery, which is situated beneath the Aurelian Wall, is profoundly moving. As implied by its name, non-Catholics, mainly English and German, have been buried here since 1738. In the oldest part are the graves of the poet John Keats (died 1821), whose epitaph reads "Here lies One Whose Name was writ in Water", and his friend Joseph Severn (died 1879);

not far away are the ashes of Percy Bysshe Shelley (died 1822). Goethe's son Julius is also buried here.

Monte Testaccio

📍 G10 🏛 Via Galvani Ⓜ Piramide. 🚌 23, 83, 719 🚊 3 🕐 by appt only; call 06-0608

Between about 140 BC and AD 250 this hill was created through the dumping of millions of *testae* (hence Testaccio) – pieces of the amphorae that were used to carry goods to nearby warehouses. The full archaeological significance of this 36 m-(118 ft-) high artificial hill was not realized until the late 18th century.

↑ The graves of English Romantic poets in the Protestant Cemetery

Il Mattatoio

📍 F10 🏛 Piazza Orazio Giustiniani 4 🕐 4-10pm Tue-Sun (only during exhibitions) 🌐 museo macro.org

For much of the 20th century the Testaccio neighbourhood was a gutsy working-class quarter, dominated by its vast 19th-century slaughterhouse, the Mattatoio, which is considered to be one of the industrial architectural landmarks of the city. Testaccio has become one of Rome's trendiest areas, and the Mattatoio has been trans-formed into a cutting-edge gallery hosting temporary modern and contemporary art exhibitions and art-related events.

Other parts of the complex are home to the Città dell'Altra Economia, committed to fair-trade economies, with an organic café and restaurant, a children's play area, a bookshop, crafts shops and alternative energy and recycling projects. There is

---

TESTACCIO'S FOOD TRADITIONS

Traditional Roman cuisine originated in the Testaccio area, near the old slaughterhouse, where the butchers were paid partly in cash and partly in meat - or more specifically, in offal. They received the "fifth quarter" (*quinto quarto*), which included head, trotters, tail, intestines and brain. When carefully cooked and richly flavoured with herbs and spices, these offcuts are a culinary delight, and such robust dishes still feature on the menus of many of Rome's restaurants.

Parco Savello

At the top of the Aventine Hill, Parco Savello (also known as Giardino degli Aranci) is a walled garden planted with orange trees that offers visitors incredible views across the Tiber towards St Peter's and the Vatican.

also a fairtrade market in Città dell'Altra Economia and a pop-up ice-skating rink in the winter months.

 16

Pyramid of Caius Cestius

📍H10 🏛Piazzale Ostiense 🚌23, 280, 716 🚋3 Ⓜ️Piramide 🕐by appt 10:30am first Sat & Sun of the month (call 06-574 31 93); all other Sat & Sun call 06-3996 7700

Caius Cestius, a wealthy *praetor* (senior Roman magistrate), died in 12 BC. His main claim to fame is his tomb, an imposing pyramid faced in white marble, set in the Aurelian Wall near Porta San Paolo. It stands 36 m (118 ft) high and, according to an inscription carved upon it, took 330 days to build. Unmistakable as a landmark, it must have looked almost as incongruous when it was built as it does today.

 17

San Saba

📍H9 🏛Via di San Saba 📞06-6458 0140 🚌75, 673 🚋3 🕐8am-noon & 4-7:10pm Mon-Sat, 9:30am-1pm & 4-7:30pm Sun

Tucked away in a residential street on the Little Aventine Hill, San Saba began life as an oratory for Palestinian monks fleeing from Arab invasions in the 7th century. The existing church dates from the 10th century and has undergone much restoration. The portico houses a fascinating collection of archaeological remains and a fresco depicting St Sabas.

The church has three naves in the Greek style and a short fourth 11th-century nave to the left with vestiges of 13th-century frescoes of the life of St Nicholas of Bari. Particularly intriguing is a scene of three naked young ladies lying in bed, who are saved from penury by the gift of a bag of gold from St Nicholas, the future Santa Claus. The beautiful marble inlay in the main door, the floor and the remains of the choir are all 13th-century Cosmati work.

 18

Circus Maximus

📍J8 🏛Via del Circo Massimo 🚌81, 160, 628, 715 🚋3 Ⓜ️Circo Massimo

What was once ancient Rome's largest stadium is today little more than a long grassy esplanade. Set in the valley between the Palatine and Aventine hills, the Circus Maximus was continually embellished and expanded from the 4th century BC until AD 549 when the last races were held. The grandstands held some 300,000 spectators, cheering wildly at the horse and chariot races, athletic contests and animal fights.

The Circus had a central dividing barrier *(spina)* with seven large egg-shaped objects on it for counting the laps of a race. These were joined in 33 BC by seven bronze dolphins for a similar purpose. In 10 BC Augustus built the Imperial box under the Palatine and decorated the *spina* with the obelisk that is now in the centre of Piazza del Popolo *(p50)*. A second obelisk, added in the 4th century by Constantine II, is now in Piazza di San Giovanni in Laterano *(p219)*.

← The ancient Pyramid of Caius Cestius, a striking and unusual landmark

Grass esplanade of the Circus Maximus, from where there is a good view of the Palatine Hill

A SHORT WALK

PIAZZA DELLA BOCCA DELLA VERITÀ

Distance 0.8 km (0.5 mile) **Nearest bus** 23, 44, 81, 160, 170, 280, 628, 715, 716, 780 **Time** 20 minutes

A quiet corner of the city, this area beside the Tiber is great for escaping the crowds. The site was ancient Rome's first port and its busy cattle market; substantial Classical remains include two small temples from the Republican age and the Arch of Janus from the later Empire. In the 6th century the area became home to a Greek community from Byzantium, who founded the churches of San Giorgio in Velabro and Santa Maria in Cosmedin. Follow tradition and place your hand inside the Bocca della Verità (the Mouth of Truth), a mythological stone sculpture in the portico of Santa Maria in Cosmedin.

Sant'Omobono, dating to the 16th century, stands in isolation in the middle of an important archaeological site where the remains of sacrificial altars and two temples from the 6th century BC have been discovered.

START

The 11th-century Casa dei Crescenzi has columns and capitals from ancient Roman temples (p246).

The Temples of the Forum Boarium (the tiny round Temple of Hercules and its neighbour, the Temple of Portunus) are the best preserved of Rome's Republican temples (p246).

Ponte Rotto, as this forlorn ruined arch in the Tiber is called, means simply "broken bridge". Built in the 2nd century BC, its original name was Pons Aemilius.

LUNGOTEVERE DEI PIERLEONI

Tevere

PONTE PALATINO

The Fontana dei Tritoni by Carlo Bizzaccheri was built here in 1715. The style shows the powerful influence of Bernini.

↑ The well-preserved Temple of Hercules in the Forum Boarium

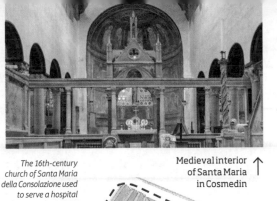

The 16th-century church of Santa Maria della Consolazione used to serve a hospital nearby (p245).

Medieval interior of Santa Maria in Cosmedin

Locator Map
For more detail see pp242–3

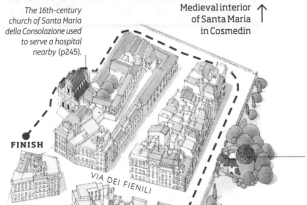

FINISH

VIA DEI FIENILI

GIOVANNI DECOLLATO

VIA DI SAN TEODORO

PIAZZA DELLA BOCCA DELLA VERITÀ

VIA DEI CERCHI

VIA DELLA GRECA

The 15th-century portal of the ancient round San Teodoro church is decorated with the insignia of Pope Nicholas V (p244).

The plain Renaissance façade of San Giovanni Decollato was completed in about 1504 (p246).

San Giorgio in Velabro's simple 12th-century portico of Ionic columns was destroyed by a bomb in 1993 but has been restored (p246).

The Arco degli Argentari, dedicated to Emperor Septimius Severus in AD 204, is decorated with scenes of religion and war.

The square Arch of Janus with arches on each side dates from the 4th century AD (p244).

The medieval church of Santa Maria in Cosmedin has a fine marble mosaic floor and a Gothic baldacchino (p244).

0 metres   100
0 yards   100

N

TRASTEVERE

The proud and aggressively independent inhabitants of Trastevere, the area "across the Tiber", consider themselves the most authentic of Romans. In one of the most picturesque old quarters of the city, it is still possible to glimpse scenes of everyday life that seem to belong to bygone centuries despite the proliferation of fashionable boutiques, cafés and restaurants that characterize the area today. Some of Rome's most fascinating medieval churches lie hidden away in the patchwork of narrow, cobbled back-streets, the only clue to their location an occasional glimpse of a Romanesque bell tower. Of these, Santa Cecilia was built on the site of the martyrdom of the patron saint of music, San Francesco a Ripa commemorates St Francis of Assisi's visit to Rome, and Santa Maria in Trastevere is the traditional centre of the spiritual and social life of the area.

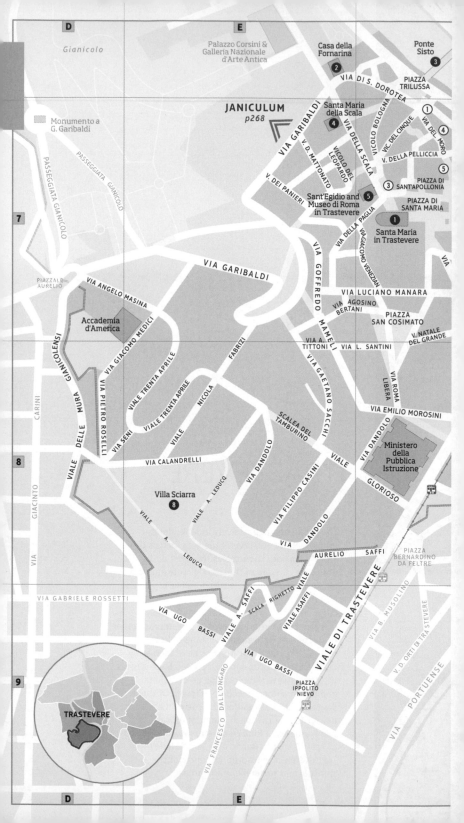

TRASTEVERE

Must See
1 Santa Maria in Trastevere

Experience More
2 Casa della Fornarina
3 Ponte Sisto
4 Santa Maria della Scala
5 Sant'Egidio and Museo di Roma in Trastevere
6 San Crisogono
7 Santa Cecilia in Trastevere
8 Villa Sciarra
9 San Michele a Ripa Grande
10 San Francesco a Ripa
11 Caserma dei Vigili della VII Coorte

Drink
1 Enoteca Ferrara
2 Big Mama
3 Ombre Rosse

Shop
4 Marta Ray
5 Pasticceria Valzani

① ⌂

SANTA MARIA IN TRASTEVERE

⚑ F7 ⌂ Piazza Santa Maria in Trastevere ☎ 06-581 4802 🚌 H & 780 to Piazza San Sonnino, 23 & 280 along Lungotevere Sanzio 🚋 8 from Piazza Venezia ⏰ 7:30am–9pm daily (8am–noon & 4–9pm Aug)

Probably the first official Christian place of worship to be built in Rome, this basilica became the focus of devotion to the Virgin Mary. Today it is famous for its splendid mosaics.

According to legend, the church was founded by Pope Callixtus I in the 3rd century, when Christianity was still a minority cult, on the site where a fountain of oil had miraculously sprung up on the day that Christ was born. Today's church is largely a 12th-century building, remarkable for its mosaics, in particular the apse mosaic of the Coronation of the Virgin and the six mosaics by Pietro Cavallini below it of the life of the Virgin, depicted with a touching realism. The 22 granite columns in the nave were taken from the ruins of ancient Roman buildings. Despite some 18th-century Baroque additions, Santa Maria has retained its medieval character.

↑ Santa Maria in Trastevere façade, with an octagonal fountain built in the late 17th century by Carlo Fontana in front

↑ Mosaic floor, relaid in the 1870s to re-create the 13th-century Cosmatesque floor mosaics

1291
▼ Pietro Cavallini adds mosaics of scenes from the life of the Virgin for his patron, Bertoldo Stefaneschi

Timeline

38 BC
Jet of mineral oil spouts from the ground on this site, later interpreted as a portent of the coming of Christ

AD 217–22
Church founded by Pope Callixtus I

c1138
Pope Innocent II starts rebuilding the church

1617
▲ Domenichino designs coffered ceiling with octagonal panel depicting the Assumption of the Virgin

1866–77
Church restored by Virginio Vespignani

Did You Know?

The glittering mosaics on the church's façade are illuminated at night.

PETRVS

The 12th-century apse mosaic and Cavallini mosaics below it ↑

Piazza di Santa Maria in Trastevere

EXPERIENCE MORE

Casa della Fornarina

◉ E6 ⌂ Via di Santa Dorotea 20 ▦ 23, 280

Not much is known about the life of Raphael's model and lover, La Fornarina, yet over the centuries she has acquired a name, Margherita Luti, and even a biography. Her father was a Sienese baker (*la fornarina* means "the baker's girl") and his shop was here in Trastevere near Raphael's frescoes in the Villa Farnesina (*p272*).

Margherita earned a reputation as a "fallen woman" and Raphael, wishing to be absolved before dying, turned her away from his deathbed. After his death she took refuge in the convent of Santa Apollonia in Trastevere.

She is assumed to have been the model for Raphael's famous portrait *La Donna Velata* housed in the Palazzo Pitti in Florence.

← *Death of the Virgin* (17th century) by Carlo Saraceni in Santa Maria della Scala

→ Ponte Sisto, with the dome of St Peter's in the background

Ponte Sisto

◉ F6 ▦ 23, 280

Named after Pope Sixtus IV della Rovere (reigned 1471–84), who commissioned it, this bridge was built by Baccio Pontelli in 1475 to replace an ancient Roman bridge. The enterprising pope also commissioned the Sistine Chapel (*p290*), the Hospital of Santo Spirito (*p298*) and had many churches and monuments restored. This put him in great financial difficulties and he had to sell personal collections in order to finance his projects.

Santa Maria della Scala

◉ E7 ⌂ Piazza della Scala 23 ☎ 06-580 6233 ▦ 23, 280 ⏱ 10am-1pm & 4-5:30pm daily

This church belongs to a time of great building activity that lasted about 30 years from the end of the 16th to the early 17th century. Its simple façade contrasts with a rich interior decorated with multicoloured marbles and a number of spirited Baroque altars and reliefs, as well as a few paintings, including Carlo Saraceni's *Death of the Virgin*. In 1849, the church was used as a hospital to treat the soldiers of Garibaldi's army.

5

Sant'Egidio and Museo di Roma in Trastevere

📍F7 🏛Piazza Sant'Egidio 1
🚌H, 23, 280 🚋8
Church: 📞06-589 5945
🔒for restoration
Museo di Roma in Trastevere: 🕐10am–8pm Tue–Sun (last adm: 7pm)
🌐museodiromain trastevere.it

Built in 1630, Sant'Egidio is the church of the adjoining Carmelite convent, one of many founded in the area to shelter the poor and destitute. The convent is now a museum, containing a wealth of material relating to the festivals, pastimes, superstitions and customs of the Romans when they lived under papal rule.

There are old paintings and prints of the city and tableaux showing scenes of everyday life in 18th- and 19th-century Rome, including reconstructions of shops and a tavern.

The museum also has manuscripts by the much-loved poets Belli and Trilussa, who wrote in local dialect.

6

San Crisogono

📍F7 🏛Piazza Sonnino 44
📞06-5810 0076 🚌H, 23, 280, 780 🚋8 🕐7–11:30am & 4–7:30pm Mon–Sat, 8am–1pm & 4–7:30pm Sun

This church was built on the site of one of the city's oldest *tituli* (private houses used for Christian worship). An 8th-century church with 11th-century frescoes can still be seen beneath the present church. It is possible to go down to see the excavations. The ground-level church dates from the early 12th century, a period of intense building activity in Rome. Most of the church's columns were taken from previous buildings, including the great porphyry columns of a triumphal arch. The mosaic floor is the result of recycled precious marble from various Roman ruins. Pietro Cavallini designed the apse mosaic. The Baroque ceiling painting is by Guercino.

> ### FESTA DE' NOANTRI
>
> Every year Trastevere hosts its very own carnival, the Festa de' Noantri, in late July. Street processions, concerts, poetry readings, theatre performances, a market and fireworks are all held in the area.

The ornate interior of Santa Cecilia in Trastevere and (inset) a detail of a fresco

7

Santa Cecilia in Trastevere

 G7 Piazza di Santa Cecilia 06-589 9289 H, 23, 44, 280 8 10am–1pm & 4–7pm daily

St Cecilia, aristocrat and patron saint of music, was martyred here in AD 230. After an attempt at scalding her to death, she was beheaded. A church was founded, perhaps in the 4th century, on the site of her house. The **excavations and crypt** beneath the church are well worth a visit. Her body turned up in the Catacombs of San Callisto (p321) and was buried here in the 9th century by Pope Paschal I, who rebuilt the church. A fine apse mosaic survives from this period.

The **fresco** of The Last Judgment by Pietro Cavallini, reached through the convent, dates from the 1200s. In front of the altar is a statue of St Cecilia by Stefano Maderno, who used her preserved remains as a model when she was briefly disinterred in 1599.

Excavations and Crypt

10am–12:30pm & 4–6pm Mon–Sat (from 11:30am public hols); **Cavallini fresco** 10am–12:30pm Mon–Fri (from 11:30am public hols)

8

Villa Sciarra

 E8 Via Calandrelli 35 44, 75 Park: 9am–sunset daily

In Roman times the site of this small, attractive public park was a nymph's sanctuary. Shaded by trees, Villa Sciarra is a tranquil place to get away from the hustle and bustle of the surrounding streets. It is especially picturesque in spring when its wisterias are in full bloom. The paths through the park are decorated with Romantic follies, fountains and statues, and there are splendid views over the bastions of the Janiculum. It also contains the headquarters of the Italian Institute for Germanic Studies.

$\rightarrow$

Bernini's *Ecstasy of Beata Ludovica Albertoni* in San Francesco a Ripa

San Michele a Ripa Grande

G8 ⌂ Via di San Michele 25 **06-6723 1440** 23, 44, 75, 280 for special exhibitions only

This huge, imposing complex, now housing the Ministry of Culture, stretches 300 m (985 ft) along the River Tiber. It was built on the initiative of Pope Innocent XII and contained a home for the abandoned elderly, a boys' reform school, a woollen mill and various chapels. Today, contemporary art exhibitions are occasionally held here.

San Francesco a Ripa

F8 ⌂ Piazza San Francesco d'Assisi 88 **06-581 9020** H, 23, 44, 75, 280 8 7:30am–1pm & 2–7pm daily

St Francis of Assisi lived here in a hospice when he visited Rome in 1219, and his stone

> **Shaded by trees, Villa Sciarra is a tranquil place to get away from the hustle and bustle of the surrounding streets.**

pillow and crucifix are preserved in his cell. The church was rebuilt by his follower, the nobleman Rodolfo Anguillara, who is portrayed on his tombstone wearing the Franciscan habit.

Entirely rebuilt in the 1680s by Cardinal Pallavicini, the church is rich in sculptures. Particularly flamboyant are the 18th-century Rospigliosi and Pallavicini monuments in the transept chapel.

The Paluzzi-Albertoni Chapel (fourth on the left, along the nave) contains Bernini's breathtaking *Ecstasy of Beata Ludovica Albertoni*, completed in 1674.

Caserma dei Vigili della VII Coorte

G7 ⌂ Via della VII Coorte 9 **06-0608** H, 23, 280, 780 8 for restoration; call for details

Not all Roman ruins are Imperial villas or grand temples; one that illustrates the daily life of a busy city is the barracks of the guards of the VII Coorte (7th Cohort), the Roman fire brigade. It was built in Augustus's reign, in the 1st century AD, and the excavated courtyard is where the men would rest while waiting for a call out.

DRINK

Enoteca Ferrara

This cosy enoteca has a vast wine list and there's a smart restaurant attached, although the wine bar's generous aperitivo buffet might leave you too full for dinner.

F7 ⌂ Piazza Trilussa 41 enotecaferrara.it

Big Mama

A basement jazz club hosting international musicians several nights a week (from 10.30pm), this is an intimate place for a nightcap. There is a €10 admission charge.

F8 ⌂ Vicolo di San Francesco a Ripa 18 bigmama.it

Ombre Rosse

The terrace of this bar is a great spot for a pre-dinner Prosecco. There's live music several nights a week.

F7 ⌂ Piazza di Sant'Egidio 12 ombrerosse intrastevere.it

A SHORT WALK
TRASTEVERE

Raphael's mistress is said to have lived at the Casa della Fornarina. There is now a flourishing restaurant in the back garden (p262).

Distance 2 km (1.2 miles) **Nearest bus** 23, 280
Time 30 minutes

It is best to appreciate the antique charm of Trastevere's narrow streets in the more tranquil atmosphere of the early morning. All year round Trastevere is a major attraction both for its restaurants, clubs and cinemas, and for its picturesque maze of narrow cobbled alleyways. On summer evenings the streets are packed with jostling groups of pleasure-seekers. Café and restaurant tables spill out over pavements, especially around Piazza di Santa Maria in Trastevere and outside the pizzerias along Viale di Trastevere. Kiosks sell slices of watermelon and *grattachecca*, a mixture of syrup and grated ice.

The Santa Maria della Scala's unassuming façade conceals a rich Baroque interior.

START

FINISH

The church of Santa Maria dei Sette Dolori (1643) is a minor work by Borromini.

Sant'Egidio and Museo di Roma in Trastevere has a 17th-century fresco of Sant'Egidio by Pomarancio in the left-hand chapel. The convent next door is a museum of Roman life and customs (p263).

Vicolo del Piede is one of the picturesque narrow streets lined with restaurant tables leading off Piazza di Santa Maria in Trastevere.

Santa Maria in Trastevere is famous for its 13th-century mosaics by Pietro Cavallini but it also has earlier works to the left of the apse (p258).

The fountain of Piazza di Santa Maria in Trastevere by Carlo Fontana (1692) is a popular meeting place. At night it is floodlit and dozens of young people sit on the steps around its octagonal base.

↑ Pretty Vicolo del Piede, off Piazza Maria in Trastevere

Ponte Sisto was built on the orders of Sixtus IV in 1474 to link Trastevere to central Rome (p262).

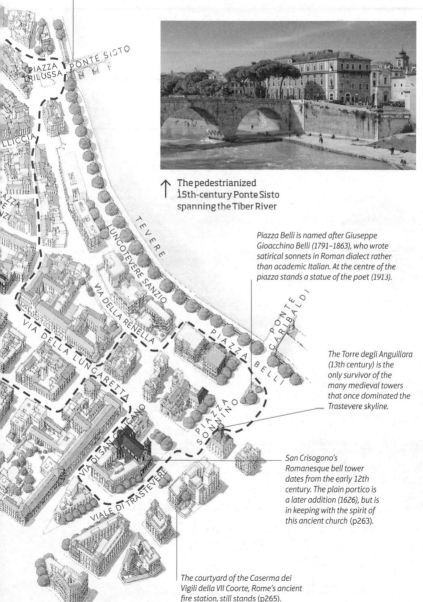

↑ The pedestrianized 15th-century Ponte Sisto spanning the Tiber River

Piazza Belli is named after Giuseppe Gioacchino Belli (1791–1863), who wrote satirical sonnets in Roman dialect rather than academic Italian. At the centre of the piazza stands a statue of the poet (1913).

The Torre degli Anguillara (13th century) is the only survivor of the many medieval towers that once dominated the Trastevere skyline.

San Crisogono's Romanesque bell tower dates from the early 12th century. The plain portico is a later addition (1626), but is in keeping with the spirit of this ancient church (p263).

The courtyard of the Caserma dei Vigili della VII Coorte, Rome's ancient fire station, still stands (p265).

JANICULUM

Overlooking the Tiber on the Trastevere side of
the river, the Janiculum Hill has often played its
part in the defence of the city. The last occasion
was in 1849 when Garibaldi held off the attacking
French troops – the park at the top of the hill is
filled with monuments to Garibaldi and his men.
A popular place for walks, the park provides a
welcome escape from the densely packed streets
of Trastevere, and you will often come across
puppet shows and other children's amusements.
In medieval times most of the hill was occupied
by monasteries and convents. Bramante built
his miniature masterpiece, the Tempietto, in
the convent of San Pietro in Montorio. The
Renaissance also saw the development of the
riverside area along Via della Lungara, where
the rich and powerful built beautiful houses
such as the Villa Farnesina.

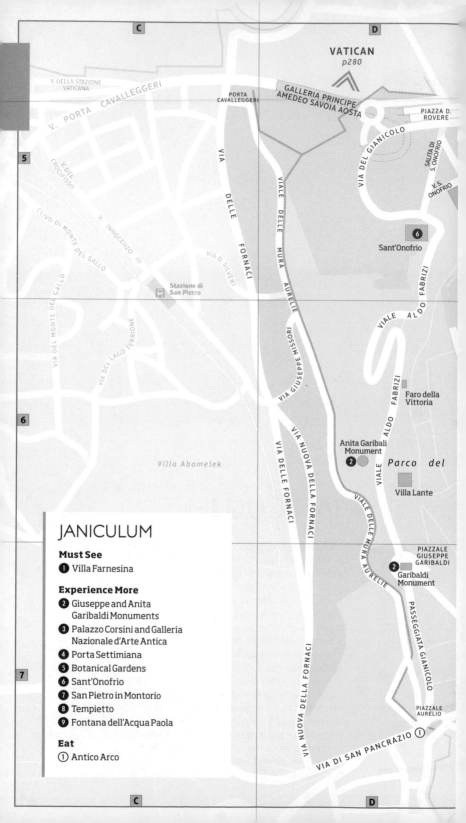

VATICAN
p280

GALLERIA PRINCIPE
AMEDEO SAVOIA AOSTA

PIAZZA D.
ROVERE

PORTA
CAVALLEGGERI

V. DELLA STAZIONE
VATICANA

V. PORTA CAVALLEGGERI

V. DEL CROCIFISSO

CLIVO DI MONTE DEL GALLO

V. INNOCENZO III

VIA D. SILVERI

VIA DELLE FORNACI

VIALE DELLE MURA AURELIE

VIA DEL GIANICOLO

SALITA DI S. ONOFRIO

V. S. ONOFRIO

6 Sant'Onofrio

VIA GIUSEPPE MISSORI

VIA DEL MONTE DEL GALLO

VIA DEL LAGO TERRIONE

Stazione di
San Pietro

Villa Abamelek

VIA DELLE FORNACI

VIA NUOVA DELLA FORNACI

VIALE ALDO FABRIZI

VIALE ALDO FABRIZI

Faro della
Vittoria

Anita Garibali
Monument
2

Parco del

Villa Lante

VIALE DELLE MURA AURELIE

PIAZZALE
GIUSEPPE
GARIBALDI

2
Garibaldi
Monument

PASSEGGIATA GIANICOLO

JANICULUM

Must See

1 Villa Farnesina

Experience More

2 Giuseppe and Anita
Garibaldi Monuments

3 Palazzo Corsini and Galleria
Nazionale d'Arte Antica

4 Porta Settimiana

5 Botanical Gardens

6 Sant'Onofrio

7 San Pietro in Montorio

8 Tempietto

9 Fontana dell'Acqua Paola

Eat

① Antico Arco

VIA NUOVA DELLA FORNACI

PIAZZALE
AURELIO

VIA DI SAN PANCRAZIO **①**

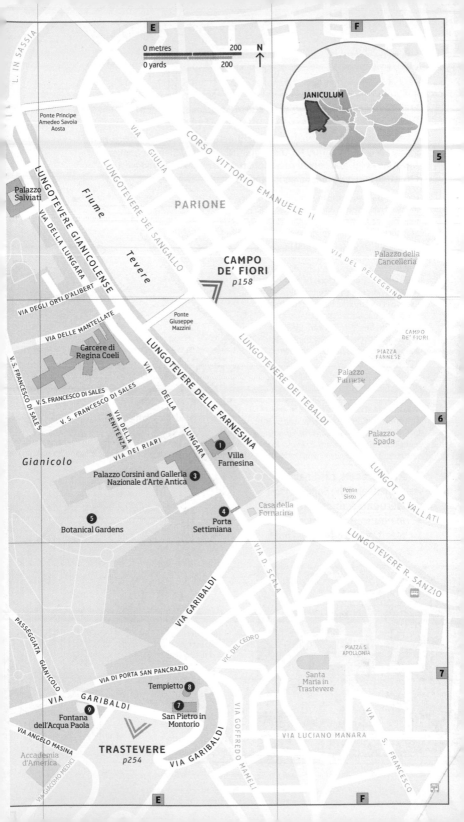

0 metres 200

0 yards 200

N

JANICULUM

L. IN SASSIA

Ponte Principe
Amedeo Savoia
Aosta

CORSO VITTORIO EMANUELE II

5

VIA GIULIA

Palazzo
Salviati

Fiume

Tevere

PARIONE

Palazzo della
Cancelleria

VIA DEL PELLEGRINO

LUNGOTEVERE GIANICOLENSE

LUNGOTEVERE DEI SANGALLO

VIA DELLA LUNGARA

**CAMPO
DE' FIORI**
p158

VIA DEGLI ORTI D'ALIBERT

Ponte
Giuseppe
Mazzini

CAMPO
DE' FIORI

VIA DELLE MANTELLATE

Carcere di
Regina Coeli

PIAZZA
FARNESE

Palazzo
Farnese

LUNGOTEVERE DELLE FARNESINA

LUNGOTEVERE DEI TEBALDI

V. S. FRANCESCO DI SALES

V.S. FRANCESCO DI SALES

V. S. FRANCESCO DI SALES

VIA DELLA

6

Palazzo
Spada

1

Villa
Farnesina

VIA DELLA PENITENZA

VIA DEI RIARI

LUNGARA

LUNGOT. D. VALLATI

Gianicolo

Palazzo Corsini and Galleria
Nazionale d'Arte Antica **3**

Ponte
Sisto

5

Botanical Gardens

4

Porta
Settimiana

Casa della
Fornarina

LUNGOTEVERE R. SANZIO

VIA D. SCALA

VIA GARIBALDI

7

PASSEGGIATA GIANICOLO

VIC. DEL CEDRO

PIAZZA S.
APOLLONIA

Santa
Maria in
Trastevere

VIA DI PORTA SAN PANCRAZIO

VIA GARIBALDI

Tempietto **8**

7
San Pietro in
Montorio

VIA
GARIBALDI

9
Fontana
dell'Acqua Paola

VIA GOFFREDO MAMELI

VIA LUCIANO MANARA

VIA

S. FRANCESCO

VIA ANGELO MASINA

Accademia
d'America

TRASTEVERE
p254

VIA GARIBALDI

VIA GIACOMO MEDICI

❶ ⌖ ⓜ 🛍

VILLA FARNESINA

📍E6 🏠 Via della Lungara 230 🚌 23, 280 to Lungotevere ⏰ 9am–2pm Mon–Sat & 9am–5pm second Sun of every month 📅 Aug 🌐 villafarnesina.it

A perfect example of Renaissance architecture, Villa Farnesina was built in the early 16th century for the fabulously wealthy Sienese banker Agostino Chigi, and served as a sophsticated retreat where he could entertain and hold magnificent banquets.

Having established the headquarters of his far-flung financial empire in Rome, Agostino Chigi commissioned the villa in 1508 from his compatriot, painter and architect Baldassare Peruzzi. The simple, harmonious design, with a central block and projecting wings, made this one of the earliest true Renaissance villas. The decoration was carried out between 1510 and 1519 and has been restored. Peruzzi frescoed some of the interiors himself. Later, Sebastiano del Piombo, Raphael and his pupils added more elaborate works. The frescoes illustrate Classical myths, and the vault of the main hall, the Sala di Galatea, is adorned with astrological scenes showing the position of the stars at the time of Chigi's birth. Artists, poets, cardinals, princes and the pope himself were entertained here in magnificent style by their wealthy and influential host. In 1577 the villa was bought by Cardinal Alessandro Farnese. Since then, it has been known as the Villa Farnesina.

> Artists, poets, cardinals, princes and the pope himself were entertained here in magnificent style by their wealthy and influential host.

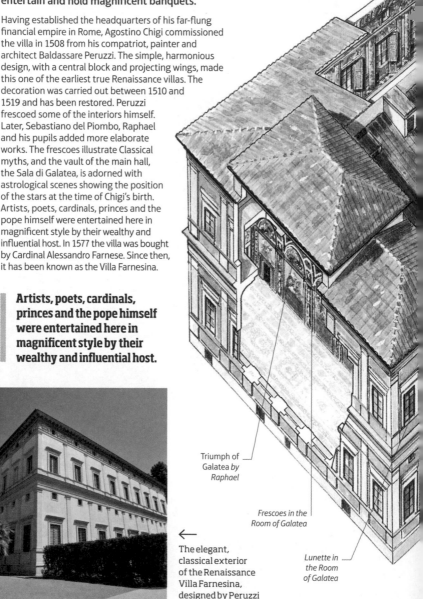

Triumph of Galatea by Raphael

Frescoes in the Room of Galatea

Lunette in the Room of Galatea

← The elegant, classical exterior of the Renaissance Villa Farnesina, designed by Peruzzi

Salone delle Prospettive

← Drawing showing the layout of the Villa Farnesina

Loggia of Cupid and Psyche

AGOSTINO CHIGI

A super-rich banking tycoon and Renaissance playboy, Agostino Chigi was fond of throwing extravagant parties. At a dinner party, held in a riverside pavilion in the grounds of Villa Farnesina, the food was served on gold and silver platters which were flung into the Tiber at the end of each course. The demonstration of wealth was not quite as reckless as it first seemed – Chigi had taken the precaution of having nets laid on the river bed so that his dinner service could be retrieved after the guests had gone home.

1 Loggia of Cupid and Psyche

2 *The Three Graces* by Raphael in the Loggia of Cupid and Psyche

3 *Perseus Beheading Medusa* fresco by Peruzzi in the Room of Galatea

EXPERIENCE MORE

2

Giuseppe and Anita Garibaldi Monuments

♀ D6 ⚑ Piazzale Giuseppe Garibaldi 🚌 870

Dominating a huge open piazza on the summit of the Janiculum Hill is an equestrian statue of Giuseppe Garibaldi, hero of the Italian Unification. The statue and piazza commemorate the weeks in 1849 when Garibaldi and his men, based on the hill, fended off attacks from highly superior French forces, before finally being overwhelmed and escaping. In 2011, to mark the 150th anniversary of the Italian Republic, a low wall was erected, inscribed with the country's constitution.

A short distance away is a dramatic monument to Garibaldi's wife Anita, who fought alongside him. She is depicted on a leaping horse, a pistol in her right hand and her baby under her left arm.

3

Palazzo Corsini and Galleria Nazionale d'Arte Antica

♀ E6 ⚑ Via della Lungara 10 🚌 23, 280 🕐 8:30am–7pm Mon, Wed–Sun 🌐 barberinicorsini.org

The history of Palazzo Corsini is intimately entwined with that of Rome. Built for Cardinal Domenico Riario in 1510–12, it has boasted among its many distinguished guests Bramante, the young Michelangelo, Erasmus and Queen Christina of Sweden, who died here in 1689. The old palazzo was completely rebuilt for Cardinal Neri Corsini by Ferdinando Fuga in 1736. As Via della Lungara is too narrow for a good frontal view, Fuga designed the façade so it could be seen from an angle.

Palazzo Corsini houses the Galleria Nazionale d'Arte Antica, also known as Galleria Corsini. This outstanding collection includes paintings by Rubens, Van Dyck, Murillo, Caravaggio and Guido Reni, together with 17th- and 18th-century Italian regional art. The palazzo is also home to the Accademia dei Lincei, a learned society founded in 1603 that once included Galileo among its members.

In 1797 French General Duphot (the fiancé of Napoleon's sister Pauline) was killed here during a skirmish between papal troops and Republicans. The consequent French occupation of the city and the deportation of Pope Pius VI

led to the proclamation of a short-lived Roman Republic (1798–9).

4

Porta Settimiana

♀ E6 ⚑ Between Via della Scala and Via della Lungara 🚌 23, 280

This gate was built in 1498 by Pope Alexander VI Borgia to replace a minor passageway in the Aurelian Wall. The Porta Settimiana marks the start of Via della Lungara, a long road built in the early 16th century.

5

Botanical Gardens

♀ 4 D5 ⚑ Largo Cristina di Svezia 24, off Via Corsini 📞 06-4991 7108 🚌 23, 280 🕐 9am–6:30pm Mon–Sat (Nov–Mar: to 5:30pm) 🚫 public hols

Sequoias, palm trees and collections of orchids and bromeliads are cultivated in Rome's Botanical Gardens (Orto Botanico). These tranquil gardens contain more than 7,000 plant species. Indigenous and exotic species are grouped to illustrate their botanical families and their adaptation to different climates and ecosystems. The gardens were originally part of the Palazzo Corsini but now belong to the University of Rome.

6

Sant'Onofrio

♀ D5 ⚑ Piazza di Sant'Onofrio 2 📞 06-686 4498 🚌 870 🕐 9am–1pm Sun–Fri 🚫 Aug

Beato Nicola da Forca Palena, whose tombstone guards the entrance, founded this church

← Dramatic equestrian statue of Anita Garibaldi riding into battle

The monumental Fontana dell'Acqua Paola, built in 1612

in 1419 in honour of the hermit St Onofrio. It retains the flavour of the 15th century in the simple shapes of the portico and the cloister. In the early 17th century the portico was decorated with frescoes by Domenichino.

The monastery next to the church has a small **museum** that is dedicated to the 16th-century Italian poet Torquato Tasso, who died there.

Museum

 by appt only (call 06-687 7341)

7

San Pietro in Montorio

E7 Piazza San Pietro in Montorio 2 06-581 3940 44, 75 8am-noon & 3-4pm daily (times may vary in summer)

San Pietro in Montorio – the church of St Peter on the Golden Hill – was founded in the Middle Ages near the spot where St Peter was presumed to have been crucified. It was rebuilt by order of Ferdinand and Isabella of Spain at the end of the 15th century, and decorated by outstanding artists of the Renaissance.

The single nave ends in a deep apse that once contained Raphael's *Transfiguration*, now in the Vatican. Two wide chapels, one on either side of the nave, were decorated by some of Michelangelo's most famous pupils. The left-hand chapel was designed by Daniele da Volterra, who was also responsible for the altar painting, *The Baptism of Christ*. The chapel on the right was the work of Giorgio Vasari, who included a self-portrait (in black, on the left) in his altar painting, *The Conversion of St Paul*.

The first chapel to the right of the entrance contains a powerful *Flagellation*, by the Venetian artist Sebastiano del Piombo (1518); Michelangelo is said to have provided the original drawings. Work by Bernini and his followers can be seen in the second chapel on the left and in the flanking De Raymondi tombs.

8

Tempietto

E7 Piazza San Pietro (in courtyard) 44, 75 10am-6pm Tue-Sun

Around 1502 Bramante completed what many consider to be the first true Renaissance building in Rome – the Tempietto, a perfectly circular Doric temple. The name means simply "little temple". Its circular shape echoes early Christian *martyria*, chapels built on the site of a saint's martyrdom. This was believed to be the place where St Peter was crucified.

Bramante chose the Doric order for the 16 columns surrounding the domed chapel. Above the columns is a Classical frieze and a delicate balustrade. Though the scale of the Tempietto is tiny, Bramante's masterly use of Classical proportions creates a satisfyingly harmonious whole. The Tempietto illustrates the great

Renaissance dream that the city of Rome would once again relive its ancient glory.

9

Fontana dell'Acqua Paola

E7 Via Garibaldi 44, 75

This fountain marks the reopening in 1612 of an aqueduct built in AD 109. It was renamed the "Acqua Paola" after Paul V, the Borghese pope who ordered its restoration. The original fountain had five small basins. In 1690 Carlo Fontana added the huge basin you can see today.

EAT

Antico Arco

This chic restaurant has a short menu of gourmet Italian dishes made with top-notch ingredients, such as sea bass with Roman broccoli and black truffle. It is the ideal dining choice for a special occasion.

D7 Piazzale Aurelio 7 anticoarco.it

€€€

The perfectly proportioned Tempietto, within the cloister of San Pietro in Montorio

A SHORT WALK
A TOUR OF THE JANICULUM

Distance 1 km (0.6 mile) **Nearest bus** 23, 280, 870 **Time** 15 minutes

The long hike to the top of the Janiculum is rewarded by wonderful views over the city. The park's monuments include a lighthouse and statues of Garibaldi and his wife Anita. There is also a cannon which is fired at noon each day. In Via della Lungara, between the Janiculum and the Tiber, stand Palazzo Corsini, with its national art collection, and the Villa Farnesina, decorated by Raphael for his friend and patron, the fabulously wealthy banker Agostino Chigi.

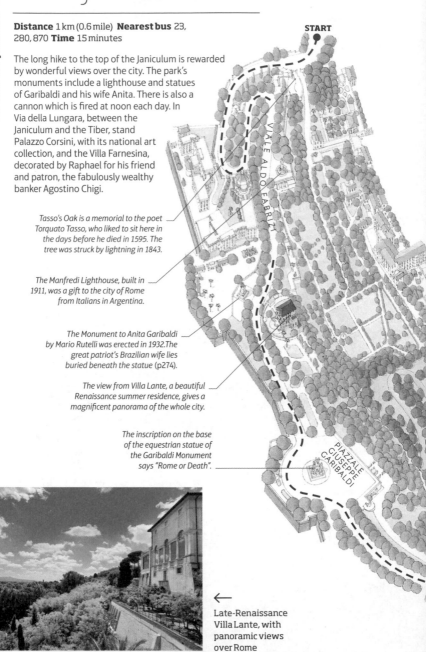

Tasso's Oak is a memorial to the poet Torquato Tasso, who liked to sit here in the days before he died in 1595. The tree was struck by lightning in 1843.

The Manfredi Lighthouse, built in 1911, was a gift to the city of Rome from Italians in Argentina.

The Monument to Anita Garibaldi by Mario Rutelli was erected in 1932. The great patriot's Brazilian wife lies buried beneath the statue (p274).

The view from Villa Lante, a beautiful Renaissance summer residence, gives a magnificent panorama of the whole city.

The inscription on the base of the equestrian statue of the Garibaldi Monument says "Rome or Death".

START

VIALE ALDO FABRIZI

PIAZZALE GIUSEPPE GARIBALDI

← Late-Renaissance Villa Lante, with panoramic views over Rome

↑ The Renaissance Porta
Settimiana, part of the
Aurelian Wall

Locator Map
For more detail see pp270–71

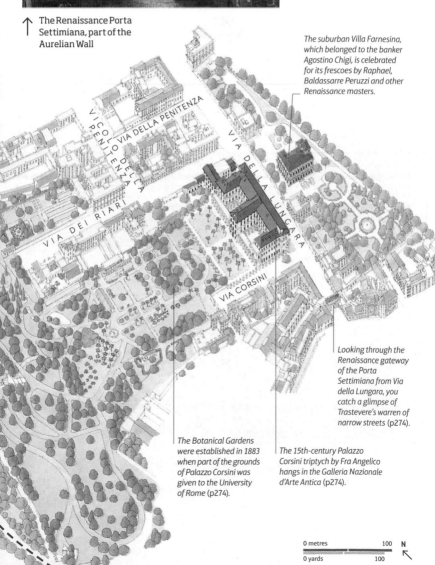

*The suburban Villa Farnesina,
which belonged to the banker
Agostino Chigi, is celebrated
for its frescoes by Raphael,
Baldassarre Peruzzi and other
Renaissance masters.*

VICOLO DELLA PENITENZA

VIA DELLA PENITENZA

VIA DEI RIARI

VIA DELLA LUNGARA

VIA CORSINI

*Looking through the
Renaissance gateway
of the Porta
Settimiana from Via
della Lungara, you
catch a glimpse of
Trastevere's warren of
narrow streets (p274).*

*The Botanical Gardens
were established in 1883
when part of the grounds
of Palazzo Corsini was
given to the University
of Rome (p274).*

*The 15th-century Palazzo
Corsini triptych by Fra Angelico
hangs in the Galleria Nazionale
d'Arte Antica (p274).*

| 0 metres | | 100 |
| 0 yards | | 100 |

N

● FINISH

VATICAN

As the site where St Peter was martyred and buried, the Vatican became the residence of the popes who succeeded him. Decisions taken here have shaped the destiny of Europe, and the great basilica of St Peter's draws pilgrims from all over the Christian world. The papal palaces beside St Peter's house the Vatican Museums. With the awe-inspiring attractions of Michelangelo's Sistine Chapel and the Raphael Rooms, their wonderful collections of Classical sculpture make them the finest museums in Rome. The Vatican's position as a state within a state was guaranteed by the Lateran Treaty of 1929, marked by the building of a new road, the Via della Conciliazione. This leads from St Peter's to Castel Sant'Angelo, a monument to a far grimmer past. Built originally as the Emperor Hadrian's mausoleum, this papal fortress and prison has witnessed many fierce battles for control of the city.

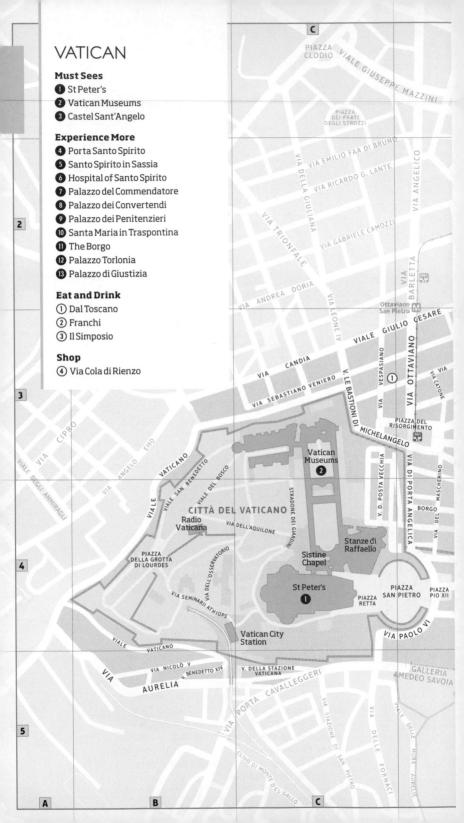

VATICAN

Must Sees
1. St Peter's
2. Vatican Museums
3. Castel Sant'Angelo

Experience More
4. Porta Santo Spirito
5. Santo Spirito in Sassia
6. Hospital of Santo Spirito
7. Palazzo del Commendatore
8. Palazzo dei Convertendi
9. Palazzo dei Penitenzieri
10. Santa Maria in Traspontina
11. The Borgo
12. Palazzo Torlonia
13. Palazzo di Giustizia

Eat and Drink
1. Dal Toscano
2. Franchi
3. Il Simposio

Shop
4. Via Cola di Rienzo

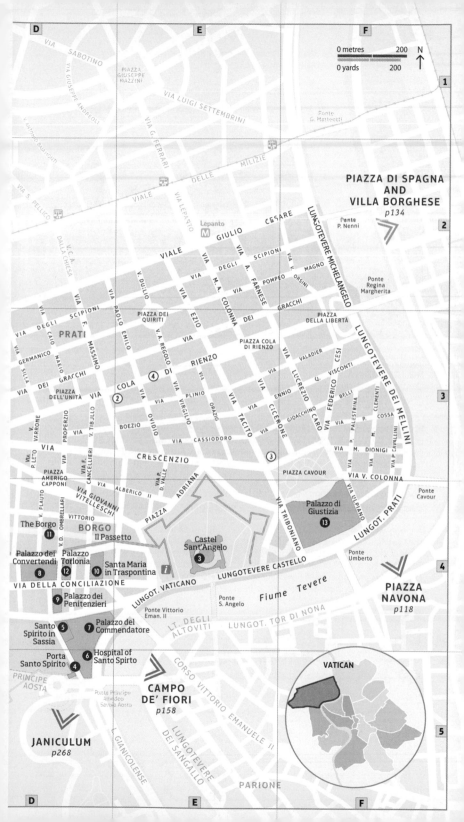

① Ⓜ 🛍

ST PETER'S

📍**C4** 🏛 **Piazza San Pietro** 📞 **06-6988 3712 (Sacristy); 0- 6988 1662 (tourist info)**
🚌 **23, 49, 70, 180, 492** Ⓜ **Ottaviano San Pietro** 🕐 **Basilica: 7am-7pm daily Apr-Sept
(to 6:30pm mid-Oct-Mar); Treasury: 8am-7:30pm daily Apr-Sep (to 6:15pm Oct-Mar);
Grottoes: 8am-6pm daily Apr-Sep (to 5:30pm Oct-Mar); Dome: 8am-6pm daily Apr-Sep
(to 5pm Oct-Mar)**

**The centre of the Roman Catholic faith, St Peter's draws pilgrims from all
over the world. The magnificent basilica holds many precious works of art.**

A shrine was erected in the 2nd century on
the site where, according to Catholic tradition,
St Peter was martyred and buried in AD 61.
The first great basilica, ordered by Emperor
Constantine, was constructed here in AD 349.
By the 15th century it was falling down, so in

1506 Pope Julius II commissioned Bramante
to replace the old church with a brand-new
basilica. It took more than a hundred years to
build and all the great architects and artists of
the Roman Renaissance and Baroque had a
hand in its design – not only Bramante, but

Timeline

AD 61
△ Burial of
St Peter

200
Altar built
marking
grave of
St Peter

324
△ Constantine
builds basilica

800
▽ Charlemagne
crowned Emperor
of the Romans in
St Peter's

1452
Nicholas V
plans restoration

1503
Pope Julius II
chooses Bramante
as architect for
new basilica

1506
Julius II lays
first stone

1514
Raphael
named
director
of works

↑ St Peter's Square with the basilica and Bernini's colonnade

Raphael, Bernini and Michelangelo. The basilica was finally completed in 1626 and is the world's second-largest church after Yamoussoukro in Côte d'Ivoire. Few are disappointed when they first enter the sumptuously decorated basilica beneath the vast dome designed by Michelangelo, the tallest dome in the world. A broad ramp followed by a spiral staircase around the inside of the dome leads from the roof to the cupola, from where there are stunning views over the city and of Bernini's colonnade. Designed by Carlo Maderno, the travertine façade features Corinthian columns and a balustrade with 13 statues.

MASS AND AUDIENCE WITH THE POPE

The Pope presides over Mass and addresses the crowds in St Peter's Square on Easter Day, Christmas Day and other major Christian festivals. General Audiences are usually held on Wednesdays (10–10.30am) in St Peter's Square (or in the Paul VI Audience Hall in bad weather). Get there very early if you want a chance of meeting or being blessed by the Pope. Tickets to Papal Masses and General Audiences are free. To apply for a ticket visit www.vatican.va/various/prefettura/index_en.html, and download the form. There is no email address and all applications must be faxed. See www.papalaudience.org/information for further details.

1538
Da Sangallo the Younger made director of works

1547
△ Michelangelo named chief architect of St Peter's

1564
Death of Michelangelo

1593
Dome completed

1606
Carlo Maderno extends basilica

1614
△ Maderno finishes the façade

1626
▽ New basilica of St Peter's consecrated

Inside St Peter's

The vast basilica's 187 m- (615 ft-) long, marble-encrusted interior contains 11 chapels, 45 altars, and a wealth of works of art. Some were salvaged from the original basilica and others commissioned from late Renaissance and Baroque artists, but much of the elaborate decoration is owed to Bernini's mid-17th-century work. The building's central focus is the Papal Altar beneath Bernini's great baldacchino, filling the space between the four piers which support the dome. From the basilica you can visit the Grottoes – where the late Pope John Paul II is buried, the Treasury and St Peter's Sacristy, or the terrace for panoramic views.

The 136.5 m- (448 ft-) high dome, designed by Michelangelo, was not completed in his lifetime.

The foot of St Peter, sculpted in the 13th century, has worn thin from the touch of pilgrims over the centuries.

The bronze doors from the old basilica were decorated with biblical reliefs by Filarete in 1439–45.

From this Library window, the pope blesses the faithful gathered in the piazza below.

Bernini's splendid bronze baldacchino stands above St Peter's tomb.

Michelangelo created the Pietà in 1499 when he was only 25.

The Papal Altar stands over the crypt where St Peter is reputedly buried.

← Michelangelo's famous marble sculpture, the *Pietà*

 HIDDEN GEM
Parco Adriano

Escape for some quiet to the green space nearest St Peter's in the small Parco Adriano, behind Castel Sant' Angelo. There is also an ice rink here in winter.

↑ The Papal Altar, with Bernini's
magnificent baldacchino
(sculpted canopy)

→ The monumental spiral staircase designed by Giuseppe Momo in 1932

2 🎨 🎧 🍴 🖥 🛍

VATICAN MUSEUMS

📍C3 🏛Città del Vaticano (entrance in Viale Vaticano) 🚌49 to entrance, 23, 81, 492, 990 Ⓜ Ottaviano San Pietro, Cipro 🕐9am–6pm Mon–Sat (last admission 4pm), 9am–2pm last Sun of month - free entry (last admission 12:30pm); low-cut or sleeveless clothing, shorts, mini-skirts and hats are not allowed 🔒religious and public hols 🌐museivaticani.va

Home to the Sistine Chapel and Raphael Rooms as well as to one of the world's most important art collections, the Vatican Museums are housed in palaces originally built for Renaissance popes Julius II, Innocent VIII and Sixtus IV. Most of the later additions were made in the 18th century, when priceless works of art accumulated by earlier popes were first put on show. Strung along 7 km (over 4 miles) of corridors, these incredible collections form one of the world's largest museums.

Among the Vatican's greatest treasures are its superlative Greek and Roman antiquities, together with the magnificent artifacts excavated from Egyptian and Etruscan tombs during the 19th century. Some of Italy's leading artists, such as Raphael, Michelangelo and Leonardo da Vinci, are represented in the Pinacoteca (art gallery) and parts of the former palaces, where they were employed by popes to decorate sumptuous apartments and galleries. The absolute highlights of this complex of museums are the Sistine Chapel and the Raphael Rooms, which should not be missed.

↑ The Cortile della Pigna, with a spherical bronze sculpture by Arnaldo Pomodoro

Book id: 9780241311875

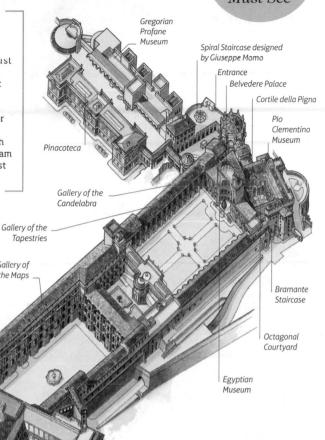

INSIDER TIP
Skipping the Queue

Book a ticket for the first slot of the day online. You can head straight to the Sistine Chapel, then make your way slowly backwards. For an extra fee, book a Breakfast Visit, which gives entry from 7:15am and includes breakfast and an audio guide.

Gregorian Profane Museum

Spiral Staircase designed by Giuseppe Momo

Entrance
Belvedere Palace

Cortile della Pigna

Pio Clementino Museum

Pinacoteca

Gallery of the Candelabra

Gallery of the Tapestries

Gallery of the Maps

Borgia Apartment

Sistine Chapel

Bramante Staircase

Octagonal Courtyard

Egyptian Museum

Raphael Rooms

↑ Hightlights of the Vatican Museums complex

Timeline

1503–13
Pope Julius II starts Classical sculpture collection

1508
▽ Raphael begins work on Rooms; Michelangelo begins painting the Sistine Chapel ceiling

1473
▲ Pope Sixtus IV builds Sistine Chapel

1541
Michelangelo's Last Judgment is unveiled

1655
▲ Bernini designs Royal Staircase

1758
Founding of Gregorian Profane Museum

1771
▲ Founding of Pio Clementino Museum

HIGHLIGHTS OF THE VATICAN COLLECTION

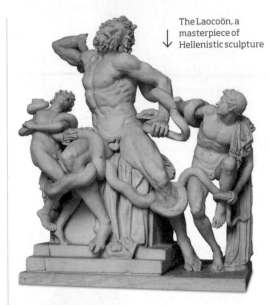

The Laocoön, a masterpiece of Hellenistic sculpture ↓

Pio Clementino Museum

The Vatican's prize pieces of Greek and Roman sculpture form the nucleus of this museum. Most of the works are Roman copies of lost ancient Greek originals, notably The Laocoön, a violenty contorted Hellenistic work showing the Trojan priest Laocoön and his two sons struggling to escape from the writhing coils of a sea serpent. Also here is the Apollo Belvedere, considered a paragon of physical perfection by Renaissance artists, and the muscular, contorted Belvedere Torso, whose influence can be seen on Michelangelo's *ignudi* (male nudes) in the Sistine Chapel. A menagerie of animal-themed sculptures and mosaics are gathered together in the Room of the Animals.

On either side of the museum are two staircases. The original spiral stairway designed by Bramante in 1505 is open only to special tours. The modern double helix stairway, commonly called the Snail or Momo Staircase, was designed by Giuseppe Momo in 1932. It was inspired by Bramante's original.

Did You Know?

Bramante designed the spiral staircase so that it could be ridden up on horseback.

Gregorian Profane Museum

In a space infused with natural light, the Gregorian Profane museum spans Classical antiquity and includes large marble fragments from the Athens Parthenon, Roman copies of Greek sculptures and a striking mosaic from the Baths of Caracalla portraying full-length figures of athletes.

Egyptian Museum

Ancient Egyptian cults and culture became extremely fashionable in Imperial Rome, and the collection here consists chiefly of Egyptian antiquities brought to the city to adorn buildings such as the Temple of Isis (which once stood near the Pantheon), Villa Adriana at Tivoli, and the Gardens of Sallust to the southeast of the Villa Borghese park. Also on display are painted mummy cases and tomb finds.

Galleries of Maps, Tapestries and Candelabra

A long corridor is divided into three contiguous galleries. The Gallery of the Maps displays 16th-century maps of Italy's regions and papal territories painted as if Rome were literally at the centre of the world, with areas south

←

Classical sculptures gallery in the Pio Clementino Museum

→
The Gallery of the Maps; detail of a map by Egnazio Danti (1580)

The modern double helix stairway, commonly called the Snail or Momo Staircase, was designed by Giuseppe Momo in 1932.

of Rome, such as Sicily and Calabria, appearing "upside down". The Gallery of the Tapestries has early 16th-century silk, gold and wool tapestries woven in Brussels to designs inspired by Raphael, while the Gallery of the Candelabra has immense marble candle holders.

Pinacoteca

There are some splendid Renaissance works from all over Italy in the 18 rooms of the art gallery. Don't miss the fragments of frescoes of apostles and angel musicians in Room IV by Melozzo da Forlì or the exquisitely romantic Madonna paintings by Filippo

Lippi and Fra Angelico in Room III. Room VI is devoted to the fabulous world of the Crivelli brothers, 16th-century Venetian artists who depicted fragile doll-like Madonnas enclosed within elaborate painted frames of fruit and flowers. Raphael has an entire room (VIII) devoted to his work, notably *The Transfiguration*, which includes a woman with red-gold hair, who is thought to have been his lover, La Fornarina. Next door in Room IX is a single, rare work by Leonardo da Vinci depicting St Jerome in the desert. There are also notable paintings by Titian, Crespi, Veronese and Caravaggio.

GALLERY GUIDE

The museum complex is vast: the Sistine Chapel is 20 to 30 minutes' walk from the entrance, so allow plenty of time. There is a strict one-way system. It is best to be selective or choose one of four colour-coded itineraries, which vary from 90 minutes to a five-hour marathon.

Michelangelo's
breathtaking
ceiling frescoes ↑

SISTINE CHAPEL: THE CEILING

Although Michelangelo had studied fresco-painting under Ghirlandaio, until 1508 he had mainly gained fame through his work as a sculptor. Nonetheless, Pope Julius II commissioned him to paint the ceiling of the Sistine Chapel, which would result in one of the greatest masterpieces of Western art.

At the time, the ceiling was painted simply blue, with golden stars. Michelangelo frescoed over the old ceiling painting between 1508 and 1512, working on specially designed scaffolding. He persuaded the pope to give him a free hand, and spent four years painting 366 figures from the Old and New Testaments, illustrating the bibilical stories of the Creation of the World, the Fall of Man and the Coming of Christ. *Ignudi* (male nudes) are depicted around these frescoes. In the spandrels surrounding the vault are sibyls, prophetesses from pagan mythology, which, in the Renaissance, were adopted by Christian artists as figures who could foresee the Coming of Christ. The central painting, *The Creation of Adam*, portraying God reaching down from a cloudy heaven to create Adam, is one of the most reproduced religious paintings of all time.

RESTORATION OF THE CEILING

From 1979 until 1994 a huge restoration programme was carried out. Five hundred years of soot, candle smoke and glue - along with breadcrumbs and retsina used by earlier restorers, and brush hairs and fingerprints left behind by Michelangelo - were removed. The faded, eggshell-cracked figures were discovered to have rose-petal skin, lustrous hair and to be wearing luscious strawberry-pink, lime-green, lemon and orange shot-silk robes. Critics were surprised that Michelangelo's palette was so bright.

The Last Judgment by Michelangelo, showing souls meeting the wrath of Christ

Hall of Constantine

The frescoes here, started in 1517, were executed mainly by Raphael's pupils and show the triumph of Christianity over paganism, focusing on key moments in the life of Emperor Constantine.

Room of Heliodorus

The theme here is divine intervention and includes *The Expulsion of Heliodorus from the Temple* and the dazzling *Liberation of St Peter*, in which an angel frees St Peter (a portrait of Julius II) from prison.

Room of the Segnatura

The frescoes here celebrate the Renaissance ideal – the ability of the intellect to discover the truth. The key work is *The School of Athens* in which Raphael painted leading Greek philosophers in a vaulted hall.

Room of the Fire in the Borgo

This celebrates a miracle in 847, when Pope Leo IV is said to have extinguished a fire in the quarter around the Vatican by making the sign of the cross.

SISTINE CHAPEL: THE WALLS

Wall Frescoes

The massive walls of the Sistine Chapel were frescoed by some of the finest artists of the 15th and 16th centuries. The twelve paintings by artists, including Perugino, Ghirlandaio, Botticelli and Signorelli, show parallel episodes from the lives of Moses and Christ. The decoration of the walls was completed between 1534 and 1541 by Michelangelo.

The Last Judgment

Twenty-four years after he had finished the Sistine ceiling, Michelangelo was commissioned by Pope Paul III Farnese to cover the altar wall of the chapel with a fresco of *The Last Judgment*. Michelangelo drew on Dante's *Inferno*. The painting is a bleak, harrowing work, showing the damned hurtling towards a putrid hell, the blessed being dragged up to heaven, and saints demanding vengeance for their martyrdoms, a theme chosen by the Pope

Did You Know?

Michelangelo's self-portrait is seen on the flayed skin held by St Bartholomew in *The Last Judgement*.

to warn Catholics to adhere to their faith in the turmoil of the Reformation.

RAPHAEL ROOMS

In 1508, Pope Julius II asked Bramante to recommend an artist to redecorate his private suite of four rooms. Bramante suggested a young artist named Raphael. The resulting frescoes swiftly established Raphael as one of the leading artists in Rome, putting him on a par with Michelangelo. Raphael and his pupils took over 16 years to fresco the rooms.

→
Detail of *The School of Athens*, with Plato and Aristotle in the centre

Hall of Constantine, a
celebration of the triumph of
Christianity over paganism

③ ⚔️ Ⓜ️ 🖥️ 🛍️

CASTEL SANT'ANGELO

📍**E4** 🏛️**Lungotevere Castello 50** 🚌**23, 40, 62 to Lungotevere Vaticano or 34, 49, 87, 280, 492, 926, 990 to Piazza Cavour** 🕐**9am-7:30pm daily (last adm: 6:30pm)** 🌐**castelsantangelo.beniculturali.it**

A massive brick cylinder rising from the banks of the Tiber, Castel Sant'Angelo began life in AD 139 as Emperor Hadrian's mausoleum. Since then it has served as a medieval citadel, a prison and as the residence of popes in times of political unrest.

The fortress takes its name from the vision that Pope Gregory the Great had of the Archangel Michael on this site. From the dank cells in the lower levels to the fine apartments of the Renaissance popes above, Castel Sant-Angelo is now a 58-room museum covering all aspects of the castle's history. Highlights include the Sala Paolina, decorated with illusionistic frescoes (1546–8) by Pellegrino Tibaldi and Perin del Vaga, and the armoury, which displays a wide range of weaponry of the times. The castle's terrace, scene of the last act of Puccini's opera *Tosca*, offers great views in every direction.

> The castle's terrace, scene of the last act of Puccini's opera *Tosca*, offers great views in every direction.

Timeline

271
Tomb is incorporated into Aurelian Wall and fortified

1527
Castle withstands siege during Sack of Rome

1870
▽ Castle used as barracks and military prison

AD 130
Hadrian begins family mausoleum

590
△ Legendary date of appearance of Archangel Michael above the castle

1542–9
Sala Paolina and apartments built for Pope Paul III

↑ Courtyard of Honour with stone cannon-balls, once the castle's ammunition store

↑ Sala Paolina, decorated with frescoes for Pope Paul III Farnese

PROTECTING THE POPE

The Vatican Corridor is an elevated 800-m (2,600-ft) passage that leads from the Vatican Palace to Castel Sant' Angelo. It was built in 1277 to provide an escape route when the pope was in danger. The pentagonal ramparts built around the castle during the 17th century improved its defences in times of siege.

← Castel Sant'Angelo and the bridge leading to it, adorned with statues by Bernini

EXPERIENCE MORE

 4

Porta Santo Spirito

📍 D5 🏛 Via dei Penitenzieri
🚌 23, 34, 46, 62, 64, 98, 870, 881, 982

This gate is situated at what was once the southern limit of the "Leonine City", the area enclosed within walls by Pope Leo IV as a defence against the Saracens, who had sacked Rome in AD 845. The walls measure 3 km (2 miles) in circumference. Work on the walls started in AD 846. Pope Leo supervised the huge army of labourers personally, and the job was completed in four years. He then consecrated his massive feat of construction.

Since the time of Pope Leo the walls have needed much reinforcement and repair. The gateway visible today at Porta Santo Spirito was built by the architect Antonio da Sangallo the Younger in 1543–4. It is framed by two huge bastions that were added in 1564 by Pope Pius IV Medici. Sadly, Sangallo's design for a monumental entrance to the Vatican was never completed; the principal columns come to an end somewhat abruptly in a modern covering of cement.

 5

Santo Spirito in Sassia

📍 D4 🏛 Via dei Penitenzieri 12 ☎ 06-687 9310 🚌 23, 34, 46, 62, 64, 98, 870, 881, 982 🕐 7:30am–noon & 3-6:30pm Mon-Sat, 9:30am-1pm & 3-6:30pm Sun

Built on the site of a church erected by King Ine of Wessex, who died in Rome in the 8th century, this church is the work of Antonio da Sangallo the Younger. It was rebuilt (1538–44) after the Sack of Rome left it in ruins in 1527. The façade was added under Pope Sixtus V (1585–90). The pretty bell tower is earlier, dating from the reign of Sixtus IV (1471–84).

 6

Hospital of Santo Spirito

📍 D5 🏛 Borgo Santo Spirito 2 🚌 23, 34, 46, 62, 64 Complex and chapel: 🕐 for events only (call 06-6835 2433)

The oldest hospital in Rome, this is reputed to have been founded as a result of a

↑ Interior of Santo Spirito in Sassia and detail of *Coronation of the Virgin Mary* by Nebbia

nightmare experienced by Pope Innocent III (1198–1216). In the dream, an angel showed him the bodies of Rome's unwanted babies dredged up from the River Tiber in fishing nets. As a result, the pope hastened to build a hospice for sick paupers. In 1475 the hospital was reorganized by Pope Sixtus IV to care for the poor pilgrims expected for the Holy Year. Sixtus's hospital was a radical building. Cloisters divided the different types of patients; one area is still reserved for orphans and their nurses.

In order to guarantee anonymity, unwanted infants were passed through a revolving barrel-like contraption called the *rota*, still visible to the left of the central entrance in Borgo Santo Spirito. Martin Luther, who visited

The richly adorned nave of the church of Santo Spirito in Sassia

in 1511, was shocked by the number of abandoned children he saw, believing them to be "the sons of the pope himself".

In the centre, under the hospital's conspicuous drum, is an octagonal chapel, where mass was said for patients. This room can be visited by prior arrangement, while the rest of the building still functions as a hospital.

---

❼

Palazzo del Commendatore

 D4 🏛 Borgo Santo Spirito 3 📞 06-6835 2353 🚌 23, 34, 46, 62, 64 🕐 courtyard open to public

As director of the Hospital of Santo Spirito, the Commendatore not only oversaw the running of the hospital, he was also responsible for its estates and revenues. This important post was originally given to members of the pope's family.

The palazzo, built next door to the hospital, has a spacious 16th-century frescoed loggia appropriate to the dignity and sobriety of its owners. The frescoes represent the story of the founding of the Hospital of Santo Spirito. To the left of the entrance is the Spezieria, or Pharmacy. This still has the wheel used for grinding the bark of the cinchona tree to produce the drug quinine, first introduced here in 1632 by Jesuits from Peru as a cure for malaria.

Above the courtyard is a splendid clock (1827). The dial is divided into six; it

→

Detail of a ceiling fresco by Pinturicchio in the Palazzo dei Penitenzieri

was not until 1846 that the familiar division of the day into two periods of 12 hours was introduced in Rome by Pope Pius IX.

---

❽

Palazzo dei Convertendi

📍 D4 🏛 Via della Conciliazione 43 🚌 23, 34, 62, 64 🕐 to the public

With the building of Via della Conciliazione in the 1930s, Palazzo dei Convertendi was taken down and later moved to this new site nearby. The house, partly attributed to the architect Bramante, is where the artist Raphael died in 1520.

---

❾

Palazzo dei Penitenzieri

📍 D4 🏛 Via della Conciliazione 33 📞 / fax 06-6989 2930 🚌 23, 34, 62, 64 🕐 2:30-5pm Mon-Fri by appt only (fax) for groups

The palazzo owes its name to the fact that the place was once home to the confessors (penitenzieri) of St Peter's. Now partly housing the Hotel

Columbus, it was originally built by Cardinal Domenico della Rovere in 1480. The palazzo still bears the family's coat of arms, the oak tree (rovere means "oak"), on its graceful courtyard well-head. On the cardinal's death, the palazzo was acquired by Cardinal Francesco Alidosi, Pope Julius II della Rovere's favourite. Suspected of treason, the cardinal was murdered in 1511 by the pope's nephew, the Duke of Urbino, who took over the palazzo. A few of the rooms of the palazzo still contain beautiful frescoes.

SHOP

Via Cola di Rienzo

Less crowded than Via del Corso, the city's main commercial thoroughfare, Rome's best choice for mid-range clothing is Via Cola di Rienzo in the Prati district. Mega-department store COIN Excelsior at No. 173 is a good place to start.

⑩ Santa Maria in Traspontina

📍 D4 📍 Via della Conciliazione 14 📞 06-6880 6451 🚌 23, 34, 62, 64 🕐 6:30am–noon & 4-7:15pm Mon-Sat, 7:30am-1pm Sun

The church occupies the site of an ancient Roman pyramid, believed in the Middle Ages to have been the Tomb of Romulus. The pyramid was destroyed by Pope Alexander VI Borgia, but representations of it survive in the bronze doors at the entrance to St Peter's and in a Giotto triptych housed in the Vatican Pinacoteca (p291).

The present church was begun in 1566 to replace an earlier one which had been in the line of fire of the cannons defending Castel Sant'Angelo during the Sack of Rome in 1527. The papal artillery officers therefore insisted that the dome of the new church should be as low as possible, so it was built without a supporting drum. The first chapel to the right is dedicated to the gunners' patron saint, Santa Barbara, and is decorated with warlike motifs. In the third chapel on the left are two columns, popularly thought to be the ones which SS Peter and Paul were bound to before going to their martyrdom nearby.

⑪ The Borgo

📍 D4 🚌 23, 34, 40, 62

The Borgo's name derives from the German *burg*, meaning "town". Rome's Borgo is where the first pilgrims to St Peter's were housed in hostels and hospices, often for quite lengthy periods. The first of these foreign colonies, called "schools", was founded in AD 725 by a Saxon, King Ine of Wessex, who wished to live a life of penance and to be buried near the Tomb of St Peter. These days hotels and hostels have made the Borgo a colony of inter-national pilgrims once again. Much of the area's character was lost after redevelopment

Did You Know?

Raphael and Michelangelo count among the Borgo area's most famous past residents.

Street lined with shops and restaurants in the historic Borgo area near the Vatican ↓

← The Palazzo di Giustizia, with the Ponte Umberto crossing the Tiber in the foreground

in the 1930s, but it is still enjoyable to stroll the old narrow streets on either side of Via della Conciliazione.

⑫

Palazzo Torlonia

📍D4 🏠Via della Conciliazione 30 🚌23, 34, 40, 62, 64 🚪to the public

The pretty palazzo was built in the late 15th century by the wealthy Cardinal Adriano Castellesi, in a style closely resembling Palazzo della Cancelleria (p168). The cardinal was a much-travelled rogue, who collected vast revenues from the bishopric of Bath and Wells which he was given by his friend King Henry VII of England. In return, he gave Henry his palazzo for use as the seat of the English ambassador to the Holy See. Castellesi was finally stripped of his cardinalate by Pope Leo X Medici and disappeared from history.

Since then the palazzo has had many owners and tenants. In the 17th century it was rented for a time by Queen Christina of Sweden. The Torlonia family, who acquired the building in 1820, owed its fortune to the financial genius of shopkeeper-turned-banker Giovanni Torlonia. He lent money to the impoverished Roman nobility and bought up their property during the Napoleonic Wars.

⑬

Palazzo di Giustizia

📍F4 🏠Piazza Cavour 🚌34, 49, 70, 87, 186, 280, 492, 913, 926, 990 🚪to the public

The monumental Palazzo di Giustizia (Palace of Justice) was built between 1889 and 1910 to house the national law courts. Its riverside façade is crowned with a bronze chariot and fronted by giant statues of the great men of Italian law.

The building was supposed to embody the new order replacing the injustices of papal rule, but it has never endeared itself to the Romans. It was soon dubbed the Palazzaccio (roughly, "the ugly old palazzo") both for its appearance and for the nature of its business. By the 1970s the building was collapsing under its own weight, but it has since been restored.

EAT & DRINK

Despite its reputation as something of a culinary wasteland, the Vatican area has a number of good places to enjoy a well-earned plate of food and a restorative glass of wine after visiting the museums.

Dal Toscano
📍C3 🏠Via Germanico 58 🌐ristorantedal toscano.it

€€€

Franchi
📍D3 🏠Via Cola di Rienzo 200 📞06-686 5564

€€€

Il Simposio
📍E3 🏠Piazza Cavour 16 🌐ilsimposioroma.it

€€€

A SHORT WALK

A TOUR OF THE VATICAN

Distance 1 km (0.6 mile) **Nearest metro**
Cipro, Ottaviano San Pietro **Time** 15 minutes

The Vatican, a centre of power for Catholics all over the world and a sovereign state since February 1929, is ruled by the pope. About 1,000 people live here, staffing the Vatican's facilities. These include a post office and shops; Vatican radio, broadcasting to the world in over 20 languages; a daily newspaper (*L'Osservatore Romano*); Vatican offices and a publishing house.

The Grotto of Lourdes is a replica of the grotto in the southwest of France, where in 1858 the Virgin appeared to St Bernadette.

Papal heliport

Radio Vatican is broadcast from this tower, part of the Leonine Wall built in 847.

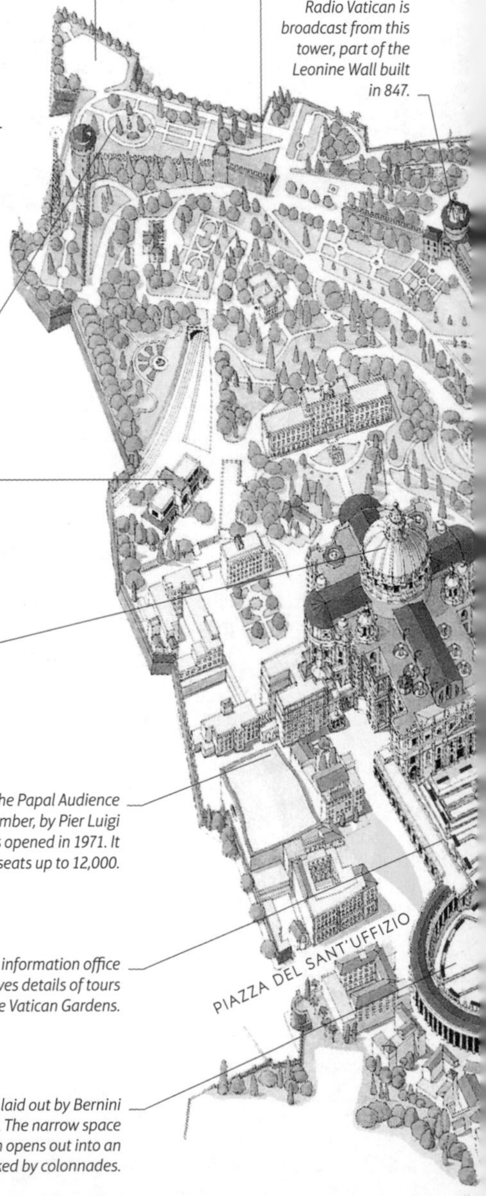

The Madonna of Guadalupe shows the miraculous image of the Madonna which appeared on the cloak of an indigenous Mexican in 1531.

The Vatican Railway Station, opened in 1930, connects with the line from Rome to Viterbo, but is now used only for freight.

The Chapel of St Peter is in the Grottoes under St Peter's basilica. The rich marble decoration was added by Clement VIII at the end of the 16th century (p284).

The Papal Audience Chamber, by Pier Luigi Nervi, was opened in 1971. It seats up to 12,000.

Did You Know?

If you visit every museum in the Vatican Museum complex you will have walked over 7 km (4 miles)

The information office gives details of tours of the Vatican Gardens.

PIAZZA DEL SANT'UFFIZIO

Piazza San Pietro was laid out by Bernini between 1656 and 1667. The narrow space in front of the church opens out into an enormous ellipse flanked by colonnades.

→

The elaborate Eagle Fountain in the Vatican Gardens

Locator Map
For more detail see pp282-3

The Eagle Fountain was built to celebrate the arrival of water from the Acqua Paola aqueduct at the Vatican. The eagle is the Borghese crest.

The Casina of Pius IV is a delightful summerhouse in the Vatican Gardens built by Pirro Ligorio in the mid-16th century.

The Cortile della Pigna is mostly the work of Bramante. The niche for the pine cone, once a Roman fountain, was added by Pirro Ligorio in 1562.

0 metres 150
0 yards 150

↗ N

Entrance to Vatican Museums

● FINISH

Raphael's Madonna of Foligno (1513) is just one of the many Renaissance masterpieces in the Vatican Museums (p288).

The Galleon Fountain is a perfect scale model of a 17th-century ship in lead, brass and copper. It was made by a Flemish artist for Pope Paul V.

VIA DI PORTA ANGELICA

PIAZZA SAN PIETRO

PIAZZA PIO XII

● START

The obelisk was erected here in 1586 with the help of 150 horses and 47 winches.

→

Piazza San Pietro and obelisk in front of St Peter's basilica

VIA VENETO

In Imperial Rome, this was a suburb where rich families owned luxurious villas and gardens. Ruins from this era can be seen in the excavations in Piazza Sallustio, named after the most extensive gardens in the area, the Horti Sallustiani. After the Sack of Rome in the 5th century, the area reverted to open countryside. Not until the 17th century did it recover its lost splendour, with the building of Palazzo Barberini and the now-vanished Villa Ludovisi. When Rome became capital of Italy in 1870, the Ludovisi sold their land for development. They kept a plot for a new house, but tax on the profits from the sale was so high, they had to sell that too. By 1900, Via Veneto had become a street of smart grand hotels and cafés. It featured prominently in Fellini's 1960 film *La Dolce Vita*, a scathing satire on the lives of film stars and the idle rich, but since then has lost its position as the meeting place of the famous.

VIA VENETO

Experience
1. Via Veneto
2. Palazzo Barberini
3. Santa Maria della Concezione and Capuchin Crypt
4. Fontana delle Api
5. Fontana del Tritone
6. Santa Susanna
7. Santa Maria della Vittoria

Drink
1. Il Giardino Hotel Eden
2. Doney Café

PIAZZA DI SPAGNA AND VILLA BORGHESE
p134

Villa Borghese

VILLA MEDICI

CAMPO MARZIO

M Spagna

PIAZZA DI SPAGNA

Scalinata della Trinità dei Monti

Museo Keats-Shelley

PIAZZA MIGNANELLI

PORTA PINCIANA

LARGO FEDERICO FELLINI

Veneto/Sardegna

Casino dell'Aurora

Palazzo Margherita

Via Veneto

Santa Maria della Concezione and Capuchin Cryt

Fontana delle Api

Barberini M

PIAZZA BARBERINI

Fontana del Tritone

Palazzo Barberini

Galleria Nazionale di Arte Antica

TREVI

Accademia di San Luca

Fontana di Trevi

Giardini del Quirinale

Palazzo del Quirinale

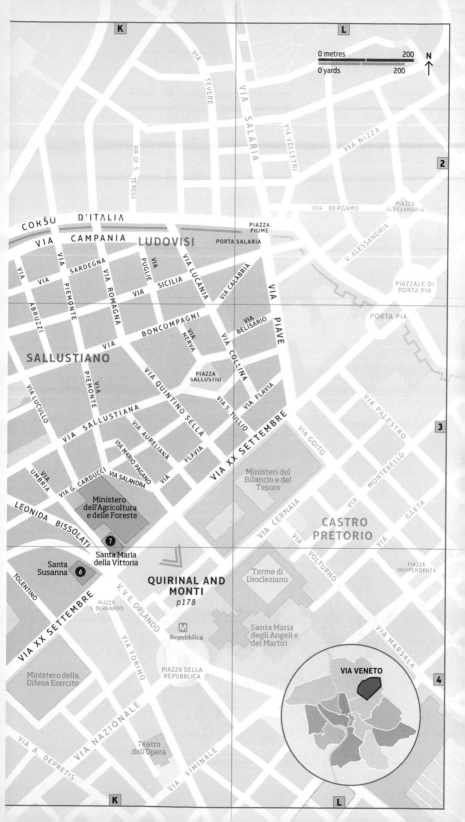

EXPERIENCE

❶ Via Veneto

QJ3 **🚌**52, 53, 63, 80, 116, 119, 160 and many routes to Piazza Barberini
ⓂBarberini

Via Veneto descends in a lazy curve from the Porta Pinciana to Piazza Barberini, lined in its upper reaches with exuberant late 19th-century hotels and canopied pavement cafés. It was laid out in 1879 over a large estate sold by the Ludovisi family in the great building boom of Rome's first years as capital of Italy. Palazzo Margherita, intended to be the new Ludovisi family palazzo, was completed in 1890. It now houses the American embassy.

In the 1960s this was the most glamorous street in Rome, its cafés patronized by film stars and plagued by paparazzi. Most of the people drinking in the cafés today are tourists, as film stars now seem to prefer the bohemian atmosphere of Trastevere or the luxury of the Parioli neighbourhood.

↑ Detail of Pietro da Cortona's ceiling fresco in Palazzo Barberini

❷   Palazzo Barberini

QJ4 **🏛**Via delle Quattro Fontane 13 **🚌**52, 53, 61, 62, 63, 80, 116, 492, 590
ⓂBarberini **🕒**8:30am-7pm Tue-Sun (last adm: 6pm)
📅1 Jan, 25 Dec **W**barberini corsini.org

When Maffeo Barberini became Pope Urban VIII in 1623 he planned a grand palace for his family on the fringes of the city. Architect Carlo Maderno designed it as a rural villa, with wings into the surrounding gardens. Maderno died in 1629 and Bernini took over, assisted by Borromini.

The pediments on some of the top-floor windows, and the oval staircase inside, are almost certainly by Borromini.

The most striking of the sumptuous rooms is the Gran Salone, with an illusionistic ceiling fresco by Pietro da Cortona. The palazzo also houses paintings from the 13th to the 16th centuries, with notable works by Filippo Lippi, El Greco and Caravaggio, as well as Guido Reni's *Beatrice Cenci*, the young woman executed for planning her father's murder *(p173)*, and *La Fornarina*, traditionally thought to be a portrait of Raphael's mistress *(p262)*, although not necessarily painted by him.

DRINK

Il Giardino Hotel Eden
A historic bar, revamped in 2017, the Eden's rooftop area has vast windows that offer stunning views of the city – to be enjoyed with an expertly mixed Negroni in hand. Service is top-notch.

QJ3 **🏛**Via Ludovisi 49
Wdorchester collection.com

Doney Café
In the heart of Via Veneto, Doney re-creates *Dolce Vita* glamour with vast chandeliers and retro furnishings. Come at aperitivo time for a cocktail and a spot of people-watching. There's a pricey restaurant, too.

QJ3 **🏛**Via Veneto 125
Wrestaurantdoney.com

Elegant Via Veneto, lined with numerous chic hotels, cafés and shops ↑

↑ Bernini's playful Fontana del Tritone in Piazza Barberini

3

Santa Maria della Concezione and Capuchin Crypt

📍 J3 🏛 Via Veneto 27 🚌 52, 53, 61, 62, 63, 80, 116, 119 Ⓜ Barberini

Pope Urban VIII's brother, Antonio Barberini was a cardinal and a Capuchin friar. In 1626 he founded this plain church at what is now the foot of the Via Veneto. When he died he was buried not, like most cardinals, in a grand marble sarcophagus, but below a simple flagstone near the altar, with the bleak epitaph in Latin: "Here lies dust, ashes, nothing".

The grim reality of death is illustrated even more graphically in the **Capuchin Crypt** beneath the church, where generations of Capuchin friars decorated the walls of the five vaulted chapels with the bones and skulls of their departed brethren. In all, some 4,000 skeletons were used over about 100 years to create this macabre *memento mori* started in the late 17th century. There are also some complete skeletons, including one of a Barberini princess who died as a child. At the exit, a Latin inscription reads: "What you are, we used to be. What we are, you will be."

Capuchin Crypt

⊘ 🕐 9am–1pm & 3–6pm daily 🚫 some religious holidays 🌐 cappucciniviaveneto.it

4

Fontana delle Api

📍 J4 🏛 Piazza Barberini 🚌 52, 53, 61, 62, 63, 80, 116, 119 Ⓜ Barberini

The fountain of the bees (*api*, symbol of the Barberini family) is one of Bernini's more modest works. Tucked away in a corner of Piazza Barberini, it is quite easy to miss. Dating from 1644, it pays homage to Pope Urban VIII Barberini, and features rather crab-like bees which appear to be sipping the water as it dribbles down into the basin.

5

Fontana del Tritone

📍 J4 🏛 Piazza Barberini 🚌 52, 53, 61, 62, 63, 80, 116, 119 Ⓜ Barberini

In the centre of busy Piazza Barberini is one of Bernini's liveliest creations, the Triton Fountain. It was created for Pope Urban VIII Barberini in 1642, shortly after the completion of his palace on the ridge above. Acrobatic dolphins stand on their heads, twisting their tails together to support a huge scallop shell on which the sea god Triton kneels, blowing a spindly column of water up into the air through a conch shell.

6

Santa Susanna

📍 K4 🏛 Via XX Settembre 14 🚌 60, 61, 62, 492, 910 Ⓜ Repubblica 🚫 for restoration

Santa Susanna's most striking feature is its vigorous Baroque façade by Carlo Maderno, finished in 1603. Christians have worshipped on the site since at least the 4th century. In the nave, there are four huge frescoes by Baldassarre Croce (1558–1628), painted to resemble tapestries. These depict scenes from the life of Susanna, an obscure Roman saint martyred here, and the rather better-known life of the Old Testament Susanna, who was spotted bathing in her husband's garden by two lecherous judges.

Santa Susanna is normally the Catholic church for Americans in Rome. It is closed for restoration until further notice, so the American church now meets at St Patrick's.

7

Santa Maria della Vittoria

📍 K3 🏛 Via XX Settembre 17 ☎ 06-4274 0571 🚌 60, 61, 62, 492, 910 Ⓜ Repubblica 🕐 8:30am–noon & 3:30–6pm daily

This intimate Baroque church has a lavishly decorated candlelit interior. It contains one of Bernini's most ambitious sculptural works, *Ecstasy of St Teresa* (1646), the centrepiece of the Cornaro Chapel, built to resemble a miniature theatre. It even has an audience: sculptures of the chapel's benefactor, Cardinal Federico Cornaro, and his ancestors sit in boxes, as if watching the scene in front of them.

Visitors may be shocked or thrilled by the apparently physical nature of St Teresa's ecstasy. She lies on a cloud, her mouth half open and her eyelids closed, with rippling drapery covering her body. Looking over her with a smile, which from different angles can appear either tender or cruel, is a curly-haired angel holding an arrow with which he is about to pierce the saint's body for a second time. The marble figures are framed and illuminated by rays of divine light materialized in bronze.

A SHORT WALK
VIA VENETO

Distance 2 km (1.2 miles) **Nearest metro** Barberini
Time 30 minutes

The streets around Via Veneto, though within the walls of ancient Rome, contain little dating from before the unification of Italy in 1861. With its hotels, restaurants, bars and travel agencies, the area is the centre of 21st-century tourism in the way that Piazza di Spagna was the hub of the tourist trade in the Rome of the 18th-century Grand Tour. However, glimpses of the old city can be seen among the modern streets. These include Santa Maria della Concezione, the church of the Capuchin friars, whose convent once stood in its own gardens. In the 17th century Palazzo Barberini was built here for the powerful papal family. Bernini's Fontana del Tritone and Fontana delle Api have stood in Piazza Barberini since it was the meeting place of cart tracks entering the city from surrounding vineyards.

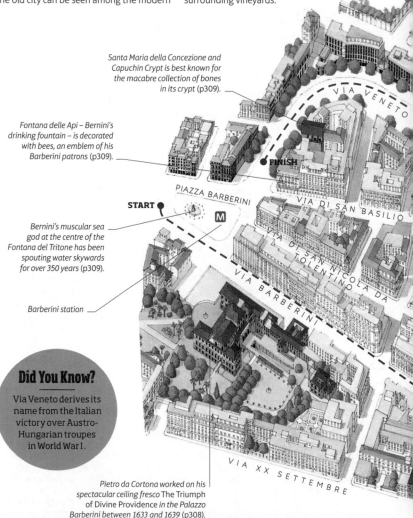

Santa Maria della Concezione and Capuchin Crypt is best known for the macabre collection of bones in its crypt (p309).

Fontana delle Api – Bernini's drinking fountain – is decorated with bees, an emblem of his Barberini patrons (p309).

FINISH

VIA VENETO

VIA DI SAN BASILIO

PIAZZA BARBERINI

START

M

VIA DI SAN NICOLA DA TOLENTINO

Bernini's muscular sea god at the centre of the Fontana del Tritone has been spouting water skywards for over 350 years (p309).

VIA BARBERINI

Barberini station

Did You Know?

Via Veneto derives its name from the Italian victory over Austro-Hungarian troupes in World War I.

VIA XX SETTEMBRE

Pietro da Cortona worked on his spectacular ceiling fresco The Triumph of Divine Providence in the Palazzo Barberini between 1633 and 1639 (p308).

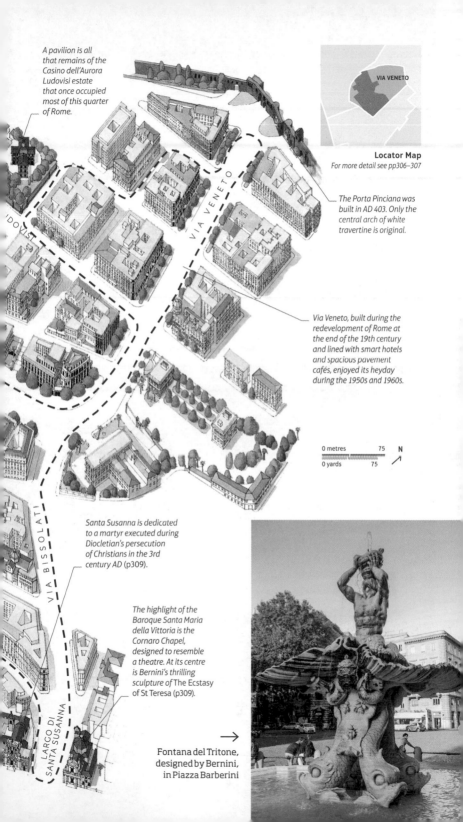

A pavilion is all that remains of the Casino dell'Aurora Ludovisi estate that once occupied most of this quarter of Rome.

VIA VENETO

The Porta Pinciana was built in AD 403. Only the central arch of white travertine is original.

Via Veneto, built during the redevelopment of Rome at the end of the 19th century and lined with smart hotels and spacious pavement cafés, enjoyed its heyday during the 1950s and 1960s.

0 metres   75

0 yards   75

N

Santa Susanna is dedicated to a martyr executed during Diocletian's persecution of Christians in the 3rd century AD (p309).

The highlight of the Baroque Santa Maria della Vittoria is the Cornaro Chapel, designed to resemble a theatre. At its centre is Bernini's thrilling sculpture of The Ecstasy of St Teresa *(p309).*

→ Fontana del Tritone, designed by Bernini, in Piazza Barberini

BEYOND
THE CENTRE

The more inquisitive visitor to Rome may wish to try a few excursions to the large parks and the catacombs on the Via Appia Antica on the outskirts of the city. With a day to spare, you can explore the villas of Tivoli and the ruins of the ancient Roman port of Ostia. More modern sights include the EUR suburb, built in the Fascist era, and the Resistance memorial at the Fosse Ardeatine.

Must See

❶ Ostia Antica

Experience More

❷ MAXXI (National Museum of 21st-Century Art)
❸ Audiorium Parco della Musica
❹ Villa Ada
❺ Catacombs of Priscilla
❻ Quartiere Coppedè
❼ Santa Costanza
❽ MACRO (Museo d'Arte Contemporanea di Roma)
❾ Sant'Agnese fuori le Mura
❿ Via Appia Antica
⓫ Catacombs of San Callisto
⓬ Catacombs of San Sebastiano
⓭ Catacombs of Domitilla
⓮ Fosse Ardeatine
⓯ Tomb of Cecilia Metella
⓰ EUR
⓱ Cinecittà Si Mostra
⓲ Foro Italico
⓳ Centrale Montemartini
⓴ San Paolo fuori le Mura
㉑ Villa Doria Pamphilj
㉒ Tivoli
㉓ Villa d'Este
㉔ Hadrian's Villa
㉕ Villa Gregoriana

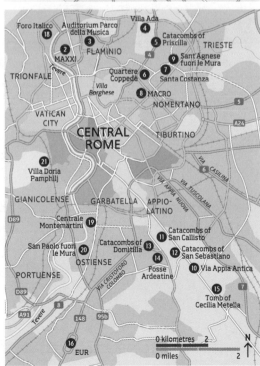

MAXXI, the national museum of contemporary art

❶ ⌗ ▭ 🛍

OSTIA ANTICA

📍 Viale dei Romagnoli 717. Site is 25 km (16 miles) southwest of Rome Ⓜ Piramide, then train from Porta San Paolo station
🕐 8:30am–1 hour before sunset 🌐 ostiaantica.beniculturali.it

With its ivy- and creeper-covered walls rising from long grass, scattered in spring with wild flowers, the remains of the ancient Roman port of Ostia are among the most extensive in Italy.

Ostia was originally built on the coast, but over the centuries silt from the Tiber has shifted the coastline further west, and the site is now several kilometres from the sea. In Republican times Ostia was Rome's main commercial port and a military base protecting the mouth of the Tiber. It continued to flourish through Imperial times until the 4th century, when the harbour began to silt up, covering the old city with sand and mud. The ruins are remarkably well preserved and give a good picture of life under the Roman Empire. People of all social classes and from all over the Mediterranean lived and worked here.

The main road through the town, the Decumanus Maximus, would have been filled with hurrying slaves and citizens, avoiding the jostling carriages and cars, while tradesmen pursued their business under the porticoes. The public buildings included bathhouses, such as the Baths of the Cisarrii (wagoners), the theatre, the Forum and temples.

↑ Mosaic of an elephant outside a shop of a North African merchant on Piazzale delle Corporazioni. The square was surrounded by businesses, each with a mosaic outside depicting a trade.

INSIDER TIP
Picnic

Still wild in parts, Ostia Antica is a lovely, relaxing site for a picnic accompanied by some ancient history. For picnic ingredients, shop at a great deli, Volpetti (Via Marmorata 47A; Tel 06-574 2352), near the Porta San Paolo station.

Ruins of shops, houses and apartment blocks
↓ at Ostia Antica

↑ A carved stone mask displayed outside the theatre. Beneath the brick arches supporting the tiers of seats were taverns and shops.

THERMOPOLIUM OF VIA DIANA

The Thermopolium was a bar that served wine and hot snacks. The ruins retain an L-shaped counter and a beautiful fresco showing carrots, onions and chickpeas.

EXPERIENCE MORE

② MAXXI (National Museum of 21st Century Arts)

⌂ Via Guido Reni 4A 🚌53, 217, 225, 910 🚇2 🕐11am–7pm Tue–Sun (to 10pm Sat) 🚫1 May, 25 Dec 🌐fondazionemaxxi.it

Along with the nearby Parco della Musica, MAXXI, the National Museum of 21st Century Arts, has put Rome on the contemporary arts map. Completed in 2009, it is located in a stunning building designed by the late architect Zaha Hadid. The museum showcases emerging Italian and international artists. An impressive amount of space is also given over to architecture. Some of the biggest names represented include Renzo Piano, Gilbert and George, and Paolo Portoghesi.

③ Auditorium Parco della Musica

⌂ Viale Pietro de Coubertin 30 🚇2 🕐11:30am–4:30pm 🌐auditorium.com

Designed by Renzo Piano and opened in 2002, the Auditorium Parco della Musica is not merely a beautiful concert venue but a multifunctional space with an outdoor amphitheatre, shops, restaurants and play area – and an ice rink in winter, a popular leisure space with Romans. Renzo Piano studied acoustics with contemporary composers Luciano Berio and Luigi Nono; guided tours of the auditoriums reveal how he applied the technology of musical instruments to architecture with the extensive use of complex geometries and fine wood.

④ Villa Ada

⌂ Via Salaria 265 🚌14 🚇3, 19

Rome's second-largest park (after Villa Doria Pamphilj, p325), Villa Ada cuts a green swathe through the north of Rome and features landscaped gardens, ornamental lakes and umbrella-pine-shaded lawns that lead the way to wilder wooded hills.

A royal hunting ground and residence belonging to the House of Savoy, the properties were sold in 1878 to a Swiss count who named them after his wife. The villa is now the Egyptian embassy. From late June to August, Villa

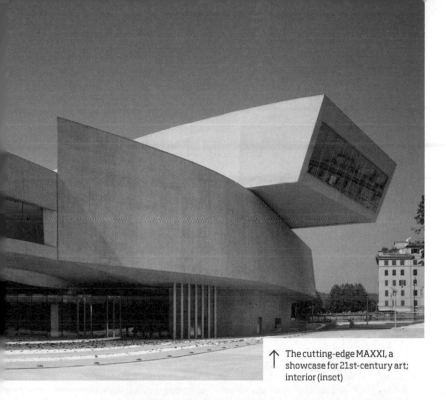

↑ The cutting-edge MAXXI, a showcase for 21st-century art; interior (inset)

Ada hosts the free world-music festival Roma Incontra il Mondo, with concerts staged on the lakeside.

⑤ Catacombs of Priscilla

🏛 Via Salaria 🚌 63, 92, 310
🕐 9am-noon & 2-5pm
Tue-Sun 🌐 catacombe priscilla.com

Tunnelling for 15 km (9 miles) on three different levels below the extensive estate of an aristocratic 1st-century AD Roman woman known only as Priscilla, these catacombs – rarely visited by tourists – are run by a small community of Benedictine sisters. They hold the tombs of more than 40,000 Christians. The sisters give personal guided tours, during which they point out tiny, telling details. The tours take in both the humble burial places of the poor and the more elaborate frescoed tombs of the wealthy. The

catacombs also contain the oldest-known image of the Madonna and Child, dating back to the late 1st or early 2nd century AD.

Quartiere Coppedè

🏛 Between Via Salaria and Via Tagliamento
🚌 3, 52, 53, 217, 360, 910, 926 🚊 3, 19

The Coppedè neighbourhood was created by Art Nouveau Florentine architect Gino Coppedè between 1913 and 1927 as a prestigious residential enclave for wealthy Ligurian bankers. Coppedè's imagination was given free rein, and the result is an architectural fantasia, a fairytale world that features Tuscan turrets, Venetian pinnacles, Moorish arches, Gothic gargoyles, medieval frescoes and gingerbread-house aesthetics. Start your visit on Via Tagliamento,

entering via a mighty archway hung with an elaborate wrought-iron lamp. This emerges onto a piazza dominated by the Fontana delle Rane, which is adorned with a dozen stone frogs. In all, there are around 40 villas and apartment buildings around the square, the highlight of which is the Villini delle Fate, a complex of three villas, embellished with everything from the signs of the zodiac and a lion of St Mark to falconers and Franciscan monks.

 HIDDEN GEM
Whimsical Architecture

Truly unique and unlike any other architectural style, the quirky Quartiere Coppedè provides quite a contrast to the classic Renaissance and Baroque styles in most of the rest of the city.

Auditorium Parco della Musica, designed by Renzo Piano

⑦

Santa Costanza

⌂ Via Nomentana 349
☎ 06-8620 5456 🚌 36, 60, 84, 90 Ⓜ S. Agnese Annibaliano ⏰ 9am-noon & 3-6pm daily

The round church of Santa Costanza was first built as a mausoleum for Emperor Constantine's daughters, Constantia and Helena, in the early 4th century. The dome and its drum are supported by a circular arcade resting on 12 magnificent pairs of granite columns. The ambulatory that runs around the outside of the central arcade has a barrel-vaulted ceiling decorated with wonderful 4th-century mosaics of flora and fauna and charming scenes of a Roman grape harvest. In a niche on the far side of the church from the entrance is a replica of Constantia's ornately carved porphyry sarcophagus. The original was moved to the Vatican Museums in 1790.

Constantia was described by the historian Marcellinus as fury incarnate and guilty of goading her equally unpleasant husband Hannibalianus to violence. Her canonization was probably the result of some confusion with a saintly nun of the same name.

⑧

Museo d'Arte Contemporanea di Roma (MACRO)

⌂ Via Nizza 138 🚌 36, 60, 90 Check website for opening times 🌐 museomacro.it

The historic Peroni beer factory is home to the MACRO gallery of contemporary art, with cutting-edge architecture featuring coloured lights, glass and exposed steel. As well as a permanent collection of late 20th-century art, with works by artists such as Carla Accardi and Mario Schifano, there are frequent interesting temporary exhibitions showcasing the latest on the local and national scene. Free screenings of oddball, experimental and arthouse short films are held in a niche just off the atrium.

> You can still walk along the Via Appia Antica in the footsteps of many ancient Romans.

⑨

Sant'Agnese fuori le Mura

⌂ Via Nomentana 349 ☎ 06-8620 5456 🚌 36, 60, 84, 90 Ⓜ S. Agnese Annibaliano ⏰ 8am-7pm Mon-Sat, between services Sun & public hols

The church of Sant'Agnese stands among a group of early Christian buildings which includes the ruins of a covered cemetery, some extensive **catacombs** and the crypt where the 13-year-old martyr St Agnes was buried in AD 304. Agnes was exposed naked by order of Emperor Diocletian, furious that she should have rejected the advances of a young man at his court, but her hair miraculously grew to protect her modesty.

The interior of Rome's contemporary art museum, MACRO, on Via Nizza ↑

Though considerably altered over the centuries, the form and much of the structure of the 4th-century basilica remain intact. In the 7th-century apse mosaic St Agnes appears as a bejewelled Byzantine empress. According to tradition she appeared like this eight days after her death, holding a white lamb. Every year on 21 January two lambs are blessed on the church altar and a vestment called the *pallium* is woven from their wool. Every newly appointed archbishop is sent a *pallium* by the pope.

Catacombs
9am–noon & 3–5pm daily ⊘Nov

10
Via Appia Antica
🚌118, 218 🌐parcoappia antica.it

The first part of the Via Appia was built in 312 BC by the Censor Appius Claudius Caecus. When it was extended to the ports of Benevento, Taranto and Brindisi in 190 BC, the road became Rome's link with its empire in the East. It was the route taken by the funeral processions of the dictator Sulla (78 BC) and Emperor Augustus (AD 14) and it was along this road that St Paul was led as a prisoner to Rome in AD 56. Abandoned in the Middle Ages, the road was restored by Pope Pius IV in the mid-16th century. It is lined with ruined family tombs and collective burial places. Beneath the fields on each side is a vast maze of catacombs. You can still walk along the Via Appia Antica in the footsteps of many ancient Romans. Today the road starts at Porta San Sebastiano (p236). Major Christian sights include the church of Domine Quo Vadis, built where St Peter is said to have met Christ while fleeing from Rome, and the Catacombs of San Callisto and San Sebastiano. The tombs

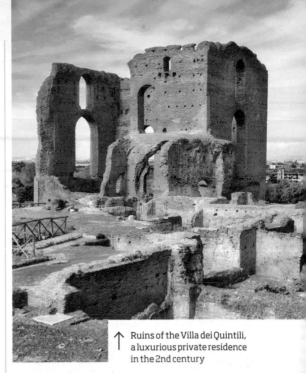

↑ Ruins of the Villa dei Quintili, a luxurious private residence in the 2nd century

lining the road include those of Cecilia Metella (p323) and Romulus (son of Emperor Maxentius) who died in 309. The remains of an ancient sumptuous private residence and baths, **Villa dei Quintili**, are nearby. It has some impressive mosaic floors, and the guided tour of the archaeological site includes entry to a small museum.

Villa dei Quintili
Via Appia Nuova 1092 📞06-3996 7700 🕐Tue–Sun.

11
Catacombs of San Callisto
Via Appia Antica 126 🚌118, 218 🕐9am–noon & 2–5pm Thu–Tue ⊘1 Jan, late Jan–late Feb, Easter Sun & 25 Dec 🌐catacombe. roma.it

In burying their dead in underground cemeteries outside the city walls, the early Christians were simply obeying the laws of the time rather than doing so because of persecution. So many saints were buried in the various catacombs that they went on to become shrines and places of pilgrimage.

The vast Catacombs of San Callisto are laid out over four different levels, and only certain parts may be explored by visitors. The rooms and connecting passageways are hewn out of volcanic tufa. The dead were placed in niches known as *loculi*, which were able to hold two or three bodies. The most important rooms were decorated with stucco and frescoes.

The area that can be visited includes the Crypt of the Popes, where many of the early popes were buried (16 pontiffs in all), and the Crypt of Santa Cecilia, where the saint's body was discovered in 820 before being moved to her church in Trastevere (p264). Dozens of martyrs were also buried in these catacombs.

Ancient frescoes in the Catacombs of Domitilla, the largest catacombs in Rome ↑

Catacombs of San Sebastiano

☖ Via Appia Antica 136
☏ 06-785 0350   🚌 118, 218
🕐 10am–4:30pm Mon–Sat
🚫 1 Jan, mid-Nov–mid-Dec,
25 Dec   🌐 catacombe.org

The 17th-century church of San Sebastiano, situated above the catacombs, occupies the site of a basilica. Preserved at the entrance to the catacombs is the *triclia*, a building that once stood above ground and was used by mourners for taking funeral refreshments. Its walls are covered with graffiti that invokes St Peter and St Paul, whose remains may have been moved here during one of the periods of persecution.

Catacombs of Domitilla

☖ Via delle Sette Chiese 282   🚌 218, 716   🕐 9am–noon & 2–5pm Wed–Mon (summer: 5:30pm)   🚫 mid-Dec–mid-Jan, Easter Sun
🌐 domitilla.info

This network of catacombs is the largest in Rome. Many of the tombs from the 1st and 2nd centuries AD have no Christian connection. In the burial chambers there are frescoes depicting both Classical and Christian scenes, including one of the earliest depictions of Christ as the *Good Shepherd*. Above the catacombs stands the basilica of Santi Nereo e Achilleo. After centuries of rebuilding and restoration, little remains of the original 4th-century church structure.

Fosse Ardeatine

☖ Via Ardeatina 174
☏ 06-513 6742   🚌 218, 716
🕐 8:15am–3:15pm Mon–Fri,
8:15am–4:45pm Sat & Sun
(museum closes 15 minutes earlier)   🚫 public hols

On the evening of 24 March 1944, Nazi forces took 335 prisoners to this abandoned quarry south of Rome and shot them at point blank range. The execution was in reprisal for a bomb attack that had killed 32 German soldiers. The victims included various political prisoners, 73 Jews and ten other civilians, among them a priest and a 14-year-old boy. The Germans blew up the tunnels where the massacre had taken place, but a local peasant had witnessed the scene and later helped find the corpses. The site is now a memorial to the values of the Resistance against the Nazi occupation, which gave birth to the modern Italian Republic (*p58*). A forbidding bunker-like monument houses the rows of identical tombs containing the victims.

Beside it is a museum of the Resistance with interesting works of modern sculpture including *The Martyrs*, by Francesco Coccia, and the gates shaped like a wall of thorns by Mirko Basaldella.

EAT

Eataly

This cathedral to gastronomy is a must for anyone who loves to eat or cook. As well as a huge number of niche producers of everything from handmade pasta to biodynamic wine, there are bars, restaurants, tastings and a packed calendar of events.

☖ Piazzale 12 Ottobre 1492

Tomb of Cecilia Metella

🅰 Via Appia Antica, km 3
📞 06-3996 7700 🚌 118,
660 🕐 9am-approx 1 hr
before sunset Tue-Sun

One of the most famous
landmarks on the Via Appia
Antica is the huge tomb built
for the noblewoman Cecilia
Metella. Her father and
husband were rich patricians
and successful generals of late
Republican Rome, but hardly
anything is known about the
woman herself.

In 1302 Pope Boniface VIII
donated the tomb to his family,
the Caetani. They incorporated
it in a fortified castle that
blocked the Via Appia, allowing
them to control the traffic on
the road and exact tolls.

Across the road are the
remains of the early 14th-
century church of San Nicola.

EUR

🚌 170, 671, 714 and other
routes Ⓜ EUR Fermi, EUR
Palasport

The Esposizione Universale di
Roma (EUR), a suburb south
of the city, was built for an
international exhibition, a
kind of "Work Olympics", that
was planned by Mussolini for
1942 to celebrate Fascist
Italy but never took place
because of World War II. The
architecture was intended to
glorify Fascism and the style
of the buildings is very over-
blown and rhetorical. The
eerie Palazzo della Civiltà del
Lavoro (The Palace of the
Civilization of Work) is an
unmistakable landmark.

The scheme was completed
in the 1950s. In terms of town
planning, EUR has been quite
successful and people are still
keen to live here owing to
its modern amenities. Many
businesses have offices in the
area. The great marble halls
and large austere buildings
inspired by ancient Imperial
Roman architecture house
government offices and a
number of museums.

The library of the SIAE
building houses the **Burcardo
Theatre Museum**, featuring
theatre literature, Chinese
masks and puppets from all
over Italy. The fascinating
**MUCIV (Museo della Civiltà
Romana)** complex brings
together the collections of
several different museums:
the Museum of Prehistory and
Ethnography "Luigi Pigorini"
features exhibits from
different cultures and some
important prehistoric remains,
such as a Neanderthal
cranium, prehistoric fauna
and some well-preserved
Neolithic boats; the Museum
of Traditional and Folk Art
explores Italian regional
culture; while the National
Museum of the Early Middle
Ages presents a wealth of
early medieval Italian objects.
The next addition to the
complex will be the collection
of the National Museum of
Oriental Art "Giuseppe Tucci",
formerly situated in Palazzo
Brancaccio in Via Merulana,
which is expected to open in
late 2019.

In the southern part of
the district is a lake and
park, and the huge domed
Palazzo dello Sport built for
the 1960 Olympics.

**Burcardo Theatre
Museum**

🅰 Viale della Letteratura 24
📞 06-5990 3814 🕐 9:15am-
1:15pm Mon-Fri

**MUCIV (Museo della
Civiltà Romana)**

🅰 Piazza G. Marconi 14
🕐 8am-7pm Tue-Sun (free
first Sun of month) 🌐 museo
civilta.beniculturali.it

The Marconi Obelisk,
towering over the central
square of EUR district

Cinecittà Si Mostra

⌂ Via Tuscolana 1055
Ⓜ Cinecittà 🕐 9:30am–5:30pm Wed-Mon
Ⓦ cinecittasimostra.it

Cinecittà Si Mostra (literally translated as "Cinecittà Shows Off") offers the chance to step behind the scenes of Italy's most famous film studio. Props and costumes are exhibited, including the dress worn by Elizabeth Taylor in *Cleopatra* (1963). Tours include film sets, such as a replica Broadway created for the Martin Scorsese film *Gangs of New York* (2002) and a mock ancient Rome (which stood in for ancient Pompeii in a 2008 episode of *Doctor Who*), along with the working film studio.

> The Stadio dei Marmi is ringed by 60 colossal marble statues of idealized male athletes, each one sculpted by a young, unknown artist.

Foro Italico

⌂ Piazza Lauro de Bosis
🚌 32, 69, 186, 224, 271, 280

The Foro Italico sports complex was created by Mussolini (and originally named the Foro Mussolini) between 1928 and 1938 in the hope of securing the 1944 Olympic Games for the city; in the event, that year's Games were cancelled due to World War II. Inspired by the Fora of Imperial Rome, it still features a huge obelisk inscribed with the words "Mussolini Dux" (*dux* being the Latin for leader). The swimming pool is pure marble, with stone mosaic decorations. The Stadio dei Marmi is ringed by 60 colossal marble statues of idealized male athletes, each one sculpted by a young, unknown artist and donated by one of the 60 provinces of Italy. Overlooking it is a building that once housed the Fascist Male Academy of Physical Education, now the headquarters of the Italian Olympic Committee. Also within the complex is the Stadio Olimpico; rebuilt for the 1990 FIFA World Cup, it is the home stadium of both the Roma and Lazio football teams and is also used for international rugby and athletics and occasional big rock concerts. International tennis tournaments are staged at the complex's Campo Centrale.

→ The 17th-century Villa Doria Pamphilj with its tranquil formal gardens

19

Centrale Montemartini

⌂ Via Ostiense 106 ☎ 06-0608 🚌 23, 769 ⏰ 9am-7pm Tue-Sun (last adm: 6:30pm)

An enormous old industrial site was restored in 1997 to house part of the collections of the Capitoline Museums (p66). Originally, the building was used as Rome's first thermo-electric power station and its two huge generators still occupy the central machine room, creating quite an intriguing contrast to the exhibits of Classical ancient Roman statuary and artifacts. Many of the statues were discovered during excavations in the late 19th and early 20th centuries and include finds from the Area Sacra di Largo Argentina (p169).

20

San Paolo fuori le Mura

⌂ Via Ostiense 186 ☎ 06-6988 0800 🚌 23, 128, 170, 670, 707, 761, 769 Ⓜ San Paolo ⏰ 7am-6:30pm daily Cloister and museum: ⏰ 8am-6:15pm daily

Today's church is a faithful reconstruction of the great 4th-century basilica destroyed by fire on 15 July 1823. Few fragments of the original church survived. The triumphal arch over the nave is decorated on one side with restored 5th-century mosaics. On the other side are mosaics by Pietro Cavallini, originally on the façade. The splendid Venetian apse mosaics (1220) depict the figures of Christ with St Peter, St Andrew, St Paul and St Luke.

The fine marble canopy over the high altar is signed by the sculptor Arnolfo di Cambio (1285) "together with his partner Pietro", who may have been Pietro Cavallini. Below the altar is the *confessio*, the tomb of St Paul. To the right is an impressive Paschal candlestick by Nicolò di Angelo and Pietro Vassalletto.

The cloister of San Paolo, with its pairs of colourful inlaid columns supporting the arcade, was spared completely by the fire. Completed around 1214, it is considered one of the most beautiful in Rome.

21

Villa Doria Pamphilj

⌂ Via di San Pancrazio 🚌 31, 44, 75, 710, 870 Park: ⏰ dawn-dusk daily

One of Rome's largest public parks, the Villa Doria Pamphilj was laid out in the mid-17th century for Prince Camillo Pamphilj. His uncle, Pope Innocent X, paid for the magnificent summer residence, the Casino del Bel Respiro, and the fountains and summerhouses, some of which still survive.

← Mosaics adorning the walls of the swimming pool in the Foro Italico, and (inset) detail of one of the marble figures around the Stadio dei Marmi

↑ Picturesque ruins in Hadrian's Villa

㉒ Tivoli

 31 km (20 miles) north-east of Rome ⓕⓢ from Tiburtina 🚌 COTRAL from Ponte Mammolo (on Metro line B)

Tivoli has been a popular summer resort since the days of the Roman Republic. Among the famous men who owned villas here were the poets Catullus and Horace, Caesar's assassins Brutus and Cassius, and the Emperors Trajan and Hadrian. Tivoli's main attractions were its clean air and beautiful situation on the slopes of the Tiburtini hills, its healthy sulphur springs and the waterfalls of the Aniene. The Romans' luxurious lifestyle was revived in Renaissance times by the owners of the Villa d'Este, the town's most famous sight.

In the Middle Ages Tivoli suffered frequent invasions as its position made it an ideal base for an advance on Rome.

The town's cobbled streets are still lined with medieval houses. The cathedral contains a lovely 13th-century life-size wooden group representing the *Deposition from the Cross*.

㉓ Villa d'Este

 Piazza Trento 5, Tivoli 🚌 COTRAL from Ponte Mammolo (on Metro line B) ⏱ 8:30am–approx 1 hour before sunset Tue–Sun 📅 1 Jan, 25 Dec (free 1st Sun in month) 🌐 villadeste tivoli.info

The Villa d'Este occupies the site of an old Benedictine convent. In the 16th century the estate was developed by Cardinal Ippolito d'Este, son of Lucrezia Borgia. A palace was designed by Pirro Ligorio to make the most of its hill-top situation, but the villa's fame rests more on the terraced gardens and fountains laid out by Ligorio and Giacomo della Porta.

The grottoes and fountains still give a vivid impression of the luxury enjoyed by the princes of the church. From the loggia of the palace you descend to the Grotto of Diana and Bernini's Fontana del Bicchierone. Below to the right is the Rometta (little Rome), a model of Tiber Island with allegorical figures and the legendary she-wolf. The Fontana dell'Organo is a

water-organ, in which the force of the water pumps air through the pipes. The garden's lowest level has flower beds and fountains and splendid views.

㉔ Hadrian's Villa

 Villa Adriana, Largo M Yourcenar 1, 6 km (4 miles) southwest of Tivoli ⓕⓢ Tivoli, then local bus No. 4 🚌 COTRAL from Ponte Mammolo (on Metro line B) ⏱ 9am–approx 1 hour before sunset daily 🌐 villaadriana.beni culturali.it

Built as a private summer retreat between AD 118 and 134, Hadrian's Villa was a vast open-air museum of the finest architecture of the Roman world. The grounds of the Imperial Palace were filled with full-scale reproductions of the emperor's favourite buildings from Greece and Egypt. Although excavations on this site began in the 16th century, many of the ruins scattered in the surrounding fields have yet to be identified with any certainty. The grounds make a very picturesque site for a picnic. The most notable buildings are signposted and several have been partially restored or reconstructed. One of the most impressive is the so-called Maritime Theatre. This is a round pool with an island in the middle, surrounded by columns. The island, reached by means of a swing bridge, was probably Hadrian's private studio, where he withdrew from the cares of the Empire to indulge in his two favourite pastimes, painting and architecture. There were also theatres, Greek and Latin libraries, two bathhouses, extensive housing for guests and the palace staff, and formal gardens with fountains, statues and pools.

Hadrian also loved Greek philosophy. One part of the gardens is thought to have been Hadrian's reproduction of the Grove of Academe, where Plato lectured to his students. He also had a replica made of the Stoà Poikile, a beautiful painted colonnade in Athens, from which the Stoic philosophers took their name. The so-called Hall of the Philosophers, close to the Poikile, was probably a library.

The most ambitious of Hadrian's replicas was the Canopus, a sanctuary of the god Serapis near Alexandria. For this a canal 119 metres (130 yards) long was dug and Egyptian statues were imported to decorate the temple and its grounds.

Below ground the emperor even built a fanciful re-creation of the underworld, Hades, reached through underground tunnels, of which there were many linking the various parts of the villa.

Plundered by barbarians, who camped here in the 6th and 8th centuries, the villa fell into disrepair and Renaissance antiquarians contributed even further to its destruction. Statues unearthed in the grounds are on display in museums around Europe. The Vatican's Egyptian Collection (p290) has many fine works that were found here.

25

Villa Gregoriana

🅐 Largo Sant'Angelo, Tivoli
🄵🄢 🚌 Tivoli, then short walk
📞 0774-332 650 🕐 Mar & mid-Oct-mid-Dec: 10am-4pm Tue-Sun; Apr-mid-Oct: 10am-6:30pm Tue-Sun

The main attractions of this steeply sloping park are the waterfalls and grottoes

←

The Grande Cascata waterfall and Villa Gregoriana above

created by the River Aniene. The park is named after Pope Gregory XVI, who in the 1830s ordered the building of a tunnel to ward against flooding. This tunnel created a new waterfall, the Grande Cascata, plunging 160 m (525 ft) into the valley behind the town.

NEED TO KNOW

Victor Emmanuel Monument

BEFORE
YOU GO

Forward planning is essential to any successful trip. Be prepared for all eventualities by considering the following points before you travel.

AT A GLANCE

CURRENCY
Euro (EUR)

AVERAGE DAILY SPEND

SAVE	SPEND	SPLURGE
€50	**€100**	**€200+**

BOTTLED WATER	COFFEE	BEER	DINNER FOR TWO
€1.30	**€1**	**€5**	**€60**

ESSENTIAL PHRASES

Hello	Buongiorno/Ciao
Goodbye	Arrivederci
Please	Per favore
Thank you	Grazie
Do you speak English?	Parla inglese?
I don't understand	Non ho capito

ELECTRICITY SUPPLY

Power sockets are type F and L, fitting two- and three-pronged plugs. Standard voltage is 220–230v.

Passports and Visas

EU nationals and citizens of the UK, US, Canada, Australia and New Zealand do not need visas for stays of up to three months. Consult your nearest Italian embassy or check the **Polizia di Stato** website if you are travelling from outside these areas.
Polizia di Stato
W poliziadistato.it

Travel Safety Advice

Visitors can get up-to-date travel safety information from the **UK Foreign and Commonwealth Office**, the **US State Department** and the **Australian Department of Foreign Affairs and Trade**.
AUS
W smartraveller.gov.au
UK
W gov.uk/foreign-travel-advice
US
W travel.state.gov

Customs Information

An individual is permitted to carry the following within the EU for personal use:
Tobacco products: 800 cigarettes, 400 cigarillos, 200 cigars or 1 kg of smoking tobacco.
Alcohol: 10 litres of alcoholic beverages above 22% strength, 20 litres of alcoholic beverages below 22% strength, 90 litres of wine (60 litres of which can be sparkling wine) and 110 litres of beer.
Cash: if you plan to enter or leave the EU with €10,000 or more in cash (or the equivalent in other currencies) you must declare it to the customs authorities.
If travelling outside the EU limits vary, so check restrictions before departing.

Insurance

It is wise to take out an insurance policy covering theft, loss of belongings, medical problems, cancellation and delays.

EU citizens are eligible for free emergency medical care in Italy provided they have a valid **EHIC** (European Health Insurance Card). Visitors from outside the EU must arrange their own private medical insurance.
EHIC
🅦 gov.uk/european-health-insurance-card

Vaccinations

No inoculations are needed for Italy.

Booking Accommodation

Rome offers a huge variety of accommodation, comprising luxury five-star hotels, family-run B&Bs, budget hostels and private apartment rentals. A list of accommodation to suit all needs can be found on the ENIT (Italy's national tourist board) website (p337).

During peak season lodgings fill up and prices become inflated, so book in advance.

All accommodation adds the city tourist tax to its rates. This varies between €3 and €7 per night (depending on the hotel category) for a maximum of 10 nights. Always check if the city tax is included in the rate quoted to you.

Under Italian law, hotels are required to register guests at police headquarters and issue a receipt of payment (ricevuta fiscale), which you must keep until you leave Italy.

Money

Most establishments accept major credit, debit and prepaid currency cards. Contactless payments are becoming increasingly common in Rome, but it's always a good idea to carry some cash for smaller items such as coffee, gelato, pizza-by-the-slice, and when visiting markets or more remote areas.

Travellers with Specific Needs

Rome's historic towns and cobbled streets are ill-equipped for disabled access. Many buildings do not have wheelchair access or lifts. Always call ahead to ensure that your needs will be met.
CO.IN. Sociale provides information and general assistance for travellers with mobility issues.

Assistance at airports can be arranged by notifying your airline company or travel agent of your particular needs in advance of your trip.
ADR Assistance can coordinate assistance at Rome's Ciampino or Fiumicino or airports. Train travellers with Trenitalia (p332) can arrange special reservations and assistance at stations.
ADR Assistance
🅦 adr.it
CO.IN.Sociale
🅦 coinsociale.it

Language

The level of English spoken in Rome varies. Many of those working in the city's major tourist areas speak good English. However, a little knowledge of the local language goes a long way, and locals appreciate visitors' efforts to speak Italian, even if only a few words.

Closures

Lunchtime Most shops, churches and some small businesses shut for a few hours in the afternoon.
Monday Many museums and restaurants close all day.
Sunday Restaurants usually close for lunch. Churches and cathedrals forbid tourists from visiting during Mass, and public transport runs a reduced service.
Public holidays Shops, churches and museums either close early or for the day.

PUBLIC HOLIDAYS 2019	
1 Jan	New Year's Day
6 Jan	Epiphany
21 Apr	Easter Sunday
22 Apr	Easter Monday
25 Apr	Liberation Day
1 May	Labour Day
2 Jun	Republic Day
15 Aug	Ferragosto
1 Nov	All Saints' Day
8 Dec	Feast of the Immaculate Conception
25 Dec	Christmas Day
26 Dec	St Stephen's Day

GETTING
AROUND

Whether exploring Rome's historic centre by foot or making use of the city's public transport, here is all you need to know to navigate the city.

AT A GLANCE

PUBLIC TRANSPORT COSTS
Tickets are valid on all forms of public transport in Rome.

ONE-WAY

€1.50

75 mins transfers included

DAY TICKET

€7

Unlimited travel

3-DAY TICKET

€18

Unlimited travel

SPEED LIMIT

MOTORWAY

130 km/h (80 mph)

DUAL CARRIAGEWAYS

110 km/h (70 mph)

SECONDARY ROAD

90 km/h (50 mph)

URBAN AREAS

50 km/h (30 mph)

Arriving by Air

Rome has two airports, Fiumicino and Ciampino, both served by international flights and with excellent transport links to the city centre.

For journey times and ticket pricing for transport between the airport and the city centre, see the table opposite.

Train Travel

International Train Travel
Regular high-speed international trains connect Italy to the main towns and cities in Austria, Germany, France and Eastern Europe. Reservations for these services are essential and tickets are booked up quickly.

You can buy tickets and passes for multiple international journeys via **Eurail** or **Interrail**; however, you may still need to pay an additional reservation fee depending on which rail service you travel with. Always check that your pass is valid before boarding.
Eurail
W eurail.com
Interrail
W interrail.eu

Regional and Local Trains
Trenitalia is the main operator in Italy. Tickets can be bought online but there are only a fixed number available so book ahead.

For travelling between cities, **Italo Treno** (NTV) and **Trenitalia** (FS) also offer a high-speed rail service. Reservations are essential. Rome's main stations are Termini and Tiburtina.

There is a useful city line to Ostia Antica and Ostia Lido from Stazione Porta San Paolo, next to the Piramide Metro station.

Tickets must be validated by stamping them before boarding. Machines are positioned at the entrance to platforms in railway stations for this purpose. Heavy fines are levied if you are caught with an unvalidated ticket.
Italo Treno
W italotreno.it
Trenitalia
W trenitalia.com

GETTING TO AND FROM THE AIRPORT

Airport	Transport	Journey time	Price
Ciampino	Bus (Siti/Terravision)	40 mins	€5
	Taxi	30 mins	€30
Fiumicino	Train (Leonardo da Vinci Express)	35 mins	€14
	Train (regionale)	50 mins	€8
	Bus (ATRAL/COTRAL/Siti/Terravision)	1 hr	€5
	Taxi	45 mins	€48

Public Transport

ATAC is Rome's main public transport authority. Timetables, ticket information, transport maps, and more can be obtained from ATAC kiosks, the customer service office or the ATAC website.
ATAC
w atac.roma.it

Tickets

Tickets *(biglietti)* are available from kiosks, stations, bars, newsstands, or any shop with the ATAC sticker in the window. Tickets cannot be bought on board – they must be bought in advance (there are automatic ticket machines at main bus stops and Metro stations that take coins) and must be validated on the day of travel.

Tickets are valid on all modes of public transport, including buses, trams, Metro, and local train lines. Regular one-way tickets (BIT) valid for 75 minutes cost €1.50, day tickets (BIG) cost €7, three-day tickets (BTI) cost €18 and weekly passes (CIS) are €24. Children under 10 travel for free with an adult.

Metro

Rome's Metro *(Metropolitana)* has three lines – A, B and C. Line A runs from west to southeast and Line B runs from northeast to south. A and B meet at Termini station, and A and C at San Giovanni. Regional rail services connect with the Metro to serve the surrounding areas and the airports. Line C runs from Pantano station to Luni and links with Line A at San Giovanni.

Trains run every 4–10 minutes from 5:30am–11:30pm daily, and 5:30am–1:30am on Friday and Saturday nights.

On street level, Metro stations are clearly marked by red and white "M" signs. Use the

Metro maps in stations to identify which line you need and the terminus you will be heading for, then follow the signs in the station.

At the station, insert your ticket through the barrier to access the platform. Keep your ticket for inspection. Screens on the platform show the waiting time for the next train. Look out for your stop, as it may not be announced.

Trams

Trams cover the outskirts of the city centre and are a good way to get to the main sights while avoiding the crowded centre. The most useful are No. 2 (to MAXXI) and No. 19 (connecting Vatican City with Villa Borghese).

Tram stops display the tram numbers that serve them and a list of stops on each route. Approaching trams display the route number and their destination. Useful routes include Route 2 (along Via Flaminio) and Route 8 (between Largo Argentina and Trastevere).

Trams operate 5:30am–10:30pm or midnight daily, depending on the route (Route 8 runs until 3am on Friday and Saturday nights). Tickets must be stamped on board in the yellow machines.

Buses

Buses cover most of the city. When not stuck in traffic they are a quick way to reach the main sights and attractions of Rome.

The main bus terminus is on Piazza dei Cinquecento outside Termini station, but there are other major route hubs throughout the city, most usefully those at Piazza del Risorgimento and Piazza Venezia.

Bus stops display the bus numbers that serve them and a list of stops on each route. Regular services generally run every 10 to 20 minutes.

After 11:30pm a night bus service operates until 5.15am. Night buses are marked with the letter "N" (for *notturno*) before the route number.

Buses must be flagged down. Enter at the front or back doors and exit via the middle door (although people may not always adhere to this system). Tickets must be stamped in the yellow machines located at the front or back of the bus. Press the button to request a stop.

For day trips, COTRAL (*see below*) blue buses run from several Rome terminals out into the suburbs and surrounding countryside.

Long-Distance Bus Travel

Long-distance coaches terminate at Tiburtina, which is the city's main coach station. Tickets and information for coaches to European cities are available from the **Eurolines**, **Baltour** or **Italybus** websites.

Local buses, serving villages and towns within the Lazio region, are run by **COTRAL**. All bus stations used by COTRAL in Rome are linked to Metro stations. Tickets are purchased on the spot and cannot be booked in advance.

Baltour
w baltour.it
Eurolines
w eurolines.com
Italybus
w italybus.it

Guided Bus Tours

City Sightseeing Roma offers hop-on-hop-off tours of the city aboard double-decker buses with audio guides in eight languages. Tours run daily with a first departure at 9am and a last departure at 7pm. The full tour lasts 1 hour 40 minutes, and buses run with a frequency of 15 to 20 minutes. Buses can be boarded at any of the eight stops, which include the Colosseum, Trevi Fountain, Piazza Barberini and the Vatican. You can also buy "combo" tickets that include the Colosseum and the Vatican, or night tours.

The **Roma Cristiana** bus is a tour with a Christian emphasis. It runs from Termini to Piazza San Pietro with stops close to religious sights, and includes audio guides.

City Sightseeing Roma
w roma.city-sightseeing. it
Roma Cristiana
w operaromanapellegrinaggi.org

Taxis

Taxis in Rome are some of the most expensive in Europe and not all accept credit cards. They cannot be hailed; take one at an official taxi stand at stations, main piazzas or close to key tourist sights – the most useful are at Termini, Piazza Venezia, Piazza di Spagna, Piazza del Popolo and Piazza Barberini. You can also reserve online or by phone. When you order a taxi by phone, the meter will run from your call.

Official taxis are white, have a "taxi" sign on the roof and their official taxi license number on the doors. Alternatively, well-known taxi apps such as UBER also operate in Rome.

Extra charges are added for each piece of luggage placed in the boot, for rides between 10pm and 7am, on Sundays and public holidays, and for journeys to and from airports. Report any problems with taxi drivers by calling 060608.

Chiama Taxi
060609
Radiotaxi 3570
w 3570.it

Driving

Driving in Rome is not recommended – roads are congested and parking is extremely difficult, even for locals.

Driving to Rome

Rome is easily reachable from other European countries via E-roads, the International European Road Network connecting major roads across national borders within Europe, or by national (N) and secondary (SS) roads from neighbouring France, Switzerland, Austria and Slovenia.

Tolls are payable on most motorways (*autostrade*), and payment is made at the end of the journey in cash, by credit card or pre-paid magnetic VIA cards, available from tobacconists and the **ACI** (*Automobile Club d'Italia*). If you wish to avoid toll roads, there is almost always an alternative route signposted.

If you bring your own foreign-registered car to Italy, you must carry a Green Card, the vehicle's registration documents and a valid driver's licence.

ACI
w aci.it

Car Rental

To rent a car in Italy you must be over 21 and have held a valid driver's licence with no points for at least one year.

Driving licences issued by any of the European Union member states are valid throughout the EU, including Italy.

If visiting from outside the EU, you may need to apply for an International Driving Permit (IDP). Check with your local automobile association before you travel.

Driving in Rome

City centre streets are designated ZTL (*Zona a Traffico Limitato*) which means that only residents can drive and park there.

Those arriving by car are advised to leave it in a car park outside the city centre. The **European Car Parking Guide** and **Saba** list free car parks on Rome's periphery. There are also car parks located near Villa Borghese and Piazza Partigiani. Look for a white "P" sign on a blue background. Metered parking is permitted in parking spaces identified by a white line from 8am until 8pm.

If your vehicle is towed, call the municipal police. You can reach them by dialling 06-0606. Tell them where you parked and they will direct you to the nearest tow lot. Once you have located your vehicle, you will have to pay a fee to retrieve it as well as pay for the parking violation.

European Car Parking Guide
🅦 car-parking.eu/italy/rome/pr
Saba
🅦 sabait.it

Rules of the Road

Drive on the right, use the left lane only for passing, and yield to traffic from the right. Seat belts are required for all passengers in the front and back, and heavy fines are levied for using a mobile phone while driving.

During the day dipped headlights are compulsory when driving on motorways, dual carriageways and on all out-of-town roads. A red warning triangle and fluorescent vests must be carried at all times, for use in the event of an emergency.

If you have an accident or breakdown, switch on your hazard warning lights and place a warning triangle 50 m (55 yd) behind your vehicle. In the event of a breakdown, call the ACI emergency number (803 116) or the emergency services (112 or 113). The ACI will tow any foreign-registered car to the nearest ACI-affiliated garage for free.

The legal drink-drive limit is strictly enforced (p336). If you are drinking alcohol, use public transport or take a taxi.

Hitchhiking

Hitchhiking (*autostop*) is illegal on motorways, and is not commonplace in large cities such as Rome. In more rural areas it is a common transport method for travellers on a budget. Always consider your own safety before entering an unknown vehicle.

Cycle and Scooter Hire

Cycling in Rome can be a challenging task due to the city's hilly nature, the heavy traffic and the lack of bike paths. If you are not up for urban cycling, a ride in Villa Borghese park can be a healthier and more enjoyable alternative. Bikes, tandems and rickshaws can all be hired by the entrance of the Pincio Gardens.

You can rent bicycles, motorcycles and scooters hourly or by the day. You may have to leave your passport with the rental shop as a deposit, and you must have a valid licence to hire a scooter or motorcycle. **Bici & Baci** and **Barberini Scooters for Rent** offer bike and scooter rental by the hour and by the day.

Motorcyclists, scooter drivers and their passengers must wear helmets by law; these can be rented from most hire shops. Unless you are an experienced moped or scooter rider, it is wiser not to ride in Rome.

Barberini Scooters for Rent
🅦 rentscooter.it
Bici & Baci
🅦 bicibaci.com

Boats and Ferries

In summer, **Battelli di Roma** runs hop-on-hop-off cruises on the Tiber between Isola Tiberina and Ponte Nenni. Boats leave hourly from 10am until 2pm, and 4pm until 8pm (summer only). Ponte Sant' Angelo and Isola Tiberina are the boarding points. Tickets are valid 24 hours.

Battelli di Roma
🅦 battellidiroma.it

PRACTICAL
INFORMATION

A little local know-how goes a long way in Rome. Here you can find all the essential advice and information you will need during your stay.

AT A GLANCE

EMERGENCY NUMBERS

GENERAL EMERGENCY

112

AMBULANCE

118

FIRE SERVICE

115

POLICE

113

TIME ZONE
CET/CEST
Central European Summer Time (CEST) runs 31 Mar–27 Oct 2019

TAP WATER
Unless otherwise stated, tap water in Rome is safe to drink.

TIPPING

Waiter	Not expected
Hotel Porter	€1 per bag
Housekeeping	€1 per day
Concierge	€1–2
Taxi Driver	Not expected

Personal Security

Bag-snatching scooter drivers are a problem, so hold bags on the inside of the pavement where possible, especially in crowded tourist areas.

Pickpockets are common on public transport, so be careful on popular bus routes such as 23, 40 and 64. Keep your belongings in a safe place and with you at all times.

If you have anything stolen, report the crime within 24 hours to the nearest police station and take ID with you. Get a copy of the crime report (*denuncia*) to make an insurance claim.

Contact your embassy if you have your passport stolen, or in the event of a serious crime or accident.

Health

Seek medicinal supplies and advice for minor ailments from pharmacies (*farmacia*). You can find details of the nearest 24-hour service on all pharmacy doors.

Emergency medical care in Italy is free for all EU and Australian citizens. If you have an EHIC card (*p331*), be sure to present this as soon as possible. You may have to pay after treatment and reclaim the money later.

For visitors coming from outside the EU and Australia, payment of hospital and other medical expenses is the patient's responsibility. It is therefore important to arrange comprehensive medical insurance before travelling.

Smoking, Alcohol and Drugs

Smoking is banned in enclosed public places. Possession of narcotics is prohibited and could result in a prison sentence.

Italians tend to drink only with meals and are unlikely to be seen drunk – obvious drunkenness is frowned upon.

Italy has a strict limit of 0.05 per cent BAC (blood alcohol content) for drivers. This means that you cannot drink more than a small beer or a small glass of wine if you plan to drive. For drivers with less than three years' driving experience the limit is 0.

ID

By law you must carry identification with you at all times in Italy. A photocopy of your passport photo page (and visa if applicable) should suffice. If you are stopped by the police you may be asked to present the original document within 12 hours.

Local Customs

You can be fined for dropping litter, sitting on monument steps or eating or drinking outside churches, historic monuments and public buildings. It is an offence to swim or bathe in public fountains.

Illegal street traders operate in many of Rome's main tourist areas; avoid buying from them as you could be fined by the local police.

Visiting Churches and Cathedrals

Entrance to churches is free, but you may be charged a small fee to see a certain area, such as a chapel, cloister or underground ruins.

Strict dress codes apply: cover your torso and upper arms, and ensure shorts and skirts cover your knees. Shoes must be worn.

Mobile Phones and Wi-Fi

Wi-Fi is generally widely available, and cafés, bars, restaurants and some cultural venues will usually allow you to use their Wi-Fi on the condition that you make a purchase.

Visitors travelling to Italy with EU tariffs will be able to use their devices abroad without being affected by roaming charges. Users will be charged the same rates for data, voice calls and SMS services as they would pay at home.

Post

Stamps are sold in kiosks and tobacconists. The Vatican City and San Marino have their own post systems and stamps. Only letters bearing San Marino or Vatican stamps can be posted in San Marino and Vatican postboxes.

Italian post is notorious for its unreliability. Letters and postcards can take anything between four days and two weeks to arrive.

Taxes and Refunds

VAT (IVA) is usually 22%. Under certain conditions, non-EU citizens can claim a rebate.

Either claim the rebate before you buy (show your passport to the shop assistant and complete a form), or claim it retrospectively by presenting a customs officer with your receipts as you leave. Stamped receipts will be sent back to the vendor to issue a refund.

Discount Cards

There are a number of visitor passes and discount cards available for Rome. It is worth considering carefully how many of the offers you are likely to take advantage of before purchasing one of these.

The two-day or three-day **Roma Pass** (€28/€38.50) includes public transport, entry to two museums or archaeological sites and discounts for various exhibitions and events. The **Omnia Rome and Vatican Pass** (€113 for three days) offers a similar package, but also includes the Vatican Museums.

Many national and city museums offer free entry to under 18s, and discounts for students.

During the *Beni Culturali* (Ministry for Culture and Heritage week) in April, admission to all state-run sites is free.

Roma Pass
🌐 romapass.it
Omnia Rome and Vatican Pass
🌐 romeandvaticanpass.com

WEBSITES AND APPS

www.italia.it
The official website of ENIT, Itay's national tourist board
Chiama Taxi App
Roma Servizi's handy taxi app
ProntoTreno
Buy train tickets, get live updates and check journey times
WiFi°Italia°
Connect quickly and easily to free Wi-Fi hotspots throughout Rome and Italy

INDEX

PHRASE BOOK

IN EMERGENCY

English	Italian	Pronunciation
Help!	Aiuto!	eye-yoo-toh
Stop!	Ferma!	fair-mah
Call a doctor	Chiama un medico	kee-ah-mah oon meh-dee-koh
Call an ambulance	Chiama un' ambulanza	kee-ah-mah oon am-boo-lan-tsa
Call the police	Chiama la polizia	kee-ah-mah lah pol-ee-tsee-ah
Call the fire brigade	Chiama i pompieri	kee-ah-mah ee pom-pee-air-ee
Where is the telephone?	Dov'è il telefono?	dov-eheel teh-leh-foh-noh?
The nearest hospital?	L'ospedale più vicino?	loss-peh-dah-leh pee-oovee-chee-noh?

COMMUNICATION ESSENTIALS

English	Italian	Pronunciation
Yes/No	Sì/No	see/noh
Please	Per favore	pair fah-vor-eh
Thank you	Grazie	grah-tsee-eh
Excuse me	Mi scusi	mee skoo-zee
Hello	Buon giorno	bwon jor-noh
Goodbye	Arrivederci	ah-ree-veh-dair-chee
Good evening	Buona sera	bwon-ah sair-ah
morning	la mattina	lah mah-tee-nah
afternoon	il pomeriggio	eel poh-meh-ree-joh
evening	la sera	lah sair-ah
yesterday	ieri	ee-air-ee
today	oggi	oh-jee
tomorrow	domani	doh-mah-nee
here	qui	kwee
there	la	lah
What?	Quale?	kwah-leh?
When?	Quando?	kwan-doh?
Why?	Perchè?	pair-keh?
Where?	Dove?	doh-veh

USEFUL PHRASES

English	Italian	Pronunciation
How are you?	Come sta?	koh-meh stah?
Very well, thank you.	Molto bene, grazie	moll-toh beh-neh grah-tsee-eh
Pleased to meet you.	Piacere di conoscerla.	pee-ah-chair-eh dee coh-noh-shair-lah
See you soon.	A più tardi.	ah pee-oo tar-dee
That's fine.	Va bene.	va beh-neh
Where is/are ...?	Dov'è/Dove sono...?	dov-eh/dovehsoh noh?
How long does it take to get to ...?	Quanto tempo ci vuole per andare a ...?	kwan-toh tem-poh chee voo-oh-leh pair an-dar-eh ah...?
How do I get to ...?	Come faccio per arrivare a ...?	koh-meh fah-choh pair arri-var-eh ah...?
Do you speak English?	Parla inglese?	par-lah een-gleh-zeh?
I don't understand.	Non capisco.	non ka-pee-skoh
Could you speak more slowly, please?	Può parlare più lentamente, per favore?	pwoh par-lah-reh pee-oo len-ta-men-teh pair fah-vor-eh?
I'm sorry.	Mi dispiace.	mee dee-spee-ah-cheh

USEFUL WORDS

English	Italian	Pronunciation
big	grande	gran-deh
small	piccolo	pee-koh-loh
hot	caldo	kal-doh
cold	freddo	fred-doh
good	buono	bwoh-noh
bad	cattivo	kat-tee-voh
enough	basta	bas-tah
well	bene	beh-neh
open	aperto	ah-pair-toh
closed	chiuso	kee-oo-zoh
left	a sinistra	ah see-nee-strah
right	a destra	ah dess-trah
straight on	sempre dritto	sem-preh dree-toh
near	vicino	vee-chee-noh
far	lontano	lon-tah-noh
up	su	soo
down	giù	joo
early	presto	press-toh
late	tardi	tar-dee
entrance	entrata	en-trah-tah
exit	uscita	oo-shee-ta
toilet	il gabinetto	eel gah-bee-net-toh
free, unoccupied	libero	lee-bair-oh
free, no charge	gratuito	grah-too-ee-toh

MAKING A TELEPHONE CALL

English	Italian	Pronunciation
I'd like to place a long-distance call.	Vorrei fare una interurbana.	vor-ray far-eh oona in-tair-oor-bah-nah.
I'd like to make a reverse-charge call.	Vorrei fare una telefonata a carico del destinatario.	vor-ray far-eh oona teh-leh-fon-ah-tah ah kar-ee-koh dell dess-tee-nah-tar-ree-oh.
I'll try again later.	Ritelefono più tardi.	ree-teh-leh-foh-noh pee-oo tar-dee.
Can I leave a message?	Posso lasciare un messaggio?	poss-oh lash-ah-reh oon mess-sah-joh?
Hold on	Un attimo, per favore	oon ah-tee-moh, pair fah-vor-eh.
Could you speak up a little please?	Può parlare più forte, per favore?	pwoh par-lah-reh pee-oo for-teh, pair fah-vor-eh?
local call	la telefonata locale	lah teh-leh-fon-ah-ta loh-kah-leh

SHOPPING

English	Italian	Pronunciation
How much does this cost?	Quant'è, per favore?	kwan-teh, pair fah-vor-eh?
I would like ...	Vorrei ...	vor-ray...
Do you have ...?	Avete ...?	ah-veh-teh...?
I'm just looking.	Sto soltanto guardando	stoh sol-tan-toh gwar-dan-doh
Do you take credit cards?	Accettate carte di credito?	ah-chet-tah-teh kar-teh dee creh-dee-toh?
What time do you open/close?	A che ora apre/chiude?	ah keh or-ah ah-preh/kee-oo-deh?
this one	questo	kweh-stoh
that one	quello	kwell-oh
expensive	caro	kar-oh
cheap	a buon prezzo	ah bwon pret-soh
size, clothes	la taglia	lah tah-lee-ah
size, shoes	il numero	eel noo-mair-oh
white	bianco	bee-ang-koh
black	nero	neh-roh
red	rosso	ross-oh
yellow	giallo	jal-loh
green	verde	vair-deh
blue	blu	bloo
brown	marrone	mar-roh-neh

TYPES OF SHOP

English	Italian	Pronunciation
antique dealer	l'antiquario	lan-tee-kwah-ree-oh
bakery	la panetteria	lahpah-net-tair-ree-ah
bank	la banca	lah bang-kah
bookshop	la libreria	lah lee-breh-ree-ah
butcher's	la macelleria	lah mah-chell-eh-ree-ah
cake shop	la pasticceria	lahpas-tee-chair-ee-ah
chemist's	la farmacia	lah far-mah-chee-ah
department store	il grande magazzino	eel gran-deh mag-gad-zee-noh
delicatessen	la salumeria	lah sah-loo-meh-ree-ah
fishmonger's	la pescheria	lah pess-keh-ree-ah
florist	il fioraio	eel fee-or-eye-oh
greengrocer	il fruttivendolo	eel froo-tee-ven-doh-loh
grocery	alimentari	ah-lee-men-tah-ree
hairdresser	il parrucchiere	eel par-oo-kee-air-eh
ice cream parlour	la gelateria	lah jel-lah-tair-ree-ah
market	il mercato	eel mair-kah-toh
news-stand	l'edicola	leh-dee-koh-lah
post office	l'ufficio postale	loo-fee-choh pos-tah-leh
shoe shop	il negozio di scarpe	eel neh-goh-tsioh dee skar-peh
supermarket	il supermercato	eel su-pair-mair-kah-toh
tobacconist	il tabaccaio	eel tah-bak-eye-oh
travel agency	l'agenzia di viaggi	lah-jen-tsee-ah dee vee-ad-jee

SIGHTSEEING

English	Italian	Pronunciation
art gallery	la pinacoteca	lahpeena-koh-teh-kah
bus stop	la fermata dell'autobus	lah fair-mah-tah dellow-toh-booss
church	la chiesa	lah kee-eh-zah
	la basilica	lah bah-seel-i-kah
garden	il giardino	eel jar-dee-no
library	la biblioteca	lah beeb-lee-oh-teh-kah
museum	il museo	eel moo-zeh-oh
railway station	la stazione	lah stah-tsee-oh-neh

| tourist information | l'ufficio turistico | loo-**fee**-choh too-**ree**-stee-koh |
| closed for the public holiday | chiuso per la festa | kee-oo-zoh pair lah **fess**-tah |

STAYING IN A HOTEL

Do you have any vacant rooms?	Avete camere libere?	ah-**veh**-teh **kah**-mair-eh **lee**-bair-eh?
double room	una camera doppia	oona **kah**-mair-ah **doh**-pee-ah
with double bed	con letto matrimoniale	kon **let**-toh mah-tree-moh-nee-**ah**-leh
twin room	una camera con due letti	oona **kah**-mair-ah kon **doo**-eh **let**-tee
single room	una camera singola	oona **kah**-mair-ah **sing**-goh-lah
room with a bath, shower	una camera con bagno, con doccia	oona **kah**-mair-ah kon **ban**-yoh, kon **dot**-chah
porter	il facchino	eel fah-**kee**-noh
key	la chiave	lah kee-**ah**-veh
I have a reservation.	Ho fatto una prenotazione.	oh **fat**-toh oona preh-noh-tah-tsee-**oh**-neh

EATING OUT

Have you got a table for ...?	Avete un tavolo per ... ?	ah-**veh**-teh oon **tah**-voh-loh pair ...?
I'd like to reserve a table.	Vorrei riservare un tavolo.	vor-**ray** ree-sair-vah-reh oon **tah**-voh-loh
breakfast	colazione	koh-lah-tsee-**oh**-neh
lunch	pranzo	**pran**-tsoh
dinner	cena	**cheh**-nah
The bill, please.	Il conto, per favore.	eel kon-toh pair fah-**vor**-eh
I am a vegetarian.	Sono vegetariano/a.	**soh**-noh veh-jeh-tar-**ee**-ah-noh/nah
waitress	cameriera	kah-mair-ee-**air**-ah
waiter	cameriere	kah-mair-ee-**air**-eh
fixed price menu	il menù a prezzo fisso	eel meh-**noo** ah **pret**-soh **fee**-soh
dish of the day	piatto del giorno	pee-**ah** toh dell**jor**-no
starter	antipasto	an-tee-**pass**-toh
first course	il primo	eel **pree**-moh
main course	il secondo	eel seh-**kon**-doh
vegetables	il contorno	eel kon-**tor**-noh
dessert	il dolce	eel **doll**-che
cover charge	il coperto	eel koh-**pair**-toh
wine list	la lista dei vini	lah **lee**-stah day **vee**-nee
rare	al sangue	al **sang**-gweh
medium	a puntino	a poon-**tee**-noh
well done	ben cotto	ben **kot**-toh
glass	il bicchiere	eel bee-kee-**air**-eh
bottle	la bottiglia	lah bot-**teel**-yah
knife	il coltello	eel kol-**tell**-oh
fork	la forchetta	lah for-**ket**-tah
spoon	il cucchiaio	eel koo-kee-**eye**-oh

MENU DECODER

apple	la mela	lah **meh**-lah
artichoke	il carciofo	eel kar-**choff**-oh
aubergine	la melanzana	lah meh-lan-**tsah**-nah
baked	al forno	al **for**-noh
beans	i fagioli	ee fah-**joh**-lee
beef	il manzo	eel **man**-tsoh
beer	la birra	lah **beer**-rah
boiled	lesso	**less**-oh
bread	il pane	eel **pah**-neh
broth	il brodo	eel **broh**-doh
butter	il burro	eel **boor**-oh
cake	la torta	lah **tor**-tah
cheese	il formaggio	eel for-**mad**-joh
chicken	il pollo	eel **poll**-oh
chips	patatine fritte	pah-tah-**teen**-eh **free**-teh
baby clams	le vongole	leh **von**-goh-leh
coffee	il caffè	eel kah-**feh**
courgettes	gli zucchini	lyee dzoo-**kee**-nee
dry	secco	**sek**-koh
duck	l'anatra	**lah**-nah-trah
egg	l'uovo	loo-**oh**-voh
fish	il pesce	eel**pesh**-eh
fresh fruit	frutta fresca	froo-tah **fress**-kah
garlic	l'aglio	**lahl**-yoh
grapes	l'uva	**loo**-vah
grilled	alla griglia	ah-lah **greel**-yah
ham	il prosciutto	eel pro-**shoo**-toh
cooked/cured	cotto/crudo	**kot**-toh/**kroo**-doh
ice cream	il gelato	eel jel-**lah**-toh
lamb	l'abbacchio	lah-**back**-kee-oh

lobster	l'aragosta	lah-rah-**goss**-tah
meat	la carne	la **kar**-neh
milk	il latte	eel **laht**-teh
mineral water fizzy/still	l'acqua minerale gasata/naturale	**lah**-kwah mee-nair-**ah**-leh gah-**zah**-tah/nah-too-**rah**-leh
mushrooms	i funghi	ee **foon**-gee
oil	l'olio	**loll**-yoh
olive	l'oliva	loh-**lee**-vah
onion	la cipolla	lah chee-**poll**-ah
orange	l'arancia	lah-ran-chah
orange/lemon juice	succo d'arancia/ di limone	**soo**-kohdah-**ran**-chah/ dee lee-**moh**-neh
peach	la pesca	lah **pess**-kah
pepper	il pepe	eel **peh**-peh
pork	carne di maiale	**kar**-neh dee mah-**yah**-leh
potatoes	le patate	leh pah-**tah**-teh
prawns	i gamberi	ee **gam**-bair-ee
rice	il riso	eel **ree**-zoh
roast	arrosto	ar-**ross**-toh
roll	il panino	eel pah-**nee**-noh
salad	l'insalata	leen-sah-**lah**-tah
salt	il sale	eel **sah**-leh
sausage	la salsiccia	lah sal-**see**-chah
seafood	frutti di mare	**froo**-tee dee **mah**-reh
soup	la zuppa, la minestra	lah **tsoo**-pah, lah mee-**ness**-trah
steak	la bistecca	lah bee-**stek**-kah
strawberries	le fragole	leh **frah**-goh-leh
sugar	lo zucchero	loh **zoo**-kair-oh
tea	il tè	eel **teh**
herb tea	la tisana	lah tee-**zah**-nah
tomato	il pomodoro	eel poh-moh-**dor**-oh
tuna	il tonno	eel **ton**-noh
veal	il vitello	eel vee-**tell**-oh
vegetables	i legumi	ee leh-**goo**-mee
vinegar	l'aceto	lah-**cheh**-toh
water	l'acqua	**lah**-kwah
red wine	vino rosso	vee-noh **ross**-oh
white wine	vino bianco	**vee**-noh bee-**ang**-koh

NUMBERS

1	uno	**oo**-noh
2	due	**doo**-eh
3	tre	treh
4	quattro	**kwat**-roh
5	cinque	**ching**-kweh
6	sei	**say**-ee
7	sette	**set**-teh
8	otto	**ot**-toh
9	nove	**noh**-veh
10	dieci	dee-**eh**-chee
11	undici	**oon**-dee-chee
12	dodici	**doh**-dee-chee
13	tredici	**treh**-dee-chee
14	quattordici	kwat-**tor**-dee-chee
15	quindici	**kwin**-dee-chee
16	sedici	**say**-dee-chee
17	diciassette	dee-chah-**set**-teh
18	diciotto	dee-**chot**-toh
19	diciannove	dee-chah-**noh**-veh
20	venti	**ven**-tee
30	trenta	**tren**-tah
40	quaranta	kwah-**ran**-tah
50	cinquanta	ching-**kwan**-tah
60	sessanta	sess-**an**-tah
70	settanta	set-**tan**-tah
80	ottanta	ot-**tan**-tah
90	novanta	noh-**van**-tah
100	cento	**chen**-toh
1,000	mille	**mee**-leh
2,000	duemila	**doo**-eh **mee**-lah
5,000	cinquemila	**ching**-kweh **mee**-lah
1,000,000	un milione	oon meel-**yoh**-neh

TIME

one minute	un minuto	oon mee-**noo**-toh
one hour	un'ora	oon or-ah
half an hour	mezz'ora	medz-**or**-ah
a day	un giorno	oon**jor**-noh
a week	una settimana	oona set-tee-**mah**-nah
Monday	lunedì	loo-neh-**dee**
Tuesday	martedì	mar-teh-**dee**
Wednesday	mercoledì	mair-koh-leh-**dee**
Thursday	giovedì	joh-veh-**dee**
Friday	venerdì	ven-air-**dee**
Saturday	sabato	**sah**-bah-toh
Sunday	domenica	doh-**meh**-nee-kah

ACKNOWLEDGMENTS

DK Travel would like to thank the following people whose help and assistance contributed to the preparation of this book

Karissa Adams, Adam Brackenbury, Elizabeth Byrne, Karen Constanti, James Davis, Sarah Dennis, Matt Dobbin, Bridget Fuller, Pauline Giacomelli-Harris, Meryl Halls, George Hamilton-Jones, Catherine Hetherington, Debbie James, Tom Morse, Chris Rushby, Mike Sansbury

Cartographic Data
ERA-Maptec Ltd (Dublin) adapted with permission from original survey and mapping by Shobunsha (Japan)

PICTURE CREDITS

284cb; Nick Fielding 186-7b; FineArt 145tr; freeartist 8-9b; Vladislav Gajic 59tr; Givaga 10cla; GL Archive 56cr, 57bc, 122cb; Godong 145br; Mikel Bilbao Gorostiaga-Travels 288br; Granger Historical Picture Archive 57cra, 58bl; Susana Guzman 8cl; Dennis Hallinan 294tl; Gary Hebding Jr. 291t; Falkenstein Heinz-Dieter 214bl; Hemis 12t; Heritage Image Partnership Ltd 32-3t; Peter Horree 259, 289clb; Scott Hortop Travel 209br; IanDagnall Computing 68bl; imageBROKER 13cr, 43tr, 262-3t; insidefoto srl 59br; Ivoha 68cr, 114tc; maurice joseph 67ftr; B.O' Kane 42tl, 55tl; Boris Karpinski 214-5; Brenda Kean 53cr; John Kellerman 216cla; Keystone Pictures USA 59bc; Kosobu 232t; Lanmas 104clb; Lautaro 163cla; Enzo Lisi 39clb; LOOK Die Bildagentur der Fotografen GmbH 37t; Dennis MacDonald 12-3b; Marka138br, 299br; Stefano Politi Markovina 26cr; mauritius images GmbH 289fcrb; Andrew Michael 295; Hercules Milas 26cl, 68t, 69tc, 95bl, 142-3t; MuseoPics - Paul Williams 187crb; ilpo musto 35cl; Niday Picture Library 54t; Nikreates 106-7c; Sérgio Nogueira 285crb; Martin Norris Travel Photography 69crb, 248t; George Oze 37cr; Pacific Press 285cr; Andrea Palma 49br; Panther Media GmbH 35tl; Stefano Paterna 26bl; Pictorial Press Ltd 58crb; J. Pie 69bc; PjrStatues 128br; Danilo Poccia 168tl; The Print Collector 89bc; RalphWilliam 84-5t; M Ramírez 144-5b; Realy Easy Star 58cr, / Daniele Bellucci 20tl, 114bl, 178-9, / Fotografia Felici 53tr; John Rees 94bl; Felipe Rodriguez 258cl; ROPI 89crb; Clemente do Rosario 123bl; rudi1976 26t; andrea sabbadini 37br; Riccardo Sala 47cb;

Science History Images 55clb; jozef sedmak 298t; Andrea Spinelli 52cra; Eckhard Supp 166-7t; Krystyna Szulecka 94br; Glyn Thomas 206-7t; Martin Thomas Photography 222t; Universal Images Group North America LLC / DeAgostini 265b; Stefano Valeri 30cr; Taras verkhovynets 55cr; valery voennyy 36tl; VPC Photo 231cra; Sebastian Wasek 129b; Gari Wyn Williams 53cl; Zoonar GmbH 297cla.

AWL Images: Marco Bottigelli 17ca, 76-7; Danita Delimont Stock 19t, 134-5; Francesco Iacobelli 2-3; Maurizio Rellini 4, 18tl, 100-1, 122-3t.

Bridgeman Images: Buyenlarge Archive / UIG 56-7t; De Agostini Picture Library / *Relief from Basilica Emilia, Rome* 87bl, / G. Nimatallah / Giotto *Boniface VIII announces Holy Year fresco* (1300) 214cla, / G. Dagli Orti / *Painted terracotta Sarcophagus of the Spouses, from Cerveteri* 146bl, / Gabinetto Comunale delle Stampe, Rome, Italy / Andrea Sacchi and Filippo Gagliardi *Saracen joust in Piazza Navona, February 25, 1634* 122clb; / Galleria Nazionale d'Arte Moderna e Contemporea, Rome, Lazio / Stefano Baldini /Giorgio de Chirico ©DACS, London 2018 *Spettacolo Misterioso* (1971) 33clb; / L. de Masi / *Close-up of a piano designed by Bartolomeo Cristofori di Francesco* 218br; / San Marco, Venice, Italy *Emperor Constantine I* mosaic 55tr.
Dorling Kindersley: Demetrio Carrasco 140cl; Mike Dunning 216crb; John Heseltine 24cb, 82tc, 106c, 164bl, 234t, 235cr, 304-5; Mockford and Bonetti 170bl.

315cr; chris-mueller 246b; fotoVoyager 24tl, 280-1; georgeclerk 284clb; Yves Grau 216-7; Imgorthand 11tc; J2R 45cl; Katharina13 203tl; KavalenkavaVolha 123cr; kenex 333tr, 335tr; Anna Kolesnikova 330bl; Lefteris_ 140clb; LightFieldStudios 38-9b; lillisphotography 183cr; lucamato 196bl; LuisPinaPhotogrpahy 47ca; MasterLu 48-9t; nejdetduzen 104cra; only_fabrizio 92tr; PaoloGaetano 274bl; pidjoe 36b; piola666 276-7; rarrarorro 38tr, 44-5t; ROMAOSLO 22t, 94cra, 240-1, 309tr; scaliger 87tr; sedmak 88cr; TatyanaGl 284-5t; Violetastock 139; walencienne 267cra; WekWek 83t; wjarek 93tr; zorazhuang 90-1t; ZU_09 284bc.

Macro - Museo d'Arte Contemporanea Roma: photo@ Luigi Filetici 320b.

Robert Harding Picture Library: Neale Clark 60-1; Cuno Images 50t; Terrance Klassen 18cb, 118-9; Andrew Michael 19bl, 158-9.

Photo Scala, Florence: Fondo Edifici di Culto - Min. dell'Interno 140br; Andrea Jemolo 126-7t; courtesy of the Ministero Beni e Att. Culturali e del Turismo 146cra.

SuperStock: agf photo 155b; age fotostock / Adam Eastland 106br, / Fabrizio Troiani / Renzo Piano © DACS, London 2018 *Auditorium Parco Della Musica* Italy 318-9, / Ken Welsh 37clb; Shirley Bowers 140cra; DeAgostini 188tr; Hemis / Patrice Hauser 130bl; Marka / Alessandro Canova 51cr.

Front flap: Alamy Stock Photo: eye35.pix br; **Dreamstime.com:** Scaliger cb; **Getty Images:** Marco Bottigelli bl; Christopher Chan cra; REDA&CO / Pino Pacifico cla; **Robert Harding Picture Library:** Neale Clark t.

Sheet Map Cover: Alamy Stock Photo: eye35.pix bc.

Cover images:
Front and spine: **Alamy Stock Photo:** eye35. pix.
Back: **Alamy Stock Photo:** AM Stock cl; eye35. pix b; **AWL Images:** Maurizio Rellini c; **iStockphoto.com:** fotoVoyager tr.

For further information see:
www.dkimages.com

MIX
Paper from
responsible sources
FSC www.fsc.org FSC™ C018179

The information in this DK Eyewitness Travel Guide is checked regularly. Every effort has been made to ensure that this book is as up-to-date as possible at the time of going to press. Some details, however, such as telephone numbers, opening hours, prices, gallery hanging arrangements and travel information are liable to change. The publishers cannot accept responsibility for any consequences arising from the use of this book, nor for any material on third party websites, and cannot guarantee that any website address in this book will be a suitable source of travel information. We value the views and suggestions of our readers very highly. Please write to: Publisher, DK Eyewitness Travel Guides, Dorling Kindersley, 80 Strand, London, WC2R 0RL, UK, or email: travelguides@dk.com

Main contributers Ros Belford,
Olivia Ercoli, Roberta Mitchell

Senior Editor Alison McGill

Senior Designer Laura O'Brien

Project Editor Rada Radojicic

Project Art Editors Tania Gomes, Bess Daly,
Ben Hinks, Hansa Babra, Stuti Tiwari Bhatia,
Ankita Sharma, Priyanka Thakur

Factchecker Daniel Mosseri

Editor Sands Publishing Ltd

Proofreader Ruth Reisenberger

Indexer Zoe Ross

Senior Picture Researcher Ellen Root

Picture Research
Harriet Whitaker, Sarah Stewart-Richardson

Illustrators Studio Illibill, Kevin Jones Associates,
Martin Woodward, Robbie Polley

Cartographic Editor James Macdonald

Cartography Subhashree Bharati, Deshpal Dabas,
Suresh Kumar, Alok Pathak, Kunal Singh

Jacket Designers
Maxine Pedliham, Bess Daly

Jacket Picture Research Susie Peachey

Senior DTP Designer Jason Little

DTP Coordinator George Nimmo

Senior Producer Stephanie McConnell

Managing Editor Rachel Fox

Art Director Maxine Pedliham

Publishing Director Georgina Dee

First published in Great Britain in 1993
by Dorling Kindersley Limited,
80 Strand, London, WC2R 0RL

A CIP catalogue record for this book
is available from the British Library.
ISBN: 978-0-2413-1187-5

Printed and bound in China.

www.dk.com